THE 100-YEAR LIFE

PRAISE FOR *THE*
100-YEAR LIFE

This playfully original book goes well beyond existing single-dimensional discussions of the major demographic transformations of our age, arguing how a different, exciting and challenging new world might be awaiting us. Blending economics, psychology and sociology, it makes a compelling case that as our lives become longer and healthier, the future might just be very very different from what we have known until now.

> DARON ACEMOGLU, *Elizabeth and James Killian*
> *Professor of Economics, Department of Economics,*
> *Massachusetts Institute of Technology*

A lifetime that lasts a century is a gift that few of us are prepared for. It will force all of us to change the way we plan and live every facet of life. Societies will have to transform and this thought-provoking book by Professors Gratton and Scott will compel leaders to think hard about how organizations can adapt to this change and make the most of it.

> N. CHANDRASEKARAN, *Chief Executive Officer,*
> *Tata Consultancy Services*

This is a timely, fascinating and thought-provoking book, full of wonderful information about the potential of a 100-year life. A brilliant read for individuals, but it should be mandatory reading for our politicians and those responsible for planning in health and social care.

> SHIRLEY CRAMER CBE, *Chief Executive,*
> *Royal Society for Public Health*

Lynda Gratton and Andrew Scott have written an important and highly readable analysis of the problem that most governments and corporations would prefer to ignore. A lot of us are going to live a lot longer than our grandparents – indeed, more than half of today's kids will live to be 100. This has implications for much more than just our personal finances. Our entire lives, they argue convincingly, will need to be reconfigured to deal with the unprecedented lifespans we are being granted. Required reading for baby boomers and millennials alike.

NIALL FERGUSON, *Laurence A. Tisch Professor of History, Harvard University*

Gratton and Scott's must-read treatise helps us see crucial patterns in modern life, where we're headed, and what we can and must do now – in both our private and public worlds – to create pathways for greater human freedom during our expanding time on earth.

STEWART FRIEDMAN, *Director, Wharton Work/Life Integration Project, Wharton School, University of Pennsylvania*

Getting the right investment of assets across a long life is not straightforward. *The 100-Year Life* presents a provocative and sophisticated analysis of both tangible and intangible assets and, in a series of fascinating scenarios, shows how it can be done. In doing so, Gratton and Scott have created a classic.

MARTIN GILBERT, *Chief Executive Officer, Aberdeen Asset Management*

This timely, important, easy-to-read and intriguing book will make you pause and think, as well as better plan your life. The lengthening of life is a very real phenomenon, bringing with it unpredictable changes and challenges, but also significant opportunities. With increased life expectancy, how do you get the most from your life? How do you leverage your abilities while at the same time taking advantage of life's opportunities? Gratton and Scott's book is a wake-up call for individuals, organizations, governments and societies. Relevant to young professionals as well as seasoned leaders, this book introduces readers to a new reality: multi-stage professional and personal lives that encompass different careers and transitions. Full of practical insights, this book helps readers to build and live a life worth living.

BORIS GROYSBERG, *Professor of Business Administration, Harvard Business School*

Longevity has been rising in rich countries at a continuing remarkable rate. How having a lot more time will affect our lives – as workers, consumers and family members – is a fundamental social, economic and psychological question that has received far too little thought. The authors discuss the implications of rising longevity for all these aspects of our lives, making sensible predictions and, at least as important, forcing all of us to think about these crucial issues.

DANIEL S. HAMERMESH, *Professor of Economics, Royal Holloway University of London and Sue Killam Professor Emeritus, University of Texas at Austin*

I found hundreds of insights in this book about the 100-year life. The authors understand implicitly that not only is the world as we know it changing beyond all recognition but the way we lead our lives is too. This book could not be more timely or necessary.

JULIA HOBSBAWM, *Founder and CEO, Editorial Intelligence Ltd and Honorary Visiting Professor in Networking, Cass Business School*

Living 100 years and working productively for the greater part of them will soon be a reality. That means that life stages as we know them have to be reinvented. Gratton and Scott's wonderful book prepares us – individuals, organizations and societies – for the possibilities of this brave new world of longevity and teaches us what it will take to thrive in it.

HERMINIA IBARRA, *The Cora Chaired Professor of Leadership and Learning, INSEAD*

With *The 100-Year Life* Gratton and Scott have accomplished the near impossible: a book that admirably provides both incredibly important personal advice and a public policy primer. The book delivers sound, straightforward and vital advice on both the risks and rewards of living much longer than we ever imagined would happen to us, and on how to make better decisions so that we are happier at each life stage. It also lays a strong foundation for policy makers to reconsider the unintended consequences of policies and regulations that both enable and inhibit our ability to live a century-long life to its fullest.

ALEC LEVENSON, *Senior Research Scientist, Center for Effective Organizations, Marshall School of Business, University of Southern California*

Too many books bemoan the economic problems facing ageing societies. This splendid book is quite different. It rightly sees increased rising life expectancy as a wonderful gift, but explores the multiple ways in which individuals, companies and societies must adapt if we are to seize the opportunities before us. Well written and combining insights from psychology and economics, it should be read by anyone who wants to understand how life chances and choices will be transformed in a world where living beyond 100 will become the norm.

LORD ADAIR TURNER, *Senior Research Fellow, Institute for New Economic Thinking; formerly Chairman of UK Pensions Commission*

What happens when working lives extend to 80 years? In this provocative and insightful book the economist Andrew Scott and psychologist Lynda Gratton show what it takes to make this a gift rather than a curse. This book is destined to fundamentally change the way we think about long lives.

JASMINE WHITBREAD, *Chief Executive Officer, Save the Children*

The lengthening of life is set to have just as profound an impact on our lives as did the explosion in female employment and the transformation of the nuclear family which marked the late twentieth century. To understand how and why things may change, there can be nowhere better to start than with the fascinating *100-Year Life*.

BARONESS ALISON WOLF, *Sir Roy Griffiths Professor of Public Sector Management, King's College London*

THE 100-YEAR LIFE

Living and Working in an Age of Longevity

BY LYNDA GRATTON AND ANDREW SCOTT

Bloomsbury Business

An imprint of Bloomsbury Publishing Plc

B L O O M S B U R Y

LONDON · OXFORD · NEW YORK · NEW DELHI · SYDNEY

Bloomsbury Business

An imprint of Bloomsbury Publishing Plc

50 Bedford Square	1385 Broadway
London	New York
WC1B 3DP	NY 10018
UK	USA

www.bloomsbury.com

BLOOMSBURY and the Diana logo are trademarks of Bloomsbury Publishing Plc

First published in 2016
This paperback edition published 2017

British Library Cataloguing-in-Publication Data
A catalogue record for this book is available from the British Library.

ISBN: HB: 978-1-4729-3015-6
PB: 978-1-4729-4732-1
ePDF: 978-1-4729-3017-0
ePub: 978-1-4729-3016-3

Library of Congress Cataloging-in-Publication Data
A catalog record for this book is available from the Library of Congress.

Cover design by Jason Anscomb
Cover image © Rawshock Design

Typeset by Deanta Global Publishing Services, Chennai, India
Printed and bound in Great Britain

To Nigel and Diane

CONTENTS

Introduction

We are in the midst of an extraordinary transition that few of us are prepared for. If we get it right it will be a real gift; to ignore and fail to prepare will be a curse. Just as globalization and technology changed how people lived and worked, so over the coming years increasing longevity will do the same.

Whoever you are, wherever you live and however old you are, you need to start thinking now about the decisions you will take in order to make the most of this longer life. The same holds for the companies you work for and the society in which you live.

Our lives will be much longer than has historically been the case, longer than the role models on which we currently base life decisions, and longer than is assumed in our current practices and institutional arrangements. Much will change and this process of transformation is already underway. You need to be prepared for this and adapt accordingly, hence our ambition in writing this book.

A long life could be one of the great gifts that those of us alive today enjoy. On average we are all living longer than our parents, longer still than our grandparents. Our children and their children will live even longer. This lengthening of life is happening right now and all of us will be touched by it. This is not trivial – there will be substantial gains in life expectancy. A child born in the West today has a more than 50 per cent chance of living to be over 105, while by contrast, a child born over a century ago had a less than 1 per cent chance of living to that age. This is a gift that has been accruing slowly but steadily. Over the last 200 years, life expectancy has expanded at a steady rate of more than two years every decade.[1] That means that if you are now 20 you have a 50 per cent chance of living to more than 100; if you are 40 you have an evens chance of reaching 95; if you are 60, then a 50 per cent chance of making 90 or more.

This is not science fiction. You probably won't live to 180, and we don't recommend you take up weird food fads. What is clear is that millions of people can look forward to a long life and this will create pressure on how they live and how society and businesses operate. There is no doubt that new norms and role models will emerge, and already there is plenty of evidence of people and society adapting to these changes. Looking forward, changes will be more extensive still, and this will raise the general issue in the level of public consciousness and debate.

How will you make the most of this gift? This is a question we have asked in our lectures and discussions with a variety of people of different ages. For many of them the gift of time came as a surprise, yet over the period of our discussions people realized they needed to start to alter their plans and to take action immediately. Others had already implicitly adjusted to the reality of longevity but had not realized how many others were thinking the same way.

This lengthening of life is a crucial topic, so why has so little been written about it in the popular press? This is puzzling. After all, this is not an issue that affects just a few, it affects everyone; and it is not a distant problem, it's happening right now. Neither is it unimportant; the right responses to greater longevity yield huge benefits. So why is the subject so little discussed?

Perhaps the explanation lies in Benjamin Franklin's famous remark, 'In this world nothing can be said to be certain except death and taxes,'[2] both of which are rightly seen as curses. Long life as a curse has been the centre of most of the discussions of longevity because the topic has been seen as one of death and taxes: the talk is of frailty and infirmity, of an Alzheimer's epidemic, of rising medical costs and a looming crisis.

Yet, as we will show, with foresight and planning, a long life is a gift, not a curse. It is a life full of possibilities, and the gift is the gift of time. How you choose to use and structure that time is at the heart of the response to living longer.

This question of structuring time is a major theme of this book. Over the twentieth century a three-stage view of life emerged: a first stage of education, followed by a career, and then retirement. Now imagine that life expectancy increases, but the retirement age remains fixed. This creates a significant problem: most people simply can't afford a generous pension if they live longer. The solution is to either work longer or make do with a smaller pension. No wonder a longer life feels like a curse – neither option is attractive.

The curse of Ondine

An image of a curse from a French fable comes to mind. An old tale tells the story of the nymph Ondine who discovers her husband Palemon fast asleep and snoring, having just committed an unfaithful act. In her fury she places a curse upon him: as long as he is awake he will breathe, as soon as he sleeps he will die. From that time on Palemon spends every moment in frantic activity, never resting for fear his eyes will close and death will overwhelm him.

An extended three-stage life can feel like the curse of Ondine. Like Palemon we are condemned to work forever, knowing we can't afford to stop, however weary we may be. The seventeenth-century political philosopher Thomas Hobbes famously described life as 'nasty, brutish and short'. There is only one thing worse: a life that is nasty, brutish and long.

This is the curse: constant work, boredom, diffusion of energy, missed opportunities, culminating in an old age of poverty and regret.

We see it differently. There is no doubt that many people will work longer, but work does not have to be the frantic and wearying activity of Ondine's curse. There are real opportunities to move away from the constraints of a three-stage life to a way of living that is more flexible, and more responsive – a multi-stage life with a variety of careers, with breaks and transitions. In fact, we believe this is the *only* way to make a long life a gift and avoid the curse of Ondine. However, this restructuring of life is not trivial. It will involve major changes for you as an individual, for the firms and organizations that hire you, and indeed for governments and society.

The need for restructuring is down to time: over a hundred years there are simply a great many more hours. Think about it this way. There are 168 hours in a week – across a 70-year lifespan that's 611,000 hours; across a 100-year lifespan that's 873,000 hours. How will you allocate this extra time? What will you do? How will you sequence stages and activities? Whether it be the working week or the weekend, the annual vacation or bank holidays, or indeed the three-stage life, the structuring and sequencing of time is effectively a social construct. In a longer life there will be different structures, alternative sequences and a redesigned social construct.

It is different this time

There will be a fundamental redesign of life; while the process is gradual and has already been ongoing for many years, it will culminate in a social and economic revolution. Just as technology and globalization, year by year, have transformed the way we live, so the changes needed to make the most of a 100-year life will do the same. Here are some of the ways we believe life will be changed as a result.

People will work into their 70s or even 80s

When we teach our MBA students at London Business School about the 100-year life, we ask the class to create scenarios for their own life. Very quickly their minds turn to finance and at this point we ask them: 'If you live 100 years, save around 10 per cent of your income and want to retire on 50 per cent of your final salary, at what age will you be able to retire?' (In Chapter 2 we make this calculation – the answer is: into your 80s.) At this point the room goes silent. Making the most of the gift of a long life requires everyone to face up to the truth of working into your 70s or even 80s. Simple as that.

There will be new jobs and skills

Over the coming decades there will be significant churn in the labour market as some traditional jobs disappear and new ones appear. A hundred years ago, agriculture and domestic service provided the bulk of jobs; today they have shrunk to a tiny percentage of the workforce, while the proportion of office jobs has soared. Looking forward, this churn will continue as robotics and Artificial Intelligence replace or augment a whole host of jobs, from back office processing jobs to sales and marketing, office management and administration. In shorter lives with relatively stable labour markets, the knowledge and skills a person mastered in their 20s could possibly last their career without any major reinvestment. If you now work into your 70s or 80s in a rapidly changing job market, then maintaining productivity is no longer about brushing up on knowledge – it is about setting time aside to make fundamental investments in re-learning and re-skilling.

Getting the finances right will not be everything

We authors are an economist and a psychologist, yet our different perspectives are not mutually exclusive; in fact, integrating them has been crucial for understanding the implications of a 100-year life. Living a happy and productive long life is indeed about making rational choices and dynamic plans, but it is also about the role of identity and the social factors that will shape future lives.

A life well lived requires careful planning in order to balance the financial and the non-financial, the economic and the psychological, the rational and the emotional. Getting your finances right is essential to 100-year life, but money is far from being the most important resource. Family, friendships, mental health and happiness are all crucial components.

Too much of the debate around longevity has been about finances and pensions. Preparing for a 100-year life is about more than just shoring up the finances. You can't have a long and financially successful career if your skills, health and relationships are depleted. Similarly, without sound finances, you will not be able to afford the time to invest in those crucial non-financial matters. Getting the balance right is hard in a short life – and while it is more complex in a long life, there are many more opportunities to do so.

Life will become multi-staged

While some people are already experimenting and diversifying away from the three-stage life, it remains the dominant model for most people. In this book we build a series of scenarios for the future, stretching the three-stage model from 70 years to 80 and then to 100 years. The only way a three-stage life can be made to work over 100 years is with a very long second stage of continuous employment. That might make the finances balance, but it doesn't work for the other things that matter. Stretched over time it becomes too hard, too exhausting and, quite frankly, too boring.

Instead a multi-stage life will emerge. Imagine you have two or three different careers: one perhaps when you maximize your finances and work long hours and long weeks; at another stage you balance work with family, or want to position your life around jobs that make a strong social contribution. The gift of living for longer means you don't have to be forced into either/or choices.

Transitions will become the norm

When life morphs from three stages to multiple stages, there will be more transitions. In a three-stage life there are two key transitions: from education to employment, and from employment to retirement. With more stages there will be more transitions. This is important because right now few people are able or skilled to make these multiple transitions. Making the most of a long and multi-stage life means taking transitions in your stride. Being flexible, acquiring new knowledge, exploring new ways of thinking, seeing the world from a different perspective, coming to terms with changes in power, letting go of old associates and building new networks. These are the transformational skills which call for a potentially huge shift in perspective and require real foresight.

New stages will emerge

This has happened before, in the twentieth century, with the emergence of two new stages: teenagers and retirees. We believe that the next decades will see the creation of more new stages of life. Right now a new stage of life is emerging for those aged 18–30. Just as longevity and greater schooling helped promote the concept of a teenager, so something is happening to the age group beyond adolescence. This group are already beginning to respond to the promise of a longer life and are keeping their options open and exploring new alternatives. As they do so, they are turning away from the commitments that past generations had made at this age and instead are pursuing other lifestyles and choices. The creation of these new stages of life is a real gift. These new stages create an opportunity to experiment, to build the life you want. Look around you – there are probably already family or friends who are experimenting with new stages.

Re-creation will be more important than recreation

With more transitions and new stages comes the need to invest: in shifting identity so you can take on a new role; in creating a different lifestyle; or in developing new skills. The gift of a longer life with more time creates the space for investment. Historically this investment came in the first stage of life – in a period of full-time education. When life becomes multi-staged, then this investment happens throughout life and in periods that have traditionally been seen as leisure time.

Using leisure time to invest in skills, health and relationships may not sound terribly appealing. Typically leisure has been seen as consuming time by doing nothing more than lying on the couch and watching a film, going sailing, or just having fun and playing computer games. With more hours there is more time for leisure, but balancing this with using leisure time as an investment will be crucial in a longer life. In a shorter life, using leisure primarily as a form of relaxation made sense. Over a longer life, leisure will create space for investment too. Perhaps a part of the gift of a 100-year life is to re-shape how leisure time is spent, with less focus on consumption and recreation and more on investment and re-creation.

Lockstep will end

A three-stage life with education first, employment second and then retirement can only be sequenced in a single way. Many people followed these stages and the resulting lockstep of action brought certainty and predictability. People were not faced with excessive opportunities or choices, and companies or governments were not confronted with a great deal of variety across what people wanted or needed. It is no surprise therefore that right now, the selection, development and promotion policies in many organizations are built on the assumption of three stages.

A multi-stage life with new milestones and turning points creates numerous sequencing possibilities, and the way these are sequenced will no longer be determined by the logic of the three-stage life. Instead it will be shaped by individual preferences and circumstances.

Importantly, when lockstep disappears, so does much of the predictability of age. At present, if someone tells you they are an undergraduate, you know their age – their stage of life reveals their age; if they are a senior manager, you can have a fairly good idea of their age and the arc of their career to date. In a multi-stage life this is no longer the case. You could be an undergraduate and no one could reliably predict your age from this piece of information. 'Age' is not 'stage' any longer, and these new stages will be increasingly age-agnostic.

The consequences of this are profound, as so much of society is based on the implicit assumption that age and stage are one and the same thing; it is hard-wired into so much of corporate HR practice, marketing and legislation. All of this will need to be unpicked.

Options will become more valuable

In long lives with greater change and more choices to be made, options become more important. When a person makes a choice to do something, this implicitly means they chose not to do something else. Taking decisions means closing down options. In the financial world options are valuable and priced. The value of an option depends upon how long the option is valid for and how much risk there is in the world.

The same goes for the decisions that are taken about life. As life becomes longer there is more opportunity for change and options become more important. Searching for options and keeping them open for longer will be a direct consequence of a 100-year life. This is one reason that a new stage for those aged 18–30 is emerging, one where the traditional commitments of previous generations; marriage, families, house and car purchases are all being delayed further and further. These people are keeping their options open.

Options are important right though life and all the more so in a multi-stage life. Investing and protecting these options will become an essential part of life planning.

Younger for longer

Conventionally, living for longer is seen as being older for longer. There is evidence that this convention will be reversed and people will be younger for longer.

This is playing out in three ways. First, as we have seen, some people aged 18–30 are behaving differently from past generations and are following more flexible and less committed lives by not closing down options. Secondly, as people progress through more transitions they will retain greater flexibility. Evolutionary biologists refer to this as *neoteny* – the retention into adulthood of adolescent features that help promote flexibility and adaptability and avoid being pinned down by habits. Finally, because age is no longer stage, there will be more cross-age friendships as people from different age groups pursue similar life stages. When lockstep ends, this mingling of ages will bring greater understanding across the ages and help those who are older to retain more youthful characteristics.

Home and work relationships will transform

A longer life with more years post the age of raising children has great potential to reduce gender inequality and to transform personal relationships, marriage and child-rearing.

Traditionally the home was a place of specialization – men worked and women looked after the home and children. This has changed in recent decades, as women increasingly entered the workforce and dual incomes became the norm rather than the exception. However, while family roles have changed, the narrative of the three-stage life as typical of the male career remains dominant. While women are more likely to have multi-stage lives, this is still seen as unusual and not the norm.

Relationships over long lives will transform, in part because the financial and saving requirements are easier when both members of the household work. Moreover, as both partners embark on multi-stage lives, they will have to coordinate with each other as they enter into different stages and support one another at different times. The variety of households that will emerge will be far broader than the conventional family structure, and this variety will put significant pressure on corporations and on government policy to be more responsive to this emerging reality.

This will provide additional momentum to gender equality. The three-stage life underpins an inflexible attitude towards work and career. To date, the demands for more flexible working patterns and career standards have been led primarily by women due to their role as primary carer. As the three-stage life ends, so men will also be pushing for more flexibility around the new stages they will be constructing.

Generational complexity

The three-stage life has led to an institutional separation of the young, the middle-aged and the old. The multi-stage life, new structures of family relationships and the fact that age is no longer stage will start to reverse this generational isolationism.

Even more dramatic will be the emergence of four generations within a family living at the same time. With life expectancy growing faster than the age at which women become mothers, we will see much more complicated family structures and changing generational attitudes.

There will be much experimentation

One thing is clear – there will be many pioneers. Neither individuals, nor communities, nor corporations or governments have worked out how best to support a 100-year life. There are few role models, as even those who live to 100 have rarely expected it. Those alive now have to plan with the expectation of a long life. The younger you are, the more you are likely to experiment and the greater the opportunity you have to start and plan afresh. If you are in mid-life, you may have been following in the footsteps of your parents and implicitly assuming a three-stage life. It is now becoming clearer that greater life expectancy is making that three-stage life uncomfortable.

All of us are therefore trying to figure out what will work and how best to support a 100-year life. We wrote this book to create clues and insights about what might come. But the truth is that no one knows precisely what will happen and while this is being figured out, society will witness a great deal of experimentation and diversity.

The coming HR battle

We believe a 100-year life is a gift for humanity. A redesigned multi-stage life gives everyone considerable choices and flexibility and it creates the possibility of achieving a better trade-off between work and leisure, career and family, finances and health. However for corporations, and especially their HR departments, all this sounds like a nightmare; companies like conformity, and simple, predictable systems are easy to run and implement. So don't be surprised if large numbers of institutions resist these changes. But everywhere experiments are taking place and eventually the individual's desire for flexibility and choice will overwhelm the company's need for systems and predictability. It will be a tough confrontation, however, and could take many decades to resolve.

There is no doubt that the real pressure will be put on lockstep and age and stage being synonymous. No doubt some companies, for whom attracting smart and skilled workers is crucial, will realize the commercial advantages of changing their policies. But not all will, and most won't be as flexible as we as individuals would like them to be. This promises to be a battleground akin to the battles about the length of the working week and working conditions that marked the Industrial Revolution.

The challenge for governments

A 100-year life touches all aspects of how people live and so creates an extensive agenda for governments. To date their attention has been restricted to issues of retirement, but increasingly they will have to consider education, marriage, working time and a range of broader social arrangements. Making the finances work is important over a 100-year life, but adjusting how people live and work over their whole life is even more critical and it will be this agenda that governments need to pursue.

Too much of current policy is aimed at the final stage of life and viewed through the prism of a three-stage life. The consequences of a 100-year life are for everyone, not just the old, and involve far more than adjusting the level of pensions or flexing the date at which retirement starts. Creating a regulatory and legislative framework that gives people choices over how they create the multiple stages of their life will be the priority for governments.

Perhaps the biggest challenge is health inequality and how to ensure that the poor will lead a long productive life. Life expectancy gains are not spread equally across the population and an ever-widening gap between rich and poor is developing within countries. It is also clear that many of the options we explore to make the most of a 100-year life are most easily available to those with professional or technical backgrounds and a high income. A long life requires resources, skills, flexibility, self-knowledge, planning and respectful employers. The danger is that the gift of a long life will only be open to those with the income and education to construct the changes and transitions required. It is therefore crucial that governments begin now to construct a package of measures to support those less fortunate in achieving the transitions and flexibility that a long life requires. It is unacceptable that a good long life should only be an option for a privileged minority.

Who am I?

The forces that shape the living of a long life are economic and financial, psychological and sociological, medical and demographic. Yet fundamentally this is a book about *you* and how you can plan your life. There will be more choices and you will experience many changes. These are factors that bring into focus what you stand for, what you value and what you wish to base your life around.

The Saturday edition of the *Financial Times* magazine carries a personal profile in which famous people are asked: 'What would your 20-year-old self say about you now?' In this book we aim to reverse that time perspective. Rather than ask what your 20-year-old self would think of you today, we invite you to think about what your 70, 80 or 100-year-old self would think of you now. Can you be sure that the decisions you are making now will stand up to the scrutiny of your future self?

This is not simply a linguistic puzzle. We believe it goes fundamentally to the heart of longevity. When lives are short, the concept of who you are develops without a great deal of insight or transformation. Yet when lives are long, what is the thread that connects the many transitions a person goes through? What is it that remains essentially *you*?

Issues of identity, choice and risk become central to questions of navigating a long life. A long life means more changes; more stages means more individual choices to be made; and the more change and choices you experience, the less the influence of where you started from. So you will need to think about your identity in a different way from those who came before. The longer your life, the more your identity reflects what you craft rather than a reactive response to where you began. Those that came before you did not have to think so consciously about actively navigating their lives through so many distinct changes, or indeed developing their capacity for transition. Long lives are lives of transitions; some of these transitions will be in the company of others, but for many there will be no cohort to offer support. Simply following the herd is not going to work. In a way that past generations simply didn't have to do, each one of us will need to think about who we are and how we construct our life and how this reflects our identity and values.

We wrote this book for people who understand that the past is not a predictor of the future; who want to learn about options and not just constraints; and who want to positively influence the working life they lead now and into the future. People who want to maximize their chances of making a long life a gift rather than a curse. This book is an invitation to take the first steps towards creating that gift.

1

Living

The gift of a long life

Picture for a moment a young child that you know. Perhaps your 8-year-old sister or 10-year-old daughter, perhaps a nephew or a young boy who lives nearby. You can see their wonderful childish enthusiasm and energy for life, and you can imagine their freedom from responsibilities and obligations. It is reassuring to think that, even as the world changes, children all over the world still display those life-affirming characteristics – and, of course, they help remind you of your own childhood.

Yet you can also see how their childhood will differ from your own as they take for granted, and seem to intuitively accept, many of the technological innovations that astound you. But it is not just their childhood that will differ from your own. It is also their adulthood. One of the parameters of their adult life is illustrated in Figure 1.1. These are the calculations demographers have made of their probable length of life. If the child you are thinking about was born in the US, Canada, Italy or France, there is a 50 per cent chance that they will live until at least 104. If the child you have in mind was born in Japan, then they can reasonably be expected to live to a staggering 107 years.

You probably found it fairly easy to think of an 8-year-old. But let us ask you to identify another age group. How many centenarians do you know? Perhaps you don't know any, or perhaps you can think with considerable pride of a grandmother who reached 100. But the very fact that you know so few, and feel such understandable pride about those you do, reveals how

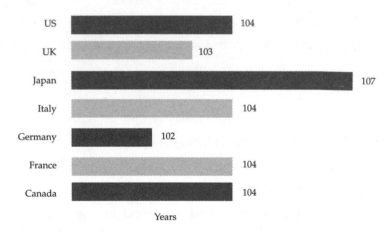

FIGURE 1.1 *Oldest age at which 50% of babies born in 2007 are predicted to still be alive.*

Source: Human Mortality Database, University of California, Berkeley (USA) and Max Planck Institute for Demographic Research (Germany). Available at www.mortality.org

exceptional it is. To understand this difference between 8-year-olds and centenarians, let's contrast the future-orientated data in Figure 1.1 with past data. Looking back to 1914, the probability that someone born that year would live to 100 was 1 per cent – and that's precisely why you found it so hard to identify centenarians alive today. The odds were simply stacked against them. But look again at Figure 1.1 – in the year 2107, being a centenarian will no longer be a rarity. In fact it will be the norm, and considerably more than half of those 8-year-olds you know will still be alive.

What is behind this extraordinary shift in longevity is neither one single simple causal factor nor indeed a sudden change. In fact, for most of the last two hundred years there has been a steady increase in life expectancy. More precisely, the best data currently available suggests that since 1840 there has been an increase in life expectancy of three months for every year. That's two to three years of life added for every decade. Figure 1.2 documents this staggering impact from the 1850s onwards. What is really extraordinary is the constancy of the gains in life expectancy over this period of time. If we focus on the highest average life expectancy around the world in any one year (what demographers refer to as *best practice* life expectancy,) it really is well characterised by a straight line. And perhaps more importantly, there is no sign that the trend is levelling off, suggesting that this phenomenon will continue into the near

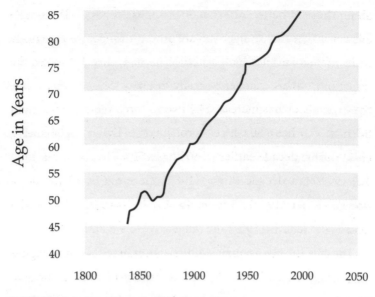

FIGURE 1.2 *Best Practice Life Expectancy.*

Source: Calculated using data from Human M ortality Database, University of California, Berkeley (USA) and Max Planck Institute for Demographic Research (Germany). Availability at www.mortality.org. For an explanation, see 'Broken Limits to Life Expectancy' by Jim Oeppen and James Vaupel, *Science*, May 2002, vol. 296.

future. So a child born in Japan in 2007 has a 50 per cent chance of living to 107. By 2014, that chance has already improved, and the new-born babies joyously received in Japanese maternity wards that year have a 50 per cent chance of living to 109 rather than 107.

A hundred years ago the chances of living to 100 were slight; for those who are 8 years old now the chances are high. What about those in between? What does it mean for you? The simple answer is that the younger you are now, the longer you are likely to live. Take another look at the curve in Figure 1.2 to see the trajectory of this change. Basically in every decade since 1840, life expectancy has increased by two to three years. So if a child born in 2007 has a 50 per cent probability of living to 104, then a child born a decade earlier (1997) has a 50% chance of reaching 101 or 102; a decade earlier (1987) the range is 98 to 100; a decade earlier (1977) 95 to 98; for 1967 it is to 92 to 96; and a decade earlier still (1957) the range is 89 to 94, and so on.

The steady improvements in life expectancy shown in Figure 1.2 have been achieved through a variety of distinct phases. The first substantial increases in life expectancy came from tackling infant mortality. If you live in a developed country now, it is almost impossible to imagine what a terrible scourge child mortality had been in the past. The classic writers of Victorian England poignantly captured these young tragedies: Little Nell dies at the end of *The Old Curiosity Shop* at the age of 14, while in *Jane Eyre*, Lowood School has a typhoid epidemic and Jane cradles her dearest friend Helen as she dies in her arms. These were not dramatic stories of exceptional events; Charles Dickens and Charlotte Brontë were simply recounting the commonplace events they saw around them. From the 1920s onwards, it was reductions in child and infant mortality that accounted for the majority of improvements in life expectancy seen in Figure 1.2.

The infectious diseases that killed Little Nell and Helen, such as TB, smallpox, diphtheria and typhoid, began to be eliminated. Governments instigated innovations in healthcare provisions, standards of nutrition improved, and people were educated into more healthy lifestyles.

The second substantial increase in life expectancy came from tackling the chronic diseases of middle age and beyond – in particular cardiovascular problems and cancer. Twentieth-century novelists no longer described the tragedy of childhood mortality, but they themselves were touched by the chronic diseases of their age. Sherlock Holmes' creator Sir Arthur Conan Doyle died of pneumonia in 1930 aged 71, while James Bond's creator Ian Fleming died in 1964 from a heart attack at 56. Over time, earlier diagnosis, better treatments and intervention, and better public education, especially around the health-related challenges of smoking, helped drive improvements in health. As Nobel Laureate Professor Angus Deaton notes, this epidemiological transition occurred as fatal diseases moved out of the bowels and chests of infants into the arteries of the elderly.[1]

The next substantial increase in life expectancy will come from tackling the diseases of old age. Indeed there have already been sharp improvements in life expectancy for the elderly. The probability of an 80-year-old man dying in England in 1950 was 14 per cent and has now fallen to 8 per cent; for a 90-year-old the probability has fallen from 30 per cent to 20 per cent. Reaching

100 years of age used to be sufficiently rare that many countries took steps to recognize it. In Japan, for example, anyone reaching 100 was entitled to receive a silver sake dish, a *sakazuki*. When this practice was introduced in 1963 there were just 153 centenarians but by 2014 more than 29,350 were issued. In the UK, a message from the Queen has been the way the country acknowledges its centenarians. A decade ago one person took responsibility for the cards; it now takes seven people, as the number of cards has increased by 70 per cent. A glance at Figure 1.2 would predict that the manufacture of *sakazuki* and the number of letter writers is set to increase significantly – indeed in 2015 the *sakazuki* tradition was discontinued.

There are, of course, myriad causal factors at work behind this increase in life expectancy: better health, better nutrition, better medical care, better education, better technology, better sanitation and better income. Demographers debate which of these factors is most important. To the extent that any consensus exists, it is probably best reflected in the influential work of Samuel Preston. He estimates that while rising income and better nutrition account for around 25 per cent of the increase, the major factors are new public health innovations around vector control, drugs and immunization.[2] The role of public health and education is a crucial factor in this improvement – consider, for, instance the impact of public awareness campaigns around smoking and life expectancy.

You will live longer wherever you are born

It's noticeable that all the data in Figures 1.1 and 1.2 are drawn from the richer and more developed countries. Right now in developing countries, fewer children born today can expect to live for 100 years. However, looking forward, the very same forces that have raised life expectancy in the developed countries are now leading to rising life expectancy in developing countries. Just as child mortality fell in the West with rising income, better nutrition and better healthcare, so too a similar phenomenon is happening around the world. Poorer countries start with lower life expectancy than rich countries, but are benefiting in general from the same increases.

Take for example India, where in 1900 life expectancy was 24 years, compared with 49 years in the US. By 1960, US life expectancy had risen to 70 years while India had only risen to 41 years; the gap in longevity between these two nations was widening. However as India's economic success picked up, the gap narrowed. By 2014, India's life expectancy was 67 years and UN demographic forecasters estimate that this should increase at the rate of around two years every decade. India may start with a lower life expectancy than the US, but it is rising in much the same way. In many countries across the world the same is true – the 100-year life is becoming a global phenomenon, although it's the rich countries that are experiencing it first.

Will you live forever?

Glance back to Figure 1.2 and let your eyes imagine how the longevity trajectory could continue upwards. You may ask yourself whether, as life expectancy has increased at the rate of two to three years every decade, there is any limit to how long people will live. The majority of children born in the West today can be expected to live beyond 100. But why stop there? Why not 150, or 200, or even beyond?

As with most scientific debates, there is a wide range of opposing views. Much discussion focuses on whether there is a natural limit to human life, and if there is, what that might be.[3] The pessimists argue that improvements in nutrition and the big breakthrough in tackling infant mortality are complete, and that the diseases of prosperity, a more sedentary lifestyle and rising obesity will curtail any further increase in life expectancy.

Others take a more optimistic view, arguing that public education will continue to be a powerful lever in boosting life expectancy and, combined with technological innovations, will continue to push longevity. Historically the combination of public education, the benefits of technology, early diagnosis and more effective treatments have all helped overcome previous barriers to life expectancy. Why wouldn't they continue to do so going forward? Indeed within this group of optimists are those who take an almost fantastical view, arguing there is no natural limit to human life, and scientific progress and technology will create life expectancies that approach many hundreds of years.

That is the view of Ray Kurzweil, who became director of engineering at Google, where he leads a team on Artificial Intelligence. In his book,[4] co-authored with his physician Terry Grossman, he describes three crucial bridges to a multi-century lifespan. The first bridge is to follow best practice medical advice so as to extend life sufficiently to benefit from the second bridge, which is created by the coming medical revolution in biotechechology, and then onwards to the third bridge, which enables one to benefit from nanotechnology innovations where Artificial Intelligence and robots rebuild ageing bodies at a molecular level. These are the optimists of gerontology, arguing that the natural limits to life are an order of magnitude greater than anything yet imagined.

Which of these schools of thought is right clearly has enormous consequences. Figure 1.2 suggests that if there is a limit, we don't seem to be close to reaching it. Best practice life expectancy would start to level off if longevity is indeed approaching a peak, but as the graph shows, the rate of progress continues at the same rate as in the past two centuries. Personally the authors tend to agree with the moderate optimists: we imagine that the rises in life expectancy will begin to slow down, perhaps at ages of 110 or 120. Of course, no one can know. But for us, the most important fact to remember is that the concept of the 100-year life it is not science fiction or some wild guess about the future, nor is it an upper limit only for a lucky few. This is such a fascinating question precisely because there is compelling evidence that babies being born today will live considerably more than a hundred years.

There is one more technical point to take into consideration before leaving this topic of longevity. If you read more about longevity, you will notice there are conflicting predictions about how long people will actually live. This conflict arises in part because there is more than one way of making the calculations of future life expectancy. By way of illustration, let's return to the 8-year-old you pictured earlier. To forecast their life expectancy, demographers have to consider their mortality risk as they grow older. In forming a view of how long an 8-year-old will live, what should be the assumptions of their life expectancy at age 55 (which is the average age of the authors right now)? Could it be that in forty-seven years' time, when these 8-year-olds actually reach the age of 55, they have the same life expectancy as we do now? Or should the assumption be that in the intervening forty-seven years the life expectancy of a 55-year-old will be much greater as a result of further innovations in public education and health technology?

Clearly the answer to that question will lead to very different estimates of their life expectancy. If demographers assume that the 8-year-old, when they are aged 55, has the same life expectancy as us now, then they are using a *period* life expectancy measure. If, however, they assume that the 8-year-old, when they reach age 55, will benefit from further improvements in life expectancy, then they are using a *cohort* estimate of life expectancy. Obviously the conclusion of life expectancy using the cohort estimate will be considerably longer than that using the period estimate, since the former takes into account likely future improvements. We have chosen here to show cohort estimates in Figures 1.1 and 1.2, both of which assume continued improvements in education and healthcare. Interestingly (and this is important) many economic estimates of life expectancy (developed, for example, for pension purposes) use the period estimates. By doing so they are effectively taking any future innovation in longevity out of the equation. It seems to us that, given historical trends, this substantially underestimates future life expectancy – which is why we have chosen to use data from cohort estimates.

You will age more healthily

Greater life expectancy is only a good thing if life itself is good. What if life expectancy increases faster than the years of good health? This would lead to the Hobbesian nightmare of 'an epidemic of frailty'. Certainly in response to rising longevity, many commentators bemoan the greater medical costs that come from looking after older people. Clearly living for longer with Alzheimer's or any number of diseases that afflict older people isn't to be welcomed.

However this is to miss the main point. It is not just that people will live for longer; a growing number of researchers also say that they will be healthier for even longer. In other words, we are beginning to witness a *compression of morbidity*.[5] If mortality refers to life expectancy and the time of death, then morbidity refers to the health-related quality of life before death.

Back in 1980, Stanford medical professor James Fries hypothesized that the initial onset of chronic diseases would be pushed back in time faster than increases in life expectancy. This would result in morbidity problems becoming compressed into shorter periods just before mortality, with chronic illnesses associated with ageing (diabetes, cirrhosis, arthritis) starting later. Fries is an optimist who believes in the power of preventive medicine, health promotion and education. In part this optimism comes from a number of studies he conducted. First he studied 1,700 University of Pennsylvania alumni over a twenty-year period and then later a group of runners. His conclusions were clear: people who have regular exercise, don't smoke and control their weight will, in general, experience a significant compression of morbidity. Since this landmark study, other studies have confirmed this – for example, the age at which people typically experience first coronaries has increased in many countries, and mobility among the older population is improving.

Morbidity is not just about disease, it is also about how people function as they age. A range of studies has examined what are called *activities of daily living* (ADL). These are activities such as bathing, continence, dressing and eating that have an important impact on daily quality of life. Data from the US based on studying the ADL of 20,000 people suggests quite striking changes over time in mobility and functionality. In the twenty years between 1984 and 2004, the number of people aged 85–89 who were classified as disabled fell from 22 per cent to 12 per cent, and for those aged over 95 from 52 per cent to 31 per cent. Older people seem to be fitter and also can achieve more as technology and public support improves. Similarly a number of studies found evidence of continual long-term declines in disability for those aged over 65 and that in recent decades the rate of decline has increased.[6]

However, although there are many studies that support the compression of morbidity, the evidence is not uncontroversial.[7] Whether you will age healthily is dependent on many factors, some of which relate to where and how you live. In the US, for example, the evidence for healthier ageing is strong; but, as a study by the Organisation for Economic Co-operation and Development (OECD)[8] has shown, while morbidity has compressed in five out of twelve countries (including the US), it has increased in three, remained unchanged in two, and has neither increased nor decreased in the remaining two countries.

The variation across countries is interesting in itself, since it would support Fries's argument that public health, education and changes in behaviour are key to achieving a healthy old age – it is not an automatic process.

Perhaps your greatest fear as you imagine how you will live over a long life is the possibility of spending the closing years with some form of dementia. This is an understandable concern. While few of us may know a centenarian, many of us have a close relative who has dementia. Indeed, in rich countries dementia is becoming the major risk of ageing: 1 per cent of 60-year-olds, 7 per cent of 75-year-olds and 30 per cent of 85-year-olds have dementia. So what will this mean for you? Inevitably this has become a topic of focused research, coupled with significant advances in brain imaging using MRI scans. One of the most exciting areas of research is cognitive enhancers, and scientists are expecting a breakthrough within twenty years.

Gerontology as a science is moving rapidly from being seen as a somewhat eccentric and alchemy-like subject into the mainstream. Several leading clinics are actively engaged in research in this area and serious commercial money is now entering the arena. Most prominently, Google has established Calico (California Life Company) with the goal of focusing, in Larry Page's words, on 'health, well-being and longevity', with initial funding of $700 million.

Much of this research starts with the idea that it is cell ageing that underlies many of the diseases that contribute to mortality and morbidity. So rather than focusing on specific diseases and illnesses, research is now considering the process of ageing itself, by encouraging cells to live longer and to continue to repair themselves. It has already proved possible to substantially improve longevity in both yeast and mice, so this nascent field has high potential for human progress. However, understandably this research is complex and human trials are some way off. Inevitably with a 100-year life it will take a very long time before the impact of different interventions is understood. This is an area where progress will be slow and landmark breakthroughs may be few and far between.

It is important to remember, however, that when science, knowledge and significant funding are focused on a challenge, then much can be achieved. In Charles Dickens' age the focus of innovation was on reducing child mortality; in Ian Fleming's age it was on tackling the diseases of middle age; now it is on confronting the diseases of old age.

So perhaps, as we leave this discussion of longevity, you would be wise not to simply think of living healthily for 100 years, but rather consider this the very minimum lifespan you can expect.

2

Financing

Working for longer

One of the themes of this book is that money, while important, really isn't everything when it comes to dealing with a long life. It is, however, the place where most people begin and so it is where we shall start. We start by calculating how much a person has to save to fund their retirement pension, using different assumptions about life expectancy and length of working life. Our focus is *only* on pensions. Yet over a long life with many stages, it is clear that life savings will also be a preoccupation and by only considering pensions we acknowledge we are taking a rather narrow view of financial planning. However, even this narrow view leads to some sobering insights.

When we share these calculations with others there is often a depressed silence. The simple truth is that if you live for longer then you need more money. This means either saving more or working for longer. That logic is both inescapable and disheartening. The greater the increase in life expectancy, the higher the savings rate, and/or the longer the working years. The gift of those extra years has swiftly turned into a curse. Most of us don't like the idea of paying the bill in return for a gift.

However this financial reality is merely the start, not the end of our analysis. It is precisely because these financial calculations are so depressing that we all need to move away from the dominant concept of a three-stage life. Once you step outside of this, as we do in the rest of this book, then even though you still have to save more or work for longer, you can do this in a way that does less harm to your non-financial assets and helps you escape Ondine's curse. This is what will create the gift.

Introducing the cast

Calculating savings rate and working years is complicated, and while the maths is relatively straightforward, the assumptions on which the calculations are based can be complex. How much will you earn, how fast will your income grow, what will be the return on savings, what will be the profile of your income over your working career, how many children will you have, what level of income do you need to be happy, and how much do you want to leave as an inheritance? These are all assumptions that lead to potentially very different conclusions.

Because so much depends on individual circumstances and aspirations, most major financial institutions use detailed software to calculate financial planning. It is the same reason that economists consider a multitude of agents when they create extremely complicated lifetime profiles.[1] The details matter.

In order to create some financial insights into the implications of a 100-year life, we decided to bypass these person-specific factors. Instead we narrate the lives of three characters: Jack, Jimmy and Jane. Born in 1945, 1971 and 1998 respectively, these three characters represent distinct generations and enable us to emphasize how longer life expectancy will impact differently on each of them. These stylized lives are designed to enable you to identify broadly with one of them so that, through their experiences, you can consider the consequences for you of the changes we outline.

The life of Jack illustrates how the three-stage life (education, work, retirement) was, with a modest life expectancy of around 70, so perfectly attuned to his generation. Jack is important, not as a description of what is happening now, but to illustrate why the success of the three-stage life for his generation was such a powerful role model for those who came afterwards.

The three-stage life is the role model for Jimmy who is now in his mid-40s, with a life expectancy of 85. He has followed the social norms of the three-stage life but now the reality is beginning to dawn that this won't work for him. In mid-life he is looking around and wondering how to make things work better. For Jimmy the curse is beginning to outweigh the gift. As we will show, a longer life can be a gift, but Jimmy will have to be prepared to change, transform and experiment in order to tip the balance.

Jane is a young woman looking forward to living for 100 years. Members of her generation know a three-stage life won't work for them and they are redesigning their life trajectory from the beginning. This is the cohort with the greatest life expectancy and also the greatest flexibility in how they design life. We expect that many will turn out to be social pioneers.

We acknowledge that, even if you do identify firmly with one of the characters, your own life will be far more complicated and unique and you will need to finesse these financial calculations as you think about your own planning. This chapter isn't meant to be a substitute for proper financial advice. However, while the simplicity of these stylized characters means the precise numerical calculations should be treated with caution, the broad results hold true. However much your own personal circumstances may differ, the broad implications will have significance for many people.

Making assumptions

Most of us are interested, perhaps very interested, in how long we should plan to work and how much we should plan to save. These decisions are important and impact on many of the day-to-day decisions you are making now. Later we will show the balance for Jack, Jimmy and Jane between the years they work and the years they retire. You may find them surprising and in order for you to take action, you need to feel completely confident that they are accurate. To build this confidence, we will describe in some detail the calculations we have made and the assumptions on which they are based.

In these stripped-down calculations, there are only four key assumptions that matter: how large a pension you are targeting; the return on your savings; how fast your income grows; and at what age you want to retire.[2] Given these assumptions, you can work out how much you need to save while you are working to produce the required pension.

In order to make these calculations as comparable as possible across Jack, Jimmy and Jane, we use the same values for each of these four key assumptions. It is, of course, very likely that because they were born at different times, our characters will face different investment returns or different earnings growth. However the key message of this book is the way that longevity will bring about change. Many other variables may shift across the generations, but forecasting these changes is treacherous and our goal is to isolate the impact of longevity.

The first assumption concerns desired pension: we assume that the goal of all three characters is an annual pension worth

50 per cent of their final salary. In Chapter 7, we will review the reasonableness of this assumption, but for now it is best to note this is a modest and conservative goal. Most people aim for a substantially higher figure and we are setting the bar relatively low; indeed, this level of savings is probably at the lower bounds of your assumptions.

The second assumption concerns your expectations of the long-term rate of return on your investments. This is a hugely important and controversial topic in finance, and one that has no single, simple answer. One variable is your appetite for risk; risky assets pay a higher return than safe assets in order to persuade investors to take on that risk. So the return on investment has three components: the risk-free rate of return (usually the interest rate on government bonds, assuming that it is a government that doesn't default); the risk premium (how much extra an investor earns from risky assets); and the balance of the portfolio between risk-free and risky assets. The risk-free rate and the risk premium often vary from one decade to another and different portfolio mixes bring about very different investment returns. Hence there is no one single 'golden' number on which everyone agrees and so a voluminous debate exists in the finance literature on this topic.

An important source of data is the work of Elroy Dimson, Paul Marsh and Mike Staunton.[3] Every year they produce estimates for a range of countries going back more than 100 years. For the US between 1900 and 2014 they report that, adjusting for inflation, the risk-free rate was 2 per cent and the risk premium 4.4 per cent – in other words, equities earn 4.4 per cent a year more than risk-free assets such as government bonds. So if an investor split their portfolio 50:50 between safe and risky assets, then they earned a return of 4.2 per cent (0.5 x 2 + 0.5 x 6.4) over and above inflation. The same calculation for the UK gives a historical return of 3.5 per cent. Taking an average of US, UK, Japan, Germany, France and Australia over this period gives a historical return above inflation of 2.8 per cent.

Will this continue? Right now many serious economists are predicting a sustained period of very low investment returns that would make these historical calculations look optimistic. However, given our focus on a 100-year life, we are more comfortable using historical averages of the past 100 years rather than 2015 forecasts that at best may get the next decade right. It's also important to realize that these calculations abstract from tax and management charges, all of which would lower returns significantly. Based on these cross-country historical calculations, we use a net return of 3 per cent above inflation for the investments of Jack, Jimmy and Jane. In some decades they will earn much more than 3 per cent, and in others much less, but assuming an average of 3 per cent real return over the long lifespans seems realistic.

The third assumption is how fast Jack, Jimmy and Jane's income grows each year. In general, as people age their income grows, as wages keep pace with inflation. Over time there are productivity gains and people get promoted and achieve greater responsibility. Obviously income won't grow at a steady rate: in recessions wages may even fall; in years of a major promotion, wages will jump dramatically. Taking this into consideration we assume a steady growth in income of 4 per cent over and above inflation a year[4] – this is optimistic but not unrealistic for those with a successful career.

The final assumption is the age at which you plan to retire. Our initial calculation is that everyone aims to retire at 65, the conventional historical retirement age. Later we investigate the extent to which working for more years helps ease the financing burden of a longer life.

The life that Jack built

Our character Jack was born in 1945, left school at 17 in 1962 and finished his college education aged 20. He entered the economy during what is known as the 'Golden Age' for developed economies. He enjoyed a successful career as an engineer and graduated into senior management. It wasn't all smooth sailing. As the richer economies wrestled with the impact of globalization and new technology as well as recessions, he lost his job a number of times and had to relocate, but the overall theme of his career was of a job well done. His was a typical traditional family structure – his wife Jill looked after the children and took a few part-time jobs, but Jack was always the main breadwinner. Jack retired at 62 and sadly passed away in 2015 aged 70.[5]

How did Jack's finances work out? The answer is 'very well'.

Jack belonged to a generation who benefited from three distinct sources of financing for his pension: a state pension, a company pension and his own private savings. Assuming Jack was a relatively high earner and received the maximum social security pension he was entitled to, he would have received from the state a pension worth around 10 per cent of his final income. Jack was fortunate enough to work during a time when most large companies provided a corporate pension. Given his length of service, we assume that this was sufficient to provide him a pension worth 20 per cent of his final salary. This leaves him to finance the rest of his pension – he needs to save enough to provide a pension worth 20 per cent of his final salary so that his total pensions account for 50 per cent of his final salary.

The other major advantage for Jack was that he worked for forty-two years and retired for eight, so he had more than five years of work to fund each year of retirement. So Jack had considerable help funding his pension and a lot of years in which to finance it.

The result is shown in Figure 2.1, which shows the level of savings Jack needed to finance his pension. Jack needed to

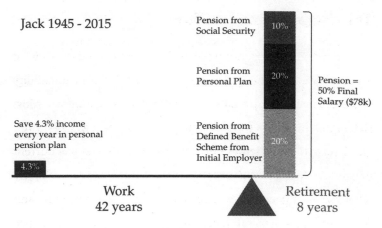

FIGURE 2.1 *Balancing Jack's financial assets.*

balance the savings during his years of working with the pension he wanted during retirement. For Jack the balancing was relatively easy. If each year he worked he saved 4.3 per cent of his income, then he could finance his desired retirement. Of course this wasn't the only saving that Jack had to do. He also needed to save to pay off his mortgage, perhaps to finance his children's education or build up a rainy-day fund, as well as saving in case he lived a longer life than was expected. However, in terms of saving for retirement, 4 per cent a year was a relatively modest and feasible amount.[6]

Given Jack's life expectancy and the support he received from the state and the companies he worked for, the three-stage life worked well financially for Jack. But as we will show, these sources of support were disappearing for Jimmy.

The disappearing pension

The most common economic issue discussed around the topic of greater life expectancy is the growing financial unsustainability of state pensions, especially in the developed economies. Most rich countries have a form of state pension known as Pay As You Go. Under these schemes current taxes are used to pay current pensions. No money is ever invested, unlike funded schemes where savings goes into a fund that accumulates over time and then pays out a pension depending on investment performance and contribution.

The problem with Pay As You Go schemes is that people are living for longer *and* birth rates are declining. When birth rates decline, there are fewer workers coming through compared to those who are retiring. The result of these trends is lower taxes but more expenditure on pensions. If pension policies remain unchanged, then the path of public finances is unsustainable and government debt is forecast to increase dramatically from its already high levels. In countries such as Japan, which has long life expectancy and where the birth rate has fallen very dramatically, the problem is already acute.

In Figure 2.2 we show the extent of the problem among the richer nations. The old age dependency ratio (the number of people of retirement age as a percentage of those of employment age) is set to at least double in many countries.

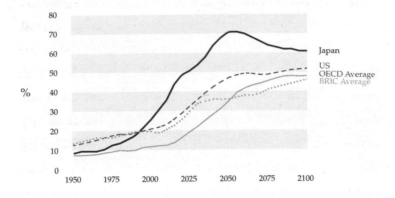

FIGURE 2.2 *Old age dependency ratio.*
Source: http://www.oecd.org/edu/ceri/SpotlightAgeing.pdf

Japan is particularly badly affected. Back in 1960, Japan had ten workers for every pensioner and the dependency ratio was 10 per cent. Under a Pay As You Go pension scheme this meant that ten workers effectively split the cost of one pension between them. In 2050 the projection is that the dependency ratio will reach 70 per cent, which means seven pensioners for every ten workers.

As a result of these trends, it is clear that Pay As You Go schemes in their current form are no longer sustainable. They were effectively designed with Jack in mind. If the state pays out a pension of 30–40 per cent of income and there are ten workers for every pensioner, then a tax rate of around 3–4 per cent on current workers pays the pension bill. However in some countries already pensions have become more generous, people retire earlier and live longer, so fewer workers pay the bill. As a result Pay As You Go has operated as a form of elaborate pyramid scheme – 'Ponzi' or 'Madoff' schemes. We have all been putting in too little relative to what we have taken out. And like all pyramid schemes, this can only continue as long as there is an ever-increasing number of new members entering the scheme. But the falling birth rates in developed economies mean this is no longer the case, and so the schemes are revealed as unsustainable.

Governments have, of course, known this for a long time and have taken a series of steps to try to improve the situation. Reform tends to be slow and as the voting population ages, it becomes increasingly resistance to pension reform. The details of reform vary considerably from country to country, but the general principles are the same: increase the retirement age so as to increase the number of years of tax paying; reduce the number of years of claiming a pension; and target pensions more to those with low incomes and assets.

Across the OECD a total of eighteen countries have raised the retirement age for women, and fourteen have done so for men. However to date these increases are at a modest pace: 2.5 years for men and 4 years for women between 2010 and 2050. That is slower than the projected increase in life expectancy and so we expect this trend of pension reform to continue or accelerate.

If you are a high earner, it is also important to realize that the state will play a smaller role in your pension provision going forward. For example, in 2000 a wealthy UK pensioner could expect a state pension worth more than 35 per cent of their final salary; by 2060 that will be only 20 per cent.

If state pension reform is slow, changes in corporations' occupational schemes have, in contrast, been rapid. Pensions are expensive to run and not something most firms are good at, and increasing longevity has made company pension schemes a major financial liability. The result is a dramatic decline in the number of such schemes, while existing schemes are already closing their membership to new workers. In 1987 in the UK, for example, there were 8.1 million members attached to occupational pension schemes in the private sector; by 2011 that number had fallen to 2.9 million.[7] In the US, the number of employees with access to defined benefit pensions declined from 62 per cent in 1983 to 17 per cent by 2013.[8] Furthermore, even among those schemes that survive, many are reducing their generosity in order to achieve financial sustainability.

With company pension schemes now scarce and state pensions becoming less generous, the overwhelming message is simple: the burden to save is being shifted increasingly to the individual. In other words, Jack had to finance 40 per cent of his overall pension, with the state and his employers funding the rest. Jimmy and Jane will have to self-finance a much greater proportion.

We have focused on the governments of developed countries and the problems they face with Pay As You Go schemes, but it's important to realize that the underlying pressures that are shifting the finance of pensions to the individual are global.

As we described in Chapter 1, life expectancy is increasing at the same rate in emerging markets as it had in developed economies; it is just that life expectancy is starting from a lower base in these emerging markets. It is also the case that fertility rates are declining in emerging markets too, but once more with a lag compared to the West. As income rises in emerging markets and as female education improves, so the fertility rate declines. In other words, emerging markets are experiencing the same combination of longer life expectancy and lower birth rates that have made Pay As You Go schemes unsustainable.

Not surprisingly, state pensions in emerging markets therefore tend to avoid using the Pay As You Go model. This is good news for those countries, as it means their public finances are not likely to be stretched in the way that developed economies are. However, while this means they won't have a pension-induced public finance crisis, it does mean that individuals will still have to rely more on themselves than the state to finance their pension. The absence of a Pay As You Go pension may mean the absence of a public finance crisis, but the result is an absence of a state-provided pension for many.

Jimmy: The three-stage life is stretched

We now turn our attention to Jimmy, who was born in 1971 and has a life expectancy of 85.[9] We are investigating the finances behind a three-stage life, so we assume that Jimmy graduated from college aged 21 in 1992 and intends to work until he reaches the age of 65 in 2036. Like Jack, he wants to achieve a pension worth 50 per cent of his final salary. However, we will make one key change for Jimmy: our calculations are based on the assumption that he does not have access to a company pension scheme. Despite the state pension reforms we mentioned above, we will continue to assume that he receives a state pension worth 10 per cent of his final salary.

Figure 2.3 shows the financing requirements for Jimmy. Whereas Jack had to save 4.3 per cent of his income every year to retire at 65, Jimmy has to save 17.2 per cent each year. Balancing is much trickier for Jimmy. He doesn't have the benefit of a company pension and so he has to finance twice as much of his pension, and, unlike Jack, he works for forty-four years and retires for twenty. So whereas Jack had a ratio of roughly 5:1 for years of work/years in retirement, Jimmy's ratio is more like 2:1. A savings rate of 17.2 per cent every year is high. Few of us can achieve that in a single year, let alone every year. Data from the UK supports this. For the period 2000 to 2005, the age group with the highest savings rate was 50–55 and they saved on

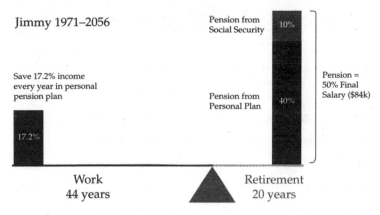

FIGURE 2.3 *Balancing Jimmy's financial assets.*

average only 5.5 per cent of their income.[10] Regardless of which country you live in, the modelling we have done for Jimmy's savings rate is high. Remember too that this is just saving for his pension. Jimmy will also have to save more than this in order to pay his mortgage and other major expenses. It's also based on a fairly conservative assumption of a pension worth only 50 per cent of final salary. This is clearly a very stressful financial model for Jimmy.

There are other options to achieve this balance and we can explore these through Jimmy. You don't have to retire at 65 but could work for longer in order to ease the financing burden. Or you could retire at 65, or even earlier, but aim for a much smaller pension. In Figure 2.4 we calculate the whole combination of outcomes that Jimmy could choose from, given the underlying assumptions. The graph shows, for a variety of different

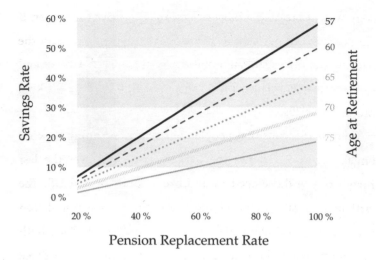

FIGURE 2.4 *Savings rate and retirement age for an 85-year life.*

retirement ages (57, 60, 65, 70 and 75), the level of savings required to achieve a given level of pension (20, 40, 60, 80 or 100 per cent of final salary), assuming life expectancy of 85 years.

For instance, what if Jimmy aspires to a pension worth 50 per cent of final salary but decides to work until he is 70, giving himself fifteen rather than twenty years of retirement? In this case his savings rate is 'only' around 13 per cent. Every year of work is another year of saving and another year less of a pension. If, instead, he would rather stick with retirement at 65, then a pension replacement rate of 30 per cent of his salary would only require savings of 8 per cent.

However, because the 50 per cent salary replacement rate assumption is already low, then looking at Figure 2.4, the more likely way of creating a balance is simply to work for longer. If you consider 10 per cent as a reasonable savings rate (and the data suggest this is still an ambitious goal for most people) and want a 50 per cent replacement ratio, then Jimmy will be working into his early 70s.

There is evidence that people are already beginning to work longer. Figure 2.5 shows the participation rates over the last thirty years of those aged 64 and over in the UK and US. The participation rate measures the proportion of the population who are economically active. In both countries, and for both men and women, there has been a significant increase in those

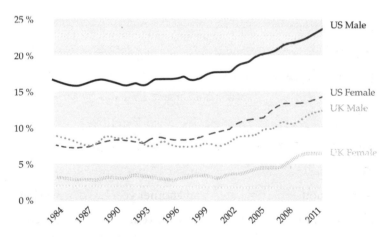

FIGURE 2.5 *Participation rates for US and UK for 64 years and over*

Source: Office for National Statistics (http://www.ons.gov.uk/ons/rel/lmac/ participation-rates-in-the-uk-labour-market/2014/art-3-older.html) and Bureau of Labor Statistics (http://www.bls.gov/emp/ep table_303.htm)

aged 64 or more who work. Nearly one in four US men aged over
64 are in work or seeking work, compared to one in six in 1984.
It is clear that this increase in participation rates will continue
into the future and involve even older age groups.

It is fascinating to note that younger retirement ages are a
relatively current phenomenon. For instance, in the UK in 1881,
73 per cent of men aged 65 and above were in work; by 1984
this had fallen to 8 per cent. In the US in 1880 nearly half of all
80-year-olds were engaged in some form of work, and 80 per
cent of those aged 65–74 were in some form of employment.
Over the course of the twentieth century there have been sharp
declines, but what the data in Figure 2.5 suggests is this process
is now going into reverse.

Jane: The three-stage life breaks

Jane was born in 1998, celebrates her 18th birthday in 2016
and is looking forward to a life expectancy of 100.[11] It's
fairly obvious intuitively that Jane, with her fifteen years of
additional life expectancy to Jimmy, is going to find a three-
stage life with retirement at 65 beyond her financial reach. As
Figure 2.6 shows, Jane will need to save 25 per cent of her
income each year to achieve a pension worth 50 per cent of
her final salary.

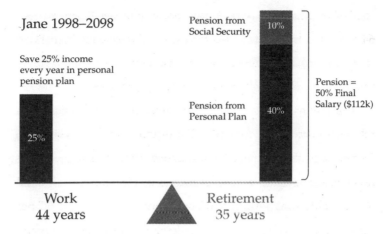

FIGURE 2.6 *Balancing Jane's financial assets.*

This just seems too high a level of savings to achieve over a lifetime. Not only is this much higher than the savings rates of most people today, but it is also only just the level of savings required to finance a pension. Jane will have to save over and above this to finance a mortgage, university fees and any other major expenditure. It is also worth pointing out that we assume in our calculations that Jane receives the same level of state pension as Jimmy. But as the earlier discussion suggested, this is unlikely to be the case. If Jane doesn't receive any state pension, then the savings rate she needs will rise to 31 per cent. Also bear in mind that because Jack's three-stage life worked so well for him financially, he probably left an inheritance for his children. If Jane's parents are like Jimmy and have a three-stage life that is proving a stretch financially, then she is unlikely to benefit from a bequest. It is clear that a three-stage life with retirement at 65 and living to 100 is financially out of reach for the majority of people.

There are, of course, other reasons why three stages with a retirement stretching for thirty-five years will not work. That's a long time on the golf course, and as studies of retired people have shown, long periods of inactivity are associated with cognitive deterioration and reduced life satisfaction.

Of course, like Jimmy, Jane could choose to work longer and spread out her savings. Figure 2.7 shows the various options available to her. If she is content with a pension worth only 30 per cent of her final salary, then she can retire at 70 if she achieves a 10 per cent savings rate throughout her working life. Remember, though, that 30 per cent is a low pension and in this case Jane would be receiving that pension for the next thirty years. Her pension will be fixed at 30 per cent of what she earned when she retired and clearly, ten or twenty years later, working salaries will have risen considerably, leaving Jane with a very low income level compared to others. A pension worth 30 per cent of a salary twenty years ago will yield a very low proportion of today's equivalent salary. So if we once again focus on at least a 50 per cent pension and a savings rate of around 10 per cent, then Jane will have to work into her 80s.[12] Compared to Jack, she has thirty more years of life, but

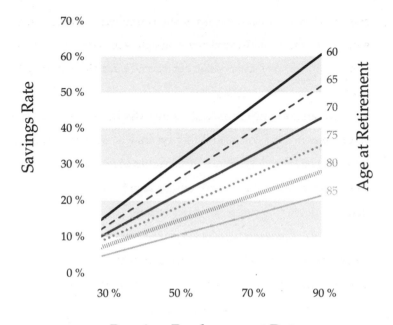

FIGURE 2.7 *Savings rate and retirement age for a 100-year life.*

Figure 2.7 suggests she may have to work an extra twenty years compared to Jack. Gift or curse?

Partnerships

We have so far looked at Jack, Jimmy and Jane as if they are in isolation and haven't considered the rest of their household. An obvious thought is that if they are part of a working couple, then financing a long life is made easier. There are two ways in which this works: there are economies of scale in a household; and, of course, the household net earnings go up.

The economies of scale occur because a house for two people isn't twice as expensive as a house for one, in the way that a meal prepared for two is not twice as expensive as a meal for one. Economists capture this effect in 'adult equivalence scales' and the OECD have calculated that a household of two adults needs only 50 per cent more income than a household of one adult to achieve the same standard of living. Therefore if both adults work, they each need to save less (25 per cent each) to achieve the same standard of living as if they were on their own. Of course, this reduces their savings burden since the household is now bringing in more income.

Later we discuss the importance of partnerships and how, over a 100-year life, their importance grows. But that does not take away the challenges of sustaining a partnership over such a long period of time. It is worth considering that though there are financial advantages to both partners working, there are also pitfalls. If both partners earn a high income, then the temptation is to develop lifestyle habits based on their current earning pattern. If they have a pension worth 50 per cent of their final salary, this can represent a sharp drop in their living standards. Both partners working only helps in terms of savings if they don't lock their consumption habits to their high earnings.

RIP the three-stage working life

Our analysis shows that when life extends, most people will have no choice but to work a great deal longer. By longer we don't mean a few years – longer for Jane means working over a decade more. Without these longer periods of work, it is very tough to accumulate sufficient savings to fund a retirement that lasts at least half as long as the total working career. This situation is exacerbated in those countries where state pensions are being scaled back, as Pay As You Go schemes become increasingly unsustainable. For most of us, these calculations show we need to save and work more than we probably thought we had to, and possibly more than we would like or feel currently capable of.

This is a conclusion that is both unwelcome and deeply unattractive. The idea of an extended working life is unappealing and sounds exhausting. However, the unappealing nature of this conclusion arises because we are simply extrapolating from the past into the future and assuming that the structure of this long working life will follow the traditional three-stage model life. If we are able to think more creatively and move away from the model of three stages, then the options are a great deal more appealing.

This will not be straightforward. It is striking how strongly embedded the model of three stages is in much career planning and long-term financial planning. Franco Modigliani of Massachusetts Institute of Technology won a Nobel Prize in economics for his work on the Life Cycle Hypothesis of consumption, and every economics textbook explains this by outlining a three-stage life. Even the word 'pension' has changed from its original meaning of a regular payment to a court favourite to reflect the three-stage model. It is clear to us that greater longevity and the financial consequences we have outlined here mean the three-stage model of life is dead. That is because the only way to make the three-stage life work financially is to create a very long second stage of working, but as we will show, the likely impact on non-financial assets such as productivity or vitality is ultimately undesirable. We will consider later in greater detail the negative impact that a relentless second stage has on non-financial assets, but even from this brief discussion it is obvious that there are challenges.

One challenge is that a long retirement, although it may sound appealing, is unlikely to provide the stimulation and camaraderie that people value and need. But if there are problems with a long drawn-out third stage, there are also problems with an extended second stage of continuous work.

The changing nature of the employment landscape will also put the three-stage model under increasing pressure. As we describe in the next chapter, over the coming decades new technologies will rise and fall, some sectors will grow and others disappear, and whole new occupations will emerge and take the place of existing jobs. Over Jack's forty-two years of work, he just managed to make the technical education he received in his early 20s relevant into his 60s. It is hard to imagine how Jane can do the same if she works into her 80s. Across the span of her life Jane will have to respond to the dynamics of the employment market by taking time out to invest in new skills and embrace new technologies. It is through this return to education throughout her life that Jane's model will morph from three stages to multiple stages.

There is also the challenge of non-financial assets. If Jane works a long and extended second stage, what does she do about her health and fitness? How does she preserve her relationships with her partner, children and wider family? It isn't just that Jane's knowledge and skills will deteriorate during this long second stage of continuous work, it could also be the quality of her relationships. Can we honestly assume that someone can work non-stop until the age of 80 – with no breaks, no sabbaticals and no flexibility? Can you imagine doing it?

What worked for Jack will be difficult to make work for Jimmy and doesn't work at all for Jane.

We think this is brilliant. We want to bury the three-stage working life and in its place consider ways of redesigning life so that long lives become a gift that is energizing, creative and fun. For most people the thread running through a long life will be work. We now turn to how the landscape of employment will change and then begin to build scenarios that demonstrate how Jimmy and Jane could have a long life that has more opportunities to be productive, energized and creative than Jack ever had.

3

Working

The employment landscape

So far we have shown that many people will live for a long time and will need to work for longer in order to finance this long life. Over this longer working career, the employment landscape will change dramatically, and making the right career choices to finance this longer life requires an understanding of this shifting employment backdrop.

Straight away this leads into a major problem of a longer life. Winston Churchill sagely remarked: 'It is always wise to look ahead, but difficult to look further than you can see.' Making predictions about the future is hard, and the further away the greater the uncertainty. With a 100-year life the range of uncertainty increases substantially.

Looking back 100 years, a present-day centenarian has seen much in their lifetime: two world wars and a shift from soldiers on horseback to nuclear weapons; the Russian Revolution and the rise and fall of communism; an end to the first wave of globalization and the emergence of the second; the collapse and subsequent ascendance of China; the advent of electricity, radio and television; the early days of the Model T; the first-ever commercial air flight; and, of course, the first manned flight to the moon, as well as the rise of the internet. At a domestic level they would have seen the advent of automatic washing machines, the widespread adoption of indoor plumbing in the house, as well as the vacuum cleaner, not to mention the introduction of the zipper and the bra!

A moment's reflection on these changes makes it obvious that being able to forecast developments for the centenarians born today is nonsensical. Dealing with this uncertainty will be a major part of living a long life. Those who live longer – assuming the pace of change will not alter – will experience a great deal more flux than past generations. If, as many technologists claim, the pace of change is increasing, then their experience of flux will be even more profound. Indeed for those destined to live a long life across a sixty-year working career, who they work for, the type of work they do and how they perform this work will change significantly.

Yet while it is foolish to make concrete predictions about the future employment landscape, it is possible to develop foresight by learning something from the past and by taking into consideration the trajectory of current forces. For those destined to live long lives, this foresight about future work is critical. We explore the future landscape first through the widest lens as we consider the industries that are likely to arise; then we examine a growing phenomenon, the smart city; and finally look in more detail at jobs and technology, and the likely winners and losers in a rapidly transforming labour market.

The new industries and ecosystems

Sectors will change

We begin with the issue of how the industrial landscape will morph. Figure 3.1 shows how the nature of employment in the US has changed over the last 100 years. In 1910, one in three workers were either farmers or farm workers, but now these occupations make up a mere 1 per cent of the workforce. Adding labourers and household service to these jobs accounted for half of US employment in 1910. By the year 2000 the employment landscape had changed dramatically, with half of US jobs becoming office-based: professional, clerical and managerial. Looking forward, there will be more shifts as the economy responds to the rise of information technology, rapid developments in robotics and Artificial Intelligence, growing environmental concerns and the impact of an ageing population.[1]

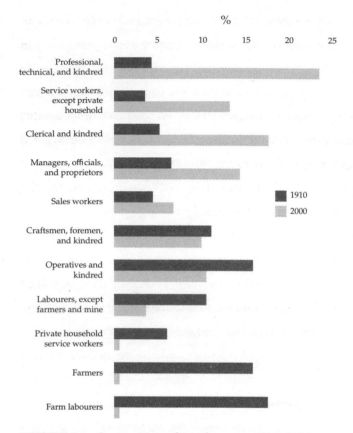

FIGURE 3.1 *Composition of Employment 1910–2000.*
Source: 'Occupational Changes during the 20th Century', I. D. Wyatt and
D. E. Hecker, Bureau of Labor Statistics Monthly Labor Review, March 2006.

Over time the structure of an economy goes through dramatic
changes in response to the primitive economic forces of supply
and demand. Some sectors fall dramatically. Consider, for
example, the agricultural sector, which in 1869 accounted for

nearly 40 per cent of US GDP and by 2013 was only 1 per cent. This was because of technological improvements, particularly in machinery and fertilizers, which led to significant increases in agricultural productivity and therefore potential supply. However, while the population became richer, their demand for food didn't increase proportionally to their income, so supply outstripped demand and food prices fell. The result of lower prices was a sharp fall in the total value of agricultural production and the laying off of many workers employed in the sector.

Other sectors rose dramatically. In contrast to agriculture, the service sector's share in the economy rose from 40 per cent in 1929 to around 65 per cent in 2013. This is explained by the fact that as people got richer they wanted to consume more services. The leisure industry illustrates this story very well. Over the twentieth century, as leisure time increased, so a substantial leisure industry grew, with far more cinemas, sports clubs, fitness centres and so on. However, unlike the agriculture sector where productivity increased substantially, productivity in the leisure industry tended not to increase – how do you substantially increase the productivity of a yoga instructor or a hairdresser? So rising demand wasn't met by rising productivity and therefore the price of services increased, drawing more workers into the sector. Higher prices, greater employment and output combined to substantially increase the share of services in terms of GDP.

Such flux is a historical constant, but precisely because it is a constant the new centenarians will experience more transitions and turnover. What of future shifts, and where will the jobs be?

One factor to consider is the impact of demography on jobs. As populations age, this has a substantial effect on the economy. Greater numbers of older people will create a demand effect to which sectors and market prices will respond. So, for example, it is likely that medical research focused on longevity and bioengineering will be significant growth sectors and the service sector will shift towards healthcare and service provision.

Environmental concerns and sustainability will also exert a substantial impact on prices and resources and the relative size of different sectors. We are on the cusp of substantial shifts in energy provision and, if energy scarcity continues and energy prices rise, then there will be significant innovations in energy creation and resource conservation. The same is true of food supply, where there is an expectation of radical innovation especially in combination with genetic engineering and health concerns. Growing water shortages will also lead to major changes in pricing and growth in the commercial importance of water efficiency, provision and recycling.

Similarly concerns about environmental sustainability and CO_2 emissions are also likely to lead to carbon taxes. This in turn will lead to substantial shifts in value and the rise of new sectors, new firms and new technologies, as abatement, capture and carbon substitution become multi-billion industries.

New Ecosystems will emerge

There will be substantial sectoral change, which will require people to be flexible in terms of their skills and possible location. There will also be substantial changes in who people work for. Richard Foster of Yale University calculates that in the 1920s the average life of a company quoted in the S&P 500 was sixty-seven years. By 2013 this had reduced to fifteen years. Looking back to 1984, only thirty of the 100 component UK firms in the FTSE 100 are still in the index today. New sectors rise and fall and new firms take over as dominant forces. So while Jack, born in 1945, would have experienced some stability in his choice of company, we can predict that Jane, born in 1998, will see more dynamism in the companies and sectors she works for and so will inevitably work for a series of different companies.

Several commentators also predict that there will be dramatic shifts in the types of company people work for. The huge growth in office-based employment shown in Figure 3.1 came about with the rise of the large modern company. These firms provided economies of scale with their organizational structure and have proved an enduring feature of the economy. There are those who view these types of firm as the dinosaurs of the organizational age and predict that they will succumb to the nimble-footed, smaller companies emerging around them. There are some signals that this could be true. Technology is making it easy for workers to coordinate among themselves and small-scale organizations have a flexibility that large firms find hard to achieve. With further developments of technology, such as the rise of 3D printing, the argument is that many of the scale advantages of large firms will disappear. At the time of writing, we see no evidence of this. Large companies such as Unilever or PepsiCo have scaling and mobilizing capabilities that enable them to deliver their products into almost every corner of the world and we believe this will remain the case. Others, like Google or Roche pharmaceuticals, have billion-dollar research budgets and the capacity to attract some of the brightest people in the world to work on developing the next generation technologies or medicines.

However, while large companies will continue to exist, there is no doubt that there will be changes in their structure. In the future corporate landscape, large firms will be increasingly surrounded by an ecosystem of smaller businesses and start-ups. These ecosystems, made up of businesses with fewer and often more specialized workers, will be places of growth. Indeed, it could be that some of the most interesting work will be in these ecosystems. This is already apparent as firms like Samsung or ARM have built incredibly complex ecosystems of alliances that enable them to partner with many hundreds of companies to deliver cutting-edge technology and sophisticated services.[2] Within the pharmaceutical sector, significant and important basic research often comes from small specialist companies that have a very narrow focus, sometimes specializing in just one specific molecule. These companies have grown in number and are able to compete as technology has reduced the barriers of entry to this type of research. We expect these ecosystems of small companies to flourish and to become more valuable. It could be that some who lead these small business set them up in order to grow into the large companies of the future, but it is likely that others will build them because they are passionate about a challenge that they want to solve.

The rise of these ecosystems will provide a variety of employment opportunities. The scale and managerial opportunities of large companies will still be there, but what will be added will be more focused and flexible employment in smaller entrepreneurial units.

In thinking of possible lives for Jane's 100 years, the flexibility that the ecosystem model offers makes the prospect of self-employment at certain stages a viable option. The technology that connects an individual to companies who want to buy their skills is becoming more global, cheaper and more sophisticated. These connecting platforms are already proliferating, leading to growing commentary about the 'gig economy' and the 'sharing economy'. Technological change reduces information costs and so enables buyers and sellers to find each other more easily as well as determine the reliability and quality of each other from independent sources.

The gig economy refers to the idea that there will be a rising number of people earning their income not through full- or part-time employment, but rather through providing a series of specific tasks and commissions to multiple sequential buyers. It's possible right now to sell your skills through platforms like Upwork, or to make a creative contribution on InnoCentive or Kaggle, which can attract top project work for cash or prize awards. These platforms will become more significant as large corporations increasingly look to small groups or individuals for their insight and innovation, and small groups look to connect with each other to build scale and reach. Corporations will engage interested individuals and teams with prizes, partner with them for a specific project, or buy them – much as Uber bought the robotics team from Carnegie Mellon. Similar to the gig economy, the sharing economy as a commercial entity provides the promise of a flexible source of income. Through renting out spare room capacity with Airbnb, the most high-profile example, individuals can generate useful income.

As well as providing a source of income, we expect these ecosystems will also help people better blend work, leisure and home. As people work more flexibly in small and focused teams where they feel passionate about what they are doing, so the barriers between work and leisure become eroded. It is also interesting to reflect that before the rise of industrialization, production took place primarily in the family home where work and leisure were blended. The rise of the factory and then the office inevitably led to a more formal separation of work and leisure. As we look forward we see more opportunities for the emerging ecosystems of work to erode this separation and enable work and life to be reintegrated.

Flexible, smart cities will rise

It is not just who you work for that will change, but also where you work. We are currently witnessing the most extraordinary migration that humanity has ever experienced. This is the migration from the countryside to the city. In 2010, 3.6 billion of the world population lived in cities. By 2050 the number is projected to be 6.3 billion – equivalent to the movement of 1.4 million people every week. Living in a city – and especially a smart city – is growing in importance and seems likely to continue.

Why are people moving to cities in such numbers? After all, the great promise of the internet was that distance would become unimportant, freeing people to live wherever they desired. In fact, while *distance* may have become unimportant, *proximity* has become ever more important. Part of the story of migration to the cities is that in the emerging markets of the world, people move from the rural sector and agriculture into the cities and industry. However, this is not the only story of migration. In advanced economies, people are also moving to the cities and this reflects the growing importance of proximity on ideas and high-level skills.

So while some industrial cities such as Detroit have suffered from decline, other 'smart cities' like San Francisco, Seattle and Boston have flourished and their population has risen. These smart cities are becoming a nexus of people who have ideas and high-level skills and who want to be close to other highly skilled people. They know that innovation is occurring at a faster pace, and they want to be close to other smart people to push and challenge one another. These clusters initially formed from groups graduating from universities and specialist colleges. Once these highly skilled groups are formed, firms naturally gravitate to them, and consequently more such workers move to the area because the job opportunities and wages are better than elsewhere. These clusters then become magnets for talent.[3] In other words, there are increasing returns to scale, or what economists call 'thick market' effects.

London is an another example of this cluster phenomenon. By 2014 the size of the highly skilled population of the city was 1.4 million people; by 2019 the estimates are that it will be 1.8 million.[4] As a capital city, London has always attracted business, government and, in turn, lawyers and financial professionals. These are historically strong cluster effects. Yet for London, beyond the location of major businesses, there is also the draw of a global design hub that is attracting creative people from across the world. What this demonstrates is that it is not just the IT industry that has the capacity to agglomerate the effects of smart people and ideas. As the economic value of ideas increases we can expect more clusters to emerge, arising wherever people want to feed off each other's ideas, support each other and build an ecosystem of start-ups.

At the centre of these creative clusters are often world-class universities. In Silicon Valley it is Stanford, Berkeley and Cal Tech; in Boston it is MIT and Harvard; the creative cluster in London is linked to the Royal College of Art and Central St Martin's, two of the top design colleges in the world. As these clusters grow, they attract companies to their burgeoning talent pools. In London, the one-million-square-foot Google Campus in King's Cross is a short walk from Central St Martin's and will grow to at least 4,500 people.

The impact on job creation of smart cities with their highly skilled workers can be significant. In fact, according to Enrico Moretti[5] of Berkeley, every one smart job creates five others. Some of these other jobs are highly skilled too, such as lawyers, accountants or consultants. Others are low paid, such as gardeners, artisanal manufacturers, baristas or yoga teachers. At this rate, smart cities will become a better place to generate employment than the old manufacturing hubs.

This growing importance of smart cities is also driven by social phenomena. The last few decades have seen a striking increase in what sociologists call *assortative mating*. In other words, marriage partners are more alike now in terms of education and income than they were in the past. This effect is also driving the growth of cities. For these highly skilled partnerships, finding interesting work for two is a great deal more difficult than finding it for one.[6] In the past, small towns were more attractive for traditional families where the husband worked and the wife was a homemaker. But living in a small town becomes more difficult when both people want to find that perfect job. So big cities begin to look more alluring – there are simply more opportunities. In fact big cities have an allure even before creating a partnership. Imagine you are dating and want to find the perfect partner who meets your growing list of partnership criteria. Will you find them in a small town? Possibly, but probably not. If you want to date someone with a similar career and earnings potential, then you are more likely to head to the city. Thick market effects work in dating too – a romantic thought.

We can expect these smart cities to lead the way in terms of the flexible workplace. Technological innovations will enable people to be more flexible about where and when they work (and therefore choose to work at home, or virtually);[7] to make matches more easily – for example, between people and jobs, or between people with similar interests (and therefore enable entry to the job market with more ease); to communicate with ease and at lower cost (and therefore work more in virtual or global teams); and to make some individual problems more collaborative (and therefore learn how to create large communities with similar skills and attitudes).

It is possible that the idea of the 'office' will come to look ridiculously traditional and expensive. Indeed, when executives at Unilever measured where and when carbon dioxide was produced, they discovered that expecting people to commute into large, central offices created an extraordinarily large carbon footprint. This and other drivers will move more people to work from home, in local hubs or in shared community centres. In part this will be supported by lower-cost technologies such as holograms and virtual meetings. It will also become the norm, as managers become more skilled at managing virtual workers and more encouraging of home working. However the move to home-based virtual working will always be balanced by the value of proximity.

A jobless future?

The history of humanity is one of continuous technological progress. Although in 1899 Charles Duell, the US commissioner of the Office of Patents, may have remarked that 'Everything that can be invented has been invented', it is clear that knowledge continues to advance. If each generation is born as smart as the previous one and inherits their stock of knowledge, then by exploring and combining different aspects of that knowledge and creating new insights, the world progresses technologically. As Isaac Newton brilliantly summarized, we stand on the shoulders of giants.

New technologies, however, mean an end to past jobs and usually the creation of new tasks and roles. At this point in time people are very aware of the jobs that are about to be lost, but of course they are not yet aware of the jobs that will be created. From the Luddites in the UK's Industrial Revolution who went on wrecking parties to destroy machinery to President Johnson's National Commission on Technology, Automation, and Economic Progress, there have been repeated concerns that automation will create a jobless future. Across the world there is an upsurge of similar concerns.[8] As we stand on the threshold of remarkable technological innovation in the field of robotics and AI,[9] will Jane be able to find work over a sixty-year career?

This is a question of deep debate and reading the conclusions of some of the participants is salutary. In his thought-provoking analysis, Silicon Valley entrepreneur Martin Ford remarks: 'The threat to overall employment is that as creative destruction unfolds the destruction will fall primarily on labor-intensive businesses in traditional areas like retail and goods preparation while the creation will generate new businesses and industries that simply don't hire many people.'[10] In the words of MIT professors Erik Brynjolfsson and Andrew McAfee, 'Computers and other digital advances are doing for mental power ... what the steam engine and its descendants did for muscle power.'[11]

The second half of the chessboard

In 1965, Intel's Geoffrey E. Moore conjectured that the processing power of semi-conductors would double roughly every two years and, to date, this has been an extraordinarily accurate prediction. As a consequence of this exponential growth, 'Second Machine Age' proponents argue that we are now in the 'second half of the chessboard'. This is a reference to a fable concerning a king in India who, bored with all his existing pastimes, set a challenge to his kingdom to come up with a better form of entertainment. When presented with an early form of chess, the king was so delighted he offered the inventor anything he wanted. The inventor requested rice: one grain on the first square, two on the second, four on the third, eight on the fourth, and so on. In other words, just as computing power doubles every two years, so the number of grains of rice doubled with the move from each square. In the fable, the king soon realized that he didn't have enough grains of rice to meet the challenge, running out before the thirtieth square (before the second half of the chessboard).

To meet the inventor's demand the king would have to provide a mountain of rice larger than Mount Everest – nearly 18.5 quintillion grains. On the first square of the chessboard there is one grain of rice, and by the 33rd square the number is 4.3 billion. The parallel with Moore's Law is obvious. Back in 1981, Bill Gates said 640K of computer memory should be enough for anyone; thirty years later not only do computers have huge processing power, but also the increase that will happen in the next two years is enormous compared to cumulative past progress. The increase in processing power going from the 32nd chess square to the 35th is worth four times the cumulative sum of processing power across the first 32 squares. In other words, if Moore's Law continues to function (discussed further below), then over the next eight years computational power will increase fourfold over and above the level of technology embedded, for example, in driverless cars.

The hollowing out of work

What will be the impact of this extraordinary trajectory? Discussions of robots and AI inevitably have a science fiction flavour to them and seem rapidly to veer into *Terminator*-like scenarios or lead to *Bladerunner*-style metaphysical considerations of the very nature of consciousness. When considering these debates it is worth staying grounded and beginning by considering the impact technology *already* has had on the labour market. From this it is easy to see why so many commentators fear a jobless future.

Figure 3.2 shows a phenomenon known as the *hollowing out of work*. While this is US data, other developed countries look similar. The data shows the percentage change in employment occupation from low-skill to high-skill work. From 1979

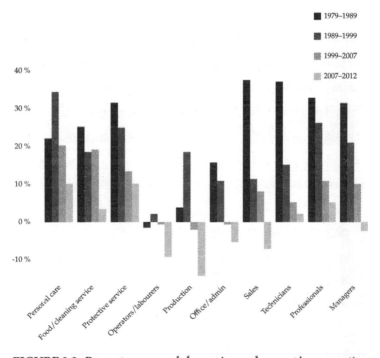

FIGURE 3.2 *Percentage annual change in employment by occupation.*
Source: David Autor, 'Why are there still so many jobs? The history and future of workplace automation', *Journal of Economic Perspectives* 29(3) (Summer 2015): 3–30.

onwards there has been an increase in employment of both skilled workers and those with low levels of skill, but in terms of medium-skill work there have been falls. The labour market has hollowed out, providing jobs at different ends of the skills spectrum, but not in the middle.

To understand why this has happened, it is useful to consider jobs as a collection of tasks. The MIT economist David Autor and his co-authors[12] do this by constructing a 2 x 2 classification of jobs: the extent to which a job requires cognitive or manual expertise; and the extent to which the tasks that define a job are routine or non-routine. By routine, Autor does not mean easy or boring, but rather that they can be described by a precise set of instructions that outline how the task should be performed. A routine cognitive task would be a bank teller, while a sorter on an assembly line would be an example of a routine manual task.

It is jobs that involve routine tasks that have already been substantially substituted by technology. Because routine tasks can be described by a specific set of instructions, they can be codified in a program for computers and robots to perform. Take a look in most Amazon warehouses, where robots move inventory from the shelves to Amazon packers while at the same time sending a constant stream of data to a central system about which products are ordered. The process takes place continually without intervention or decision-making by humans. This has been made possible by rapid technological innovations in machine learning and the accuracy of sensors. The hollowing out of the labour market has occurred because so many medium-skill jobs are of this routine form: either cognitive or manual. Technology basically provided a substitute for these jobs at a cheaper price than human labour.

However this isn't the only part of the story. In order to understand the debate on how technology will shape the future landscape for jobs, it is also necessary to consider what else happens. While technology has acted as a *substitute* for medium-skill jobs, it has served as a *complement* for skilled workers. Software and computers are complementary to skilled and educated workers. So while they have replaced medium-skill work, they have boosted the productivity and therefore the income of highly skilled workers. As the income of these skilled workers has increased, so they have increased their demand for the services produced by low-skilled workers. The net effect of these substitution, complementarity and demand effects has been the hollowing out of the labour market.

That described the first half of the chessboard. We are now entering the second half where computational power increases dramatically, so the concern is that the hollow gets wider and wider. So far technology has replaced simple routine tasks, and limits to computational power have restricted the loss of jobs. Driving a car is a routine task – it is just that the list of instructions is very long and complicated. With the innovations associated with the dramatic increase in low-cost computational power, it is now possible to develop driverless cars. When this happens it will threaten a significant number of jobs in the logistics industry. Diagnosing medical conditions is another routine task which has required knowledge and pattern recognition skills that have to date proved beyond computers. However, yet again, the implications of the second half of the chessboard is that this is no longer the case. Famously IBM's supercomputer Watson is now performing oncology diagnosis. As computing power increases, so the hollowing out of the labour market accelerates. Instead of being complementary to skilled labour, technological innovations begin to substitute for it. The fact that this is already happening is given credence in one recent economic study which found that the long-running increase in demand for skilled workers started to go into reverse in 2000.[13] In a much-quoted study, Oxford academics Carl Frey and Michael Osborne[14] calculate that a total of 47 per cent of jobs in the US are vulnerable to these forces in the next few decades – that's 60 million jobs.

The future of work

These are complex issues, yet those looking forward to a long life are faced with making some early bets about what path to go down. What would be the advice to them? What will be the future of work?

Unique human skills

From a technological perspective, the real question about the future of work concerns the limits of AI and robotic substitution. At the time of writing there is broad agreement that certain skills and capabilities are unique to humans and cannot (yet) be replicated or substituted by AI or robotics. David Autor and his co-authors point to two sets of these uniquely human capabilities. One set involves capabilities associated with complex problem solving that relies upon expertise, inductive reasoning or communication skills. Apple's iPhone tells this story. The iPhones and iPads are mostly made by Foxconn in Shenzen in China and the cost of manufacturing amounts to around 5–7 per cent of the purchase price. Apple makes between 30–60 per cent profit on each model. Moreover, the value created by each employee in Foxconn is in the order of $2,000, while in Apple the value created per employee is in excess of $640,000. The value creation is in the innovation, not the manufacture. The second set of capabilities involves interpersonal interactions and situational adaptability. These tend to be associated with more manual roles.

At the heart of the first set of capabilities is *Polyani's Paradox*, which refers to a comment made by chemist and philosopher Michael Polyani that 'We know more than we can tell'. In other words, a significant amount of human knowledge is tacit and therefore cannot be written down in the form of instructions, so cannot be replicated by AI and robotics.[15] The second set of tasks relates to *Moravec's Paradox*, which states that 'It is comparatively easy to make computers exhibit adult-level performance on intelligence tests or playing checkers, and difficult or impossible to give them the skills of a one-year-old when it comes to perception and mobility'.[16] So, for example, a robot can perform complex analytical tasks with ease, but finds it more difficult to pick up a cup or climb stairs.

Even here, however, some technology experts argue that the advantage of humans over machines will be short-lived. Fast developments in Cloud Robotics and Deep Learning could close the gap between human and machine performance. Developments in Cloud Robotics, where networks of robots have access to each others' learning through the cloud network, could result in learning at an exponential rate – certainly far faster than human learning. In Deep Learning the technology attempts to mimic the way humans make inductive reasoning through association by experience, again potentially through leveraging the experience of every other robot via the cloud.

Job Vacancies

From an economic perspective, the question is not simply one of substitution, but also one of supply. The supply side of the employment landscape will be influenced by crucial demographic forces that will substantially shape this landscape, particularly in developed countries. These demographic forces are population decline and the retirement of the Baby Boomer generation. In many developed countries, ageing and a declining birth rate have led to a falling population and a decrease in the number of people of working age. This is most noticeable in Japan, with a population predicted to decline to 87 million by 2060, from a high of 127 million. Of this population, 40 per cent will be aged over 65. This declining population is occurring alongside the retirement of a large demographic cohort known as Baby Boomers. Even if, as our analysis suggests, they will postpone their retirement, the end result is still the creation of a whole raft of vacancies. Take, for example, the UK, where the Institute of Public Policy Research predicts that the greatest driver for job vacancies comes not from the creation of new work (expansion) but rather from people leaving the workforce (replacement). Their prediction is that, as the Baby Boomers retire, millions of jobs will be vacated, particularly in low-skill work. Indeed, even in high-skill work, over the next decade replacement demand will exceed expansion demand – particularly in new technologies that require people with advanced technical skills.

So rather than worrying that robots are going to take our jobs, we should be delighted that they are arriving just in time to boost a flagging working population and maintain output, productivity and living standards.

Implementation challenges

There is also a view that while frontier technology is likely to advance rapidly, there will be substantial lags in its implementation. Driverless cars, for instance, face a significant number of regulatory and legal hurdles before they become an everyday reality. It is likely that there will come a day, almost certainly in Jane's lifetime, when cars are driverless, but it will be a while before it happens.

Some technologists also believe that, after fifty years, Moore's Law is beginning to reach physical constraints and is no longer operable. In effect, Moore's Law works by continually shrinking the size of transistors so that a greater number can be fitted on a chip. Technologists point to both physical and economic limits. Advanced nanotechnology is currently needed to produce transistors with atomic size, and these nanotechnology plants are expensive to run. Of course, fears that Moore's Law has come to an end have been proved groundless several times before and the industry is working on ways to bypass these constraints, but the physical limits are approaching. It is, of course, also possible that exponential growth is still available in many other areas of this technology even if Moore's Law is coming to an end. For instance, software has not, to date, fully exploited the hardware benefits of Moore's Law, so several decades of progress may still await.

New Jobs

There is a strong argument that technology substitutes work and therefore leads to mass unemployment. However historically, as economists point out, it is a rather more complex story. The empirical message from history is that technological progress raises productivity, boosts living standards and therefore encourages people to spend and consume more; as a consequence, these technologies do not create aggregate unemployment. For instance, although machines did take jobs from factory workers, they also created whole rafts of new jobs. These machines needed people to make, maintain and operate them. It is these complementary jobs that create employment.

However, there is a counter-argument that while this was true in the past, it will not be true in the future, and that the number of complementary jobs created this time will be relatively small. Consider Facebook's striking acquisition of WhatsApp for $19 billion in February 2014. WhatsApp had fifty-five employees at the time, but the deal valued it at almost the same as Sony with 140,000 employees. This certainly demonstrates the impact on employment – but there is another story here about income distribution. It is true that WhatsApp itself has very few employees. However, the ecosystem of partnerships supporting the WhatsApp service is much larger; for example, the product needs the internet for it to have value and the internet itself creates hundreds of thousands of jobs. The real concern is the 'winner takes all' nature of the industry, whereby a small number of individuals make large amounts of money but most employed in the industry do not.

From an economic perspective there is another factor of job creation. Factories and offices that use robots and AI tend to be more productive and so the cost of the product or service goes down. As costs go down, firms want to remain competitive and so they cut their prices. As prices are reduced, so demand for that product or service goes up and more people are therefore employed to meet this growing demand. It is true, of course, that each unit of output requires fewer people, but if output increases the result may be no loss of employment. Indeed those that remain in employment could have more income because they are more productive and this income is then spent on goods and services in other industries.

Another boost for new jobs will come as the result of technological innovation in the development of new products and services. Over the next decades there will be a host of new products that are as yet unimagined but will be seen as indispensable and will prove economically valuable. Peter Thiel, co-founder of PayPal, critically commented that we were promised flying cars and all we got was 140 characters. However that is one of the critical features of technology. No one could have foreseen how economically valuable Twitter would prove to be or how much time people would spend on it.

This is clearly an important debate with serious consequences for the coming decades. From a technological perspective the argument is that the rate of innovation is speeding up dramatically and machines will embody intelligence in a way that humans cannot compete with. Machines will replace humans in jobs and even an investment in education will no longer be sufficient to secure a safe career and a respectable income. The economic argument is more optimistic: technology will also bring complementary jobs, an increase in output and therefore increased employment; and whole new sectors will be created by as yet unforeseen products that will drive the economy forward.

What would be the advice to Jane?

Jane is now a young adult looking forward to a long life. Later we will build a number of scenarios to narrate the sort of long life she could have. What are the take-aways from this overview of the landscape of employment? While there is no agreement about the speed at which these effects will happen and what the net effect will be on employment, there is agreement that technology is shaking up the labour market and will continue to do so. The technologists argue that society as a whole will find it hard to secure jobs that pay well. The economists argue that while there will be many losers, there will also be many who gain, although they stress that the gains may be unevenly distributed across the population. Both agree that government policy will have to change in order to increase social security so as to protect the less skilled and the low paid. And both agree that many of the traditional jobs on which people have relied in the past will disappear.

So what would be the advice to Jane? In thinking of the jobs that will survive the rise of technology, consider two categories: those jobs where humans will have an *absolute advantage*, and those jobs where humans will have a *comparative advantage*. Having an absolute advantage means that humans are just better than robots or AI at performing the task. Going back to Polyani and Moravec's paradoxes, we could imagine that right now humans clearly have an advantage over robotics and AI in terms of creativity, empathy and problem solving, opening doors and much manual labour. Over the coming decades, as the labour market hollows out further, these will be the jobs that survive. No one is sure for how long. Some technologists believe that robotics and AI will eventually perform these tasks better than humans. But even if this is true, there will still be areas where humans have a comparative advantage and this is where future high-earning jobs lie.

There is also the issue of technology complementing human skills. This will continue with the rise of augmented work where humans and machines are more productive together.

This is already happening in the world of chess, where a group of amateur chess players augmented by mid-level machines were able to beat both Grand Masters and supercomputers working separately. We can expect to see a rapid development in this type of augmentation. Just as people currently bring their mobile device to work, it is possible that in future they will also bring their machine to work – chosen and programmed to best augment the individual's own unique capabilities.

We have sketched some of the changes that are likely to shape the labour market in coming decades. But it is worth recalling the force of Churchill's quote at the beginning of this chapter. For the outer years of Jane's career these projections will be of little use. This in turn raises a problem: it is hard to prepare for something if you don't know what is going to happen. Compared to Jack, in Jane's longer working career she will experience more change and face more uncertainty. So she will have to be more flexible and more aware that at some later date she will need to reorientate and reinvest. As the American novelist Paul Auster remarks: 'If you're not ready for everything, you're not ready for anything.'

4

Intangibles

Focusing on the priceless

As life elongates, periods of work become more extensive, savings more central, and across the passage of time, major transformations occur in industries and jobs. This is the broad sweep of a 100-year life. But to think about this only in terms of finances and work is to negate the very essence of being a human. The gift of a long life is fundamentally a much more intangible gift. In this chapter we focus on the priceless – on intangible assets.

Intangible assets play a crucial role in all our lives. For most of us, while money is indeed important, it is not an end in itself. We make money for what it can deliver for us. For most people, a good life would be one with a supportive family, great friends, strong skills and knowledge, and good physical and mental health. These are all intangible assets and it is not surprising they are as important as financial assets when it comes to building a productive long life.

However, these intangible assets are not independent from tangible ones; rather they play an important reciprocal role in the development of tangible assets. Take, for example, the strong skills and knowledge without which it is likely that career and earning potential will be very limited. The same is true of a network of supportive and knowledgeable friends, as it turns out that they are crucial for optimizing transitions and broadening career choice. And if you are in bad health or have an unhappy family home, then the stress that this creates significantly reduces productivity, empathy and creativity at work.

So intangible assets are key to a long and productive life – both as an end in themselves and also as an input into tangible assets. Indeed a good life needs both, as well as the balance and synergies between the two.

Asset management

Perhaps you have not thought about friendships and knowledge or health and fitness as *assets*. Most of us would not use this term in everyday life. But the idea of these as assets is a crucial framing for a 100-year life. An asset is something that can provide a flow of benefits over several periods of time. In other words, an asset is something that lasts for a while. So clearly, as life elongates, a major challenge is how these assets are managed. While assets can last for several periods, they usually suffer from some form of *depreciation* – that is, they diminish over time due to usage or neglect. This means that assets require careful maintenance and mindful investment. Viewed like this, it is clear why we would consider a friend, or knowledge, or health as an asset. Friends and knowledge don't disappear in a day, but if you fail to invest by not keeping contact with a friend or not refreshing your knowledge, then they will eventually depreciate and possibly even disappear.

Intangible assets differ significantly from tangible assets such as housing, cash, or savings in the bank. Tangible assets have a physical existence and so tend to be relatively simple to measure and define. As a result, they can be easily priced and readily traded and are therefore fairly straightforward to understand and monitor: bank statements can be checked; the price of a house verified on the internet; pensions followed carefully. Intangible assets such as friendships and family, physical and mental health, skills and knowledge lack this obvious physical existence, which creates challenges in how they are measured and whether they can be traded.

Some intangibles can be relatively easily measured. Clearly, measuring your health and vitality is reasonably straightforward and the health checks most of us have are designed to do just that and remind us whether our health has increased or depleted over a period of time. The same is true of some forms of skills and knowledge. The examinations we sit and certificates we receive are a measure of our explicit knowledge, although tacit knowledge is inherently more difficult to measure. What of friendships and relationships? Most people have some understanding of the health of their most important relationships, though would struggle to quantify this understanding. There are also growing attempts by network analysts to measure the size, variety and interconnectedness of an individual's network and, over time, to track the extent by which these are growing or depleting.[1] Rapid developments in augmented technology – which measure many aspects of daily behaviour such as miles walked, time spent talking with friends and so forth – will add to the sophistication with which intangible assets can be measured.

So some intangibles can be directly measured quantitatively or through a proxy, some only qualitatively (increasing/decreasing), while others remain elusive to measurement. Some of these measurements can be objectively compared – for example, the extent of education – while others, such as happiness, cannot. The evasive and elusive nature of intangibles and their often subjective character means that pricing them and trading them is sometimes impossible and invariably difficult. Further, as the political philosopher Michael Sandel argues, there is something even more profound about some intangible assets that make them 'priceless' and impossible to trade. Often there is something about their very essence and their history that makes intangible assets non-tradable. You simply can't buy (or indeed create) a lifelong friendship when you are in your 80s; in fact, perhaps the very definition of friendship means it can't be bought at any age.

The fact that intangibles can't be bought or sold in a marketplace makes planning and investing in them more complex. By comparison, decisions about investing in tangible assets are relatively straightforward. This is in part because these decisions are *reversible*. A house can be bought and sold at will and money can be moved from the stock market to a pension. And because tangible assets can be easily priced and bought and sold, they are easily *substitutable*: a house can be sold and another one bought, wealth can be shifted from equities into cash.

Intangibles, however, are neither substitutable nor reversible. If you move country you cannot sell one friend and buy another in a new place, and if the knowledge you have mastered is no longer valuable, it cannot simply be sold and new skills bought. The impact of this *irreversibility* is that care has to be taken when choices are made about investing in intangible assets and there has to be concern about a sudden loss in value. Just as an earthquake can render a house worthless, so external shifts can make intangible assets lose value.

Yet just because intangible assets can't be easily priced or traded doesn't mean they aren't valuable.[2] Questions about the importance of intangible assets relative to tangible assets is a recurring theme across literature and religions.[3] Take, for example, studies in the psychology of what creates a happy purposeful life. The Harvard Grant Study is particularly fascinating. It focused on a broad range of indicators for 268 male Harvard undergraduates from 1938–40 who were tracked for the following seventy-five years. The researchers discovered that tangible assets were indeed important – having little money, or less than your peer group, is a source of dissatisfaction. However, what emerged as one of the key predictors of life satisfaction were the deep and strong relationships the men had established throughout their lives.[4] In the words of George Valliant, the study's pioneer, there are two pillars to happiness: one is love; the other is finding a way of coping with life that doesn't push love away. Earning more does make you happier, but love makes you happy.

In the economics literature there is much interest in *Easterlin's Paradox,* which states that while it is true that wealthier people tend to be happier, there is no direct relationship between average happiness and average income. In other words, as a country becomes richer, happiness doesn't appear to increase and this suggests that other factors dominate in what gives people a sense of well-being.[5]

Of course, none of this means that money doesn't matter. While money can't buy intangible assets outright, you still need money and financial security to invest in your intangible assets;

money helps buy gym memberships, family holidays and peace of mind to share leisure with loved ones. And just as money helps support intangible assets, these in turn help support financial success. These are important inter-linkages and getting the balance right is crucial for planning for a 100-year life.

Asset-rich

Given this definition of intangible assets, the list of possibilities to consider is potentially huge. For instance, there is evidence that beauty is an important asset. Labour economist Daniel Hamermesh finds in his research that beautiful people get hired sooner, promoted quicker, and are paid 3–4 per cent more than their more average-looking colleagues.[6] People who are taller get paid more,[7] and there is a range of studies that document the impact of gender and racial characteristics on income.

According to the earlier definition, each of these characteristics could count as an intangible asset – they are capable of providing a flow of benefits over long periods of time and they cannot be physically separated, priced and traded. Clearly the same holds for a wide range of other individual characteristics, such as general intelligence, genetic inheritance in terms of health, being born into an educated and wealthy family, or basic personality traits such as a positive disposition, low neuroticism or sociability. The range of possible intangible assets is therefore potentially large and there are many innate or genetic factors that may influence destiny.

In our analysis, we remove those intangible assets that are part of an individual's endowment when they were born. Instead we focus on those intangible assets that are a choice variable, the factors that an individual can actually influence and affect. It is not possible, for example, to choose to become more beautiful or more intelligent, or to be born into a more educated family, or to have a more positive disposition. That is not to deny the fact that one could shape these assets through enhancements such as cosmetic surgery, or through behavioural therapy to become, for example, more sociable. However, our starting point is that for these endowed intangibles the relative ratio of what is fixed and what is malleable is such that we should consider them as predetermined.

Excluding these endowed intangibles still leaves a wide range of possible intangibles. So we then selected and grouped them in a way that makes sense to a long life, creating three distinct categories.

1   The first category of intangibles is *productive assets*. These are the assets that help an individual become productive and successful at work and should therefore boost their income. Obviously, skills and knowledge will be a major component of this category, but there is much else as well.

2   The second category is *vitality assets*. Broadly these capture mental and physical health and well-being. Included here are friendship, positive family relationships and partnerships, as well as personal fitness and health. Longitudinal studies suggest that high stocks of vitality assets are a key component in a measure of a good life.

3   The final category is *transformational assets*. Across a 100-year life, people will experience great change and many transitions. These transformational assets refer to their self-knowledge, their capacity to reach out into diverse networks and their openness to new experiences. This group of assets has been relatively under-utilized within a traditional three-stage life but will become crucial in a multi-stage life.

1. Productive assets

Productive assets are those intangibles that support productivity at work and boost income and career prospects. Of course, many intangible assets indirectly affect working capability – when you are ill or unhappy in your relationships then your work will undoubtedly suffer; however here the focus is on those assets that are directly aimed at productivity. This is not to say they should only be valued for reasons of productivity; they undoubtedly also have a hugely important role to play in creating a general sense of well-being.

Stocks of valuable skills and knowledge

The most obvious examples of productive assets are the skills and knowledge you have acquired over time. Stocks of knowledge are built as a result of the allocation of significant periods of time to education, engaging in specific types of work and learning on the job, or spending time with coaches, mentors or peers. This is crucial in view of the extraordinary speed at which both the market for jobs and the acquisition of skills is developing. This leaves some important questions about how best to invest in stocks of skills and knowledge and in particular what to focus on.

The returns on learning and education

Over a long productive life, investing in knowledge and skills is a priority. The financial benefits to be gained from learning and education are significant. At the time of writing, a 22-year-old graduate in the US is on average likely to earn $30,000 a year compared to $18,000 for someone without a college education. The gap between them continues to increase over time, reaching a peak in their mid-40s, when the college graduate earns nearly $80,000 compared to $30,000 for the high school graduate. The implied average return to education is as high as 15 per cent over and above inflation.[8] If these sorts of rates of return continue, then we can definitely expect some of the extra years that longevity brings to be spent on education. Throughout the twentieth century, average years of schooling in the US have risen from seven to fourteen years, and this could well continue to rise further.

Technological innovation will have a significant impact on the job market. Indeed the Harvard economists Claudia Goldin and Larry Katz describe a race between education and technology.[9] Technology has been, to date, a complement to education; as technology advanced, so too did the salaries awarded for skilled jobs. Those without education saw their wages fall and society saw inequality rise, but the return to education was clearly leading to rising numbers of individuals going to college. The result is that today around 25–30 per cent of the working population in the US have a degree and this proportion is rising.

With college degrees so prevalent, and with the onward march of technology, it will be very natural that some people will use these additional years of life for postgraduate study. Postgraduate qualifications tend to be about specialization, and provide a signal of commitment and a detailed knowledge that helps a person stand out in the labour market. Further, as IT continues to hollow out the labour market, more and more individuals will increasingly try to achieve the top end of the skills distribution and distinguish themselves with postgraduate qualifications.

However, as investment advisors are required to say, 'past results do not predict future performance', and there could be a turning point in terms of the returns to education and the continual growth in numbers in further education. There is no doubt that the 'what, when and how' of acquiring stocks of skills and knowledge will change substantially.

It may be that over a 100-year life substantial knowledge acquisition will no longer take place in one shot, completed early in life. Given the degree of likely technological advances, it seems impossible to imagine that a specialism learnt early in a career will sustain someone through their long working life. Either through boredom or technological obsolescence, the acquisition of new skills and new specialisms will become a lifelong endeavour. Given that across a 100-year lifespan there are 873,000 hours available and if, as is often claimed, a specialist expertise takes 10,000 hours to acquire, then mastery in more than one field is neither daunting nor impossible.

Valuing knowledge

Learning is an important part of life and has a value way beyond the income it can generate. Nelson Mandela was right when he said 'Education is the most powerful weapon which you can use to change the world', and he wasn't talking about GDP or income. There is a lot of sense in choosing to learn what one is passionate about and interested in. However, for most people, income matters – and it matters even more over the course of a 100-year life. Looking forward, is it possible to know what might be the subjects of passion and interest that will also secure a good income?

In the abstract this is an easy question to answer. The emphasis should be on acquiring stocks of skills and knowledge that are *valuable* – in other words, they are in demand as useful – and *rare*. Not many people have them, hence the earlier prediction regarding the rise in postgraduate education. These skills and knowledge also have to be *difficult to imitate*, so those who have them have a head start compared to others.[10] And they must be hard to *substitute*. It is this last characteristic that technological developments threaten the most and is the most challenging in terms of learning and educational choices.

The greatest current concern is the rise of machine learning and AI. Given these technological developments, what stocks of skills and knowledge could remain valuable and how can they be developed? In generic terms there are three key areas where education and learning and development can help support careers, given the shifts in technology: in supporting the development of ideas and creativity; in enabling human skills and empathy; and in developing core portable general skills such as mental flexibility and agility.

There is likely to be a rise in importance of education that supports the creation of ideas and the value of being *innovative and creative*. If the nineteenth century was about the Industrial Revolution and the power provided by physical capital, then the twentieth century was about the advantage of education and human capital. The twenty-first century, however, will be about adding value by coming up with ideas and innovations that can be replicated or purchased by others. Indeed this is already happening at the authors' own institution of London Business School, where there is an ever-increasing emphasis on the part of both students and firms on ideas and innovation, creativity and entrepreneurship.

Aligned to this is the growing importance of *human skills and judgement*. There are those who argue that even these skills can be performed by AI – pointing, for example, to the development of IBM's supercomputer Watson, which is able to perform detailed oncological diagnosis. This means that with diagnostic augmentation, the skill set for the medical profession will shift from information retrieval to deeper intuitive experience, more person-to- person skills and greater emphasis on team motivation and judgement. The same technological developments will occur in the education sector, where digital teaching will replace textbooks and classroom teaching and the valuable skills will move towards the intricate human skills of empathy, motivation and encouragement.

Across a long productive life there will be an increasing focus on general portable skills and capabilities such as *mental flexibility and agility*. This raises an interesting conflict between this need for general skills and the importance of valuable specialization. Specialization is important and necessary, and when developed in an area of accelerating importance then it can also be valuable. The conundrum is that no single specialization is likely to be sufficient to support productivity over long working careers. And given the rate of technological churn, any specialization runs a high risk of obsolescence. So it is more likely that people will choose to specialize at one stage in their working life and then later re-specialize as they shift into other intellectual areas and activities. As a result, formal education will increasingly create opportunities to build foundational analytical abilities and principles. Building these foundations then creates an opportunity to be flexible and innovative and to span disciplines. So while a specialist subject will require a deep dive into pools of knowledge to achieve career success and signal the ability for sustained and accurate thought, this is unlikely to be sufficient to sustain a whole career. And because people can expect to move across jobs and sectors, having portable, highly credentialized knowledge and skills will be essential.

So the debate is ongoing. Some believe that the importance of human and empathic skills and judgement and the focus on creativity and innovation all suggest that an updated form of liberal arts education may be surprisingly valuable. Others argue that in a world where technology and science is becoming ever more important, an education in science, technology, engineering or mathematics remains key and the most valuable productive asset. Of course, in a long life it need not be either/ or – perhaps it will be possible to do both.

As well as shifts in what we learn, there will also be changes in how we learn, and in particular a rise in *experiential learning*. This is the learning that goes beyond textbooks or classroom learning and is developed through action. In part, the value of experiential learning will increase as simple knowledge acquisition becomes so much easier because of the developments of web and online learning. So what will separate people is not what they know, but rather what they have experienced using this knowledge. This is a consequence of the two paradoxes (Polyani and Moravec) that we discussed earlier and the increasing importance of tacit knowledge – that which cannot be codified. This tacit knowledge, though hard to build, is very valuable. It is the basis of wisdom, insight and intuition and is built through practice, repetition and observation.

It is also likely that what is valuable from an employer's perspective is not simply being 'book smart' but also having real world savvy. While experiential learning will undoubtedly form part of the undergraduate and postgraduate experience, its development will grow in other settings. In the scenarios described later, we explicitly create a number of new stages that are focused on acquiring valuable skills and knowledge through experiential learning. As we shall show, while there are many advantages of experiential learning, one challenge is that education-based learning is much easier to certify and credentialize.

Peers

Skills and knowledge appear to be very individualistic. Education certificates reflect an individual's abilities and performance, and all academic institutions heavily penalize plagiarism or cheating. However, it turns out that how we acquire knowledge and how productive we are depends very much on others. Making knowledge productive is, in other words, a team game. The critical interdependencies in most complex high-value tasks mean that highly productivity people want to be matched with other highly productivity people. As Harvard economist Michael Kremer tartly notes,[11] Charlie Parker used to perform with Dizzy Gillespie while Donny Osmond sang with Marie Osmond.

The importance of others is clearly demonstrated in a fascinating study by Boris Groysberg of Harvard Business School.[12] His interest was in the value a person creates, and the value created by them in combination with others around them. To understand this balance, Groysberg examined the careers of more than a thousand analysts employed at Wall Street investment banks. If these star analysts' individual stocks of knowledge were directly translated into their individual productivity, then when they move to another bank their performance should remain the same. If their performance was also dependent on others, then when they left the bank for another their performance would decline. Groysberg discovered that this was indeed the case; the analysts' knowledge was not portable in its entirety and, as a consequence, their performance suffered an immediate and often lasting decline.

Why was the knowledge and skills of these analysts not portable and what lessons can be drawn from this? There are clearly firm-specific aspects – proprietary resources, organizational culture – that are important in converting an individual's stock of knowledge into productivity and performance. What is important here is Groysberg's finding that not all firms are the same in their capacity to convert an individual's skills into performance. This suggests that when you think about maximizing your stocks of knowledge, you would be wise to search carefully, since finding the right match is crucial. What was also apparent from the study is that the networks of associates and colleagues that the analysts built within the bank were crucial to their performance. These turned out to be particularly effective if the team trusted each other and had a positive regard for each other's reputation. This effect was so crucial that when an analyst's performance actually did remain the same or increase when they moved firms, it was almost always the case that their own team moved with them. Without this network effect the majority of stars that switched firms turned out to be meteors, quickly losing lustre in their new settings.

These networks and relationships are an important aspect of productive assets and we term them *professional social capital*.[13] The strong relationships you develop enable knowledge to flow easily between people and help bolster your productivity and innovation. That is because those close collaborative relationships, rich in trust and reputation, allow you to access much wider areas of knowledge and insight than your personal knowledge stocks. This creates a fertile ground for working collaboratively with others and creates the opportunity for the combining of insights. This combination effect turns out to be especially important in innovation.[14]

It would seem that what is particularly crucial to developing productive assets are small work-based networks of colleagues that have strong, trusting relationships between each other. When you have this, then you are able to share similar skills and expertise with ease and support each other in your professional development. In Lynda's studies of collaboration, she called this the *posse*. This is a network of close professional relationships with people who have mutual trust, who coach and support each other, introduce each other to their own network and are prepared to give important and valuable advice.[15]

So how does a posse develop? Like many aspects of social capital, it takes time. It happens when you are prepared and able to devote extended periods of time to building relationships with people in your similar skill and knowledge set and to spend time in face-to-face conversations. It is in these focused times that deep expertise is developed and shared.[16]

Reputation

Leaders of large corporations such as Coca-Cola or Apple know that much of the value of their company is not held in specific physical items or tangible assets, such as the factories and shops they may own. Instead it is located within intangible assets like brand or intellectual property rights. For example, the brand 'Apple' is estimated to be worth substantially more than $100 billion. Although laboratories, factories and shops are crucial for Apple to design, produce and distribute, some of their intangible value comes from their brand.

The same is true of personal brands. As far back as medieval times in Europe and Asia, artisans could value their products in part on their brand. Discussing medieval craftsmen, the sociologist Richard Sennett remarks: 'The single most pressing earthly obligation of a medieval artisan was the establishment of a good personal reputation. This was especially an urgent matter for itinerant craftsmen such as goldsmiths, who were strangers in many of the places they worked.'[17] The artisans' reputation was built over time and provided predictable quality – a customer could order an object knowing that it would meet the quality they expected. Brand and reputation are as important now as they were hundreds of years ago. When a company has a positive brand, or a person a good reputation, it is much easier for others to interact with them. If a company has a good reputation, you as a consumer don't need to monitor or investigate them closely, since their reputation is the mark of what you can expect. The same is true of a person. If they have a good reputation, then they can be trusted to behave competently under a variety of circumstances.

So in building productive assets, a good reputation can be enormously important as it enables your valuable stocks of skills and knowledge to be really utilized in a productive way. It can also have a profound impact on your professional social capital. Without a good reputation, it is unlikely you would be able to bring together a valuable group of colleagues.

Like any other intangible asset, a good reputation has to be invested in and acquired over time; it can provide a flow of value over time, it cannot be bought or sold, and it can depreciate quickly. You have a good reputation if you have historically behaved in a cooperative or trustworthy way, and a bad reputation if you have a history of behaving in a selfish or deceptive way. Reputation is, of course, in the eye of the beholder – it is others who decide whether you have a good reputation. How do they do this? In part, reputation is conferred by association. Those people who attend certain schools or work for specific companies which are thought to have a good reputation benefit from association, which signals to others they have a good reputation unless proved otherwise. The same was true for medieval artisans; their membership of a prestigious guild or fraternity conferred on them a good reputation even though they were itinerant. Throughout history, the membership of an elite community or corporation has sent out strong reputational signals. While these associations are important initially, over time reputation is conferred by the behaviours others see. Intentions and statements of principle set an expectation, but it is fundamentally actions that cement a reputation.

So what is it that others see in you? Obviously, in a community of any size, it is difficult to pay attention to the behaviours of all individuals, so people tend to notice only selective information. Some of these perceptions are first-hand reputation through direct experience, but much will inevitably be second-hand as you are described by others. So the social structure around you behaves rather like a broadcast system, constantly transmitting information to an audience, the signal multiplying as it diffuses.[18] Indeed, the importance of this social structure in the creation and dissemination of a reputation means that reputation is not an asset that you own. Instead it is created within the set of beliefs, perceptions and evaluations a community forms about you. The inevitable consequence is that although a good reputation is a valuable intangible asset, it is also a complex asset. While it is a product of your history of behaviour and can have an important impact on your capacity to be productive, it is never fully under your control.

As careers spread across more companies, sectors and different skills, one of the threads that connect intangible value over time will be a good reputation. This is particularly crucial at times when you decide to change jobs or sectors. Just as firms use their brand reputation to enter new markets, so a good reputation will be one of the assets that enable you to expand your horizons. It is the combination of portable skills and knowledge and a good reputation that will help bridge into new fields. Your reputation for fairness and integrity, for getting things done, for being flexible and trustworthy are all examples of reputations that can carry a value across many roles and jobs.

Over the coming decades it is likely that reputation will be based on a broader range of inputs. For those who pursued a three-stage career, much of their reputation depended on their specialist skills and knowledge and their track record. As future careers embrace more stages and more transitions, then inevitably this will create a broader range of information. At the same time, social media will increasingly broadcast your image and values to others and allow others to track and monitor performance. So it is inevitable that you will need to curate a brand and reputation that covers far more than just your professional behaviour.

Of course, with this public exposure comes scrutiny, and just as a good reputation will be broadcast, so too will the antisocial behaviours that result in a bad reputation. As communities become more highly connected, so people will strive to engage more thoughtfully in self-presentation to maintain and enhance their positive reputation. As life elongates, the impact of reputation is felt over a longer period. And just as a good reputation can be built over time, so too can it be lost. Social media can be a virulent and dramatic way of destroying reputation and having a lasting impact.[19]

2. Vitality assets

Physical and mental health and psychological well-being are crucial intangibles. When people are asked what makes a good life, they tend to talk about health, friendships and love. We term these intangibles *vitality assets*. They are what make us feel happy and fulfilled, motivated and positive.

Fitness and health

Many of us live in a society in which there is an increasing focus on the need to be fit and healthy. This is crucial in the context of the 100-year life, because a longer life is not an automatic right bestowed on everyone. It is true that children born today have long life expectancy as a result of better genetic and nutritional inheritance. It is also true that longevity is boosted by continual improvements in technology and increasing finances to pay for treatment. However, public knowledge and changes in behaviour play a crucial role too. So following best practice advice on healthy living is a cornerstone of making the most of the gift of longevity.

Fitness and health become more valuable over a longer life. The cost of being incapacitated from work aged 50 when life expectancy is 100 is much greater than when life expectancy was 70. The multi-stage 100-year life is simply not possible with poor health, and the consequences, both financial and non financial, can be dramatic. Just as there are habits of healthy financial planning, so to there are habits of healthy living. What you eat, how much you eat, and whether you take regular and specific exercise are all important aspects of your investment in intangible assets. Over time medical advice and knowledge will continue to shift and develop, so it will be important to invest time in learning about health developments and adjusting behaviour and habits.

Perhaps the most important insight about well being is the growing awareness of maintaining a healthy and well-functioning brain. It turns out that our actions and behaviour are important here. While studies suggest that genetic inheritance accounts for about one-third of the rate of mental decline, the rest is dependent on lifestyle: on daily actions, community involvement, strong relationships, physical fitness and diet.[20]

This is an important new insight because, until relatively recently, the consensus was that as people age their brain cells die. That was the explanation for why older people sometimes had trouble remembering and seemed less mentally adept. It turns out this is not the case and the idea of *neoplasticity* is emerging. This imagines the brain more as a muscle, where repeated use and practice can change how it operates and can aid its recovery. With lack of use, like any muscle, the brain withers and becomes feeble. So while brain cells don't die as people age, the size and weight of the brain does decrease. It seems that after the age of 50 the brain starts to shrink, and after 80 it does so more substantially. The research on what can be done to make a positive impact on brain development is in its infancy, but there are already a few and somewhat commonsensical proposals emerging. It is no surprise that physical exercise is an important factor in avoiding mental decline. Exactly why is not clear (is it more oxygen to the brain or the stimulation of growth hormones?) but several studies suggest a significant role. Other recommendations are low-fat diets, plenty of vegetables and fruit and oily fish, Omega 3 fatty acids and vitamin B12, and of course cognitive training and mental exercise. All seem relevant and all have some research to support them, although exactly how important they are remains to be established.

Balanced living

The antithesis of vitality is stress. Across the world, work-related stress levels are soaring and with this comes a plethora of health issues, from heart attacks to general disability. A recent study by the World Health Organization reported that the percentage of workers in the UK who say they are working 'very hard' or 'under a great deal of tension' had risen steadily since the 1980s. The results of this stress can be devastating. Stress at work is associated with a 20 per cent increased risk of heart disease and a range of other mental and physical health issues. And this is not just a UK phenomenon. In a 2009 global survey of 1,000 corporations across seventy-five countries, more than

60 per cent of workers reported that they had experienced increased workplace stress.[21]

What is clear is that building and sustaining vitality assets is in part about managing the triggers of stress. To understand this better, some years ago Lynda and her fellow researcher Dr Hans-Joachim Wolfran studied over 200 people employed in complex, knowledge-based work.[22] They found that being at work and being at home were not hermetically sealed existences. Rather, most people experience *emotional spillover* between the two places and the effect of this spillover could have a positive or negative impact on stress and therefore vitality.

You experience positive emotional spillover when you leave home in the morning feeling supported and relaxed and take these positive feelings into work; you leave work later in the day feeling productive, having learnt new skills and built interesting networks and bring these positive emotions and resources into the home. The emotional flow between work and home can also be negative. You leave home feeling tired and guilty, the kids are unhappy and you know that you are not giving your partner the support and encouragement they need. As you start working, these negative feelings of guilt and exhaustion immediately spill over and influence how you feel about the day ahead and the tasks you want to perform. This lack of emotional resources and vitality has a negative impact on creativity and innovation, and in the long term leads to increased stress and the erosion of vitality.

In Chapter 9 we take a close look at this balance as we consider how home and partnerships are transforming and the impact this has on emotional vitality. We describe the various ways in which you can ensure that you experience the positive aspects of home (support and relaxation) rather than the negative (exhaustion and guilt), and the positive aspects of work (productivity, new skills, interesting networks) rather than the negative (frustration and boredom). Fundamentally it comes down to the choices and decisions you make about the work you do, how you negotiate your role with your partner, and the way you allocate your time.

Regenerative friendships

The development of a posse of like-minded peers builds the professional social capital that supports us in staying productive. However, it is the network of close, positive friends who will keep you sane and happy and contribute to your vitality asset. In her book *The Shift*, Lynda called these types of long-established and rich friendships the *Regenerative Community*, to reinforce the role these people can play in regeneration.[23] Whether it is the Harvard longitudinal study mentioned earlier or studies of communities of people who enjoy vitality into their old age, they all inevitably show the same phenomenon – people who are well connected to others are more vital, energetic and positive than those who are isolated.[24]

These networks are subtly different from those that are the foundation of professional social capital. Regenerative friendships typically are built over many years; indeed it is not unusual for them to reach back into the early days of education or working, when people are at a stage of their life when they are more 'plastic' about the development of relationships. These regenerative relationships are often *multi-stranded*, in the sense that you know your friend across many different circumstances and in different roles – at home, with their family – and inevitably share some common interests. These multiple strands are crucial to prolonging your friendship and bringing it depth. As a consequence, these relationships tend to be *emotionally laden*, in the sense that you are both investing your feelings and emotions, and if the friendship breaks or changes you feel upset and sometimes baffled. It is this emotionality that brings the support that is so crucial to vitality.

These multi-stranded, emotionally laden relationships play a central role in well-being and vitality. They provide the backdrop to a working life and often, when they reach back in time, they support the narrative and commentary about life and identity.

Over 100 years, these sorts of deep, emotionally laden friendships will be both harder to keep and also more valuable. Harder to keep because, as people live for longer and go through more transitions, the ties that bind them will loosen and potentially break as their sense of identity changes. However, their value will increase as some of these friendships will continue to be the thread that defines the basis of a life identity.

Jack's intangible assets

A major challenge over a lifetime is not just achieving the right level of tangible and intangible assets but also keeping the two in balance. Over a long life, this interplay becomes even more complicated and is at the root of why a three-stage life is no longer optimal. Earlier we modelled the tangible assets of Jack, Jimmy and Jane, and considered how growing longevity affects their finances. Now we review their productivity and vitality intangible assets.

Tracking intangible assets is more complicated than financial assets because they are so difficult to measure with any accuracy and therefore to value. Stock market analysts can use a company's share price to deduce the value of its intangible assets, such as brand and reputational value. It is not so straightforward with individual intangible assets, though economists are able to infer from the choices you make how much you value different activities. But it simply isn't easy or perhaps even helpful to try and put a monetary value on intangible assets. However, although it is not possible to make a definitive value statement at any point in time, it is possible to infer the direction. Specifically we can ask: has the intangible asset decreased or increased depending on developmental activities? This is the qualitative approach we take here as we consider the state of Jack's intangible assets.

We begin by hypothetically modelling the appreciation and depreciation of Jack's tangible and intangible assets over the course of his life. We look at his asset flow over the three key working phases of his life. In Figure 4.1 we show how Jack's assets rise and fall over his life. When his assets are increasing this is a result of investment by Jack, but when his assets fall this is because of a lack of investment and focus by Jack, so that his assets depreciate – or in the case of financial assets, this occurs when Jack runs down his assets. We make the following, admittedly stylized, representation of Jack's asset flow.

The narrative we have built of Jack's life goes something like this. He made an early investment in productive assets: he took a college course and began to build his knowledge and skills – we show this by his *productive assets* rising in this first phase. During his college years, Jack is heavily investing in skills and knowledge. He is also making friends with some people in his field who could form his peer group throughout his career. Through his academic performance he is also establishing a reputation. Jack enjoys student life and has a wide circle of friends

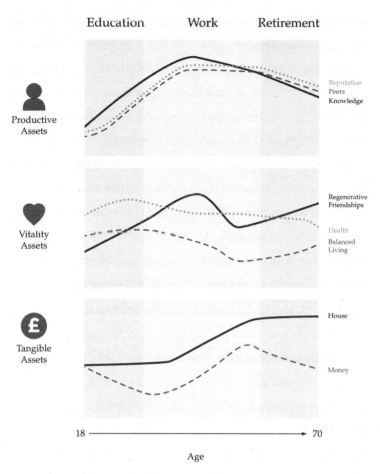

Education   Work   Retirement

Productive Assets

Reputation
Peers
Knowledge

Vitality Assets

Regenerative
Friendships

Health
Balanced
Living

Tangible Assets

House

Money

18 —————————————————→ 70

Age

FIGURE 4.1 *Jack's three-stage asset flow.*

who introduce him to new ideas (regenerative friendships) as
well as his future wife. Although he studies hard, he also has a
good social life, so he is balancing living and being young with
a social life that also incorporates sport as he builds his health.

Obviously student debt and paying rent means that his tangible assets are diminishing.

When Jack leaves college, he joins a local manufacturing company – let's call it Makewell. This is important for his productive assets as he joins a team and establishes a supportive community of peers who mentor and coach him. Notice, though, that while these peers are helpful in supporting him to do his work better, this is not a time when he is investing in building much new valuable knowledge and skills other than learning on the job. During these years, Jack gets married, starts a family and buys a house, financed with a large mortgage. His social network is narrowing to those in his new neighbourhood and the parents of friends of his children. Balanced living is becoming difficult. Jack is working hard for promotion and securing the money to finance his household, meaning his family and friends see less of him. The emotional energy flow between work and home is becoming negative; he leaves work tired after a hard day, and arrives home to find a family of small children. That is why this is a period of depletion – indeed it is a period that for many people is crowded with long working days and building a family.

In his mid-40s, Jack leaves Makewell to move to another company in the same sector – let's call it Construct – and achieves a significant promotion through the move. In this role he is shifting from his specific area of expertise and is now involved in broader general management at a senior level. In this more senior role, Jack finds it harder to construct a work-related community of peers and by now his valuable knowledge and skills are beginning to depreciate, as he has made no further major investment in these since leaving college. He hasn't learnt a new skill and acquired new knowledge, or built his professional social capital by investing time with colleagues who could push his ideas forward. This depletion continues over his career but he is buoyed by the small group of peers he established earlier in his professional life and his specialist knowledge lasts just long enough for him to retire without being completely lost in his profession. On the tangible asset side, by the time he retires Jack has achieved his financial aim of paying off the mortgage and reaching his goal in terms of the size of his pension pot.

At retirement Jack can start to invest again in his physical and mental health, take up long-postponed hobbies and spend more time with his family and friends while running down the financial assets he accumulated during his working life. For Jack, as it is for many people, this is a happy and contented period of his life.

The imbalances of a three-stage life

Stepping back and looking at this stylized vision of Jack's life reveals a number of stark realities. It is clear that this version of his life works as a whole. While various periods of life have a different focus, and so at any point in time the assets do not balance, across the three-stage life there is a balance between tangible and intangible assets.

Yet if Jack's balance works as a whole, it most definitely isn't due entirely to his efforts. Jack's primary focus is on building tangible assets, especially during his second working stage. In his 'traditional' household relationship, it is his wife Jill who is tending to the intangible assets during this period by caring for the children and connecting the family to the community and friends. The combination of both their actions and motivations together create the balance. The fact that Jack's retirement is a good one is a result of his wife's focus on their intangible assets during his second stage. Without that, Jack's life as a whole would be completely unbalanced.

Even if this traditional relationship ever existed as a norm, we have witnessed over recent decades a restructuring of marriage and household partnerships. In fact, some argue that marriage in the traditional sense is disappearing and what is emerging is a plurality of possible lifestyles. In part this reflects social justice and rising equality, as women claim the political right to a wider choice of roles in the three-stage life. As a partnership, Jack and Jill's life may have achieved a balance of tangibles and intangibles but individually there were many times when it did not. The rising numbers of dual career/job/ income households will also impact on this. As we remarked earlier, under certain conditions having both adult members of a household working helps finance savings and pensions, but of course it raises the question of how the household then maintains its intangible assets.

The other intangible imbalance that is clear from Jack's three-stage life is just how little investment is happening in the second stage. Take a look at Figure 4.1 to see how front-ended his investment is. His career succeeded because he made heavy investments in his productive assets during education and the launch stage of his career. During that period of time his sharp focus on financial accumulation meant his vitality assets were basically being neglected.

Because of these imbalances it is clear that while the three-stage life worked well for Jack, it isn't optimal over a long life. A longer second stage of relentless work will result in too much depletion of important intangible assets and, over time, a run-down in productive assets. The run-down in vitality assets brings to mind the curse of Ondine and an exhausted and zombie-like existence driven by money. A longer third stage of retirement may sound attractive, but can only be supported by significant financial accumulation and savings in the second stage, and could even turn into tedium if not managed properly.

3. A new asset class: Transformational assets

If achieving a balance of tangible and intangible assets over a 100-year life within a three-stage model is challenging, then a natural consequence is the emergence of a multi-stage life. We cannot know exactly what this multi-stage life will look like, but there are some broad predictions we can make. It is likely that the first stage of education will last longer. This will give people more time to acquire and accumulate the intangible assets that will act as a buffer for a longer second stage. It will also create the opportunity to develop the greater specialization that will be so important in facing up to the threat of technological obsolescence. We predict that the second stage of work will fragment. To avoid knowledge stocks hitting zero, fitness and motivation disappearing, and friends and family disconnecting, most people will want to split their career into various stages, each with its own character and purpose. Technological innovations and sectoral shifts will bring flux, and being able to refresh and reskill at more points than Jack will become crucial.

So if a multi-stage life is the way to achieve balance between tangibles and intangibles, then it will require the development of a new asset class. We call these *transformational assets* and they reflect the capacity and motivation to successfully achieve change and transitions.

What sort of transitions will you face? Some transitions will be forced upon you by external circumstances: your skills could become technologically obsolete or the business you work for could close. There will also be those that you will have to initiate: you have to leave a job to go into full-time education, or transition from an exploration phase to a high-powered corporate role. Some of these changes will be difficult and unsettling, and of course the more difficult they are, the less likely you are to prepare for them. Transformational assets assist this process. They increase the ability to deal with the uncertainty of transition.

In some traditional tribal societies, these transitions – for example, from childhood to adulthood – are achieved through a series of rituals. Anthropologists who study these tribal rituals observe that the passage across the threshold of childhood and adulthood is often crucial. They use the term *liminality* to describe the ambiguity and disorientation they observe in the middle stage, when participants no longer hold their pre-ritual status but have not yet begun the transition to the status they will hold when the ritual is complete.[25] This liminality can also be seen in studies of transitions in modern societies. Professor Herminia Ibarra has spent the last two decades watching people make transitions. She has found that, like tribal rituals, there is often an intermediate point when those in transition are 'betwixt and between'.[26] This is an uncomfortable place where past identity is beginning to disappear, but a new one has not yet been established – where the security of the past is left, but the success of the future remains unknown.

Transformational assets are those that help increase the success of transitions and reduce the uncertainty and costs of change. Jack had little need for transformational assets and limited stock of them. He started his working life in the 1960s imagining a linear path, working in two companies most of his life and settling into a series of comfortable roles that involved very little stretch. For Jack, and most others of his age, the *psychological contract* between the employer and employee was clear: the corporation would provide full-time work and a wage, and the employee would be prepared to work diligently,[27] ideally in the same firm, until they retired. In this scenario, the qualities of seniority and maturity would be valued and respected.

In the late 1980s, when Jack was in his mid-40s, this all began to change.[28] Those who studied employment patterns reported seeing a significant rise in mobility – businesses no longer offered a job for life and employees wanted more flexibility. The contract had shifted from relational to transactional and was becoming more short-term and performance-based. The external environment also became more challenging as the rising importance of globalization led to significant job losses, forcing transition on many of Jack's peers.

This shift caught Jack unaware and unprepared. He had to scramble to find another job, but his financial strength was such that he had enough assets to see him through. Given the stability Jack had expected and his limited amount of transformational assets, these changes caused him some anxiety at the time. But he was not called upon to make any significant transitions in terms of skills, role or identity and over time the anxiety subsided.

By contrast, Jimmy was born into a world where job mobility was becoming the norm. As he grew up, Jimmy heard more and more about what this flexibility meant.[29] So if the old contract was with the organization, in the new career the contract was with the self and one's work. Organizations had become the context, a medium in which an individual could pursue their personal aspirations. By the time Jimmy was in his 30s there was an avalanche of books about how to manage your career.

If Jimmy's career involved more transitions and change than Jack's, then Jane will see even more. As we will show later when we develop a range of scenarios for Jimmy and Jane, there are sure to be more stages and more changes. Jane won't simply be changing employers but also probably sector. The most significant transitions in her life will not be forced upon her by external market circumstances, but rather she will instigate them in order to maintain her intangible asset base.

Understanding how people make successful transitions has become a priority for groups of psychologists and sociologists.

While there are a number of studies, ideas and theories, there are three interrelated elements of transformation that have come to the fore. The first is the idea that successful transformation only happens when people have some understanding of themselves, both as they are now, and how they might be in the future. This becomes what the sociologist Anthony Giddens describes as the 'reflexive project', a more or less continuous interrogation of the past, present and future, and this requires *self-knowledge*.[30] Next, those who have observed people in transition discovered that, in the process, they reach out into new communities and those who had already created these *dynamic/diverse networks* found transitions easier. With these networks they were able to draw from a wider social context for role models, images and symbols of what they could be. Third, what became very clear from these studies is that making a transition is not a passive experience. People do not *think* their way into change – as Ibarra so powerfully reminds us – they *act* their way into change. It is this *openness to experience* that brings dynamism to the transformational asset.

Self-knowledge

In traditional working lives like the one we sketched for Jack, the sense of self was in part conferred by his status and roles. With a longer life, identity will be based more on what you do than on where you started, and the more roles you take the less useful any one role will be in determining your identity. Now identity is being crafted rather than assumed or inherited and, for this process of crafting, self-knowledge plays an important role.

You understand and learn about yourself better when you are prepared to receive feedback, to seek out and hear what others think, and then reflect on this. This reflection is important. All of us are able to add information to the way we think about ourselves and our world. What differentiates those who are actively building transformational assets is that they are not simply adding information, they are changing their sense of themselves and the way they see the world. Their understanding of themselves is becoming larger, more complex, and more able to deal with multiple demands and uncertainty. Transformation occurs, argues the psychologist Robert Kegan, when people are able to step back and reflect on something and make decisions about it. It occurs when someone changes not just the way they behave, not just the way they feel, but the way they know – not just what they know, but how.[31]

As crafting becomes more important in our identity, then our sense of self reaches deep into the future as we develop what psychologists Hazel Markus and Paula Nurius call *possible selves*. These possible selves are future articulations of who we might be and what we might do. They represent alternatively an ideal of what we might become, what we would like to become or what we are afraid of becoming. Some stand as symbols of hope, others as reminders of bleak, sad or tragic futures that we would want to avoid.[32] Combined with self-knowledge, these possible selves serve as a powerful incentive to future behaviour, what is to be approached and avoided, and by doing so frame behaviour and guide its course. We utilize this idea of possible selves when we consider the scenarios for Jimmy and Jane and how they can make the most of a longer life.

Self-knowledge is needed to plot a path through change and transitions and, above all, to provide a sense of identity and coherence. When we know something of ourselves then we are more able to choose a path that provides a sense of purpose and integrity to our life. That means we are able to avoid a life path characterized by flux, whether induced through external circumstances or periodic shifts in job and location. This self-knowledge helps make sure that future stages are more likely to succeed and that change is viewed as less threatening to a sense of identity. Shifts in identity are troubling and, if something changes, this raises the issue of what remains the same. The anthropologist Charlotte Linde has listened to many life stories.[33] What she found particularly striking was the energy people put into building a life narrative that had coherence. To shape this, there has to be both *continuity* (what is it about me that remains the same) and *causality* (what is it that has happened to me that explains the change). She discovered that deep self-knowledge plays a crucial role in shaping both these features.

Diverse networks

For Jack, his reference groups remained the same throughout much of his life. Later we build a scenario for Jane that is characterized by frequent shifts in reference groups, role models and relevant points of comparison. This shifting of perspective is a necessary component of transformation.

You begin to shift your perspective when you interact in ever wider and more diverse networks. Since your identity is fundamentally embedded in relationships and friendships, as you begin to make a transition you inevitably begin to shift connections. You are searching for new role models and kindred spirits who are on the same transition and with whom you can begin to understand the rules of the game. As a consequence, transformation does not occur in isolation, nor does it typically occur within the same group of friends. As you make these new connections, you inevitably let go of some from the past. This is important, because the people who know you best are the very ones most likely to hinder transformation rather than help it. It is they who are often most invested in you staying the same. These new peer groups to which you are reaching out come with their new values, norms, attitudes and expectations. They are also likely to be experiencing similar doubts and it is these points of comparison that can create the 'tipping points' of transformation.

These new, diverse networks are unlikely to be found in the posse or the regenerative relationship networks described earlier. Both of those networks are too small (so there is insufficient diversity) and too homogenous (so people support others to be like them rather than to change). It is within larger and more diverse networks of friendship and associates that variety is found. Somewhere in this large diverse network are people who are doing or behaving in a way that you admire and believe could be appropriate to your own transformation.

We rate these big diverse networks as an important intangible asset because of the value they bring over time. Take for instance the issue of how people find a job. Conventional wisdom suggests people find jobs because they use their intangible asset of stocks of knowledge; they get a job because of *what* they know. In a powerful study, Mark Granovetter[34] found that it is not just what they know, it is also *who* they know that matters. But here is the twist: people don't hear about new opportunities through their friends (what sociologists refer to as strong ties); they hear about new opportunities from weak ties, the friends of a friend. That is because there is much redundant information within circles of friends – they all know much of the same. However, when these networks extend to people who aren't known well, then this provides access to novel information. In her multi-stage life, Jane will experience many transitions and shifts in sector. These big diverse networks will be all the more important if Jane wishes to change sector and role.

Openness to new experience

The combination of self-knowledge and diverse networks creates the foundations for transformation. But what brings dynamism to this asset are actions, a preparedness to be open to creative solutions, to question old habits and routines, to challenge stereotypes and experiment with new models for integrating the different parts of life; being curious about how others are working and living, and feeling comfortable with the ambiguity that novelty brings.[35]

Much of everyday life is substantially made up of routines. Most of us have regular modes of activity that we repeat from day to day. These routines are important, since they give form to our lives and identity as well as context to how we work. Inevitably, during the process of transformation, these routines are threatened and as a result we often feel anxiety. While this anxiety may not be a pleasant feeling, it helps to mobilize our adaptive responses and preparedness to jump into embracing novel initiatives. Taking charge of your life involves risk, because it means confronting a diversity of open possibilities. There will be occasions when you will have to make a more or less complete break with the past, and to contemplate novel courses of action that cannot be guided by established habits.[36]

These routines are interrupted by triggers from self-knowledge or from the environment, which can herald a conscious exploration of alternative ways of being. It is what Douglas Hall and Philip Mirvis call *routine-busting* that leads to new cycles of learning. When these experiments of busting routines lead to changes in our behaviour that we believe to be successful, then we are likely to integrate them into our identity and may even be prepared to engage with more explorations and adaptations.[37] Later we will explore the new emerging stages of life: becoming an explorer, an independent producer, or creating a portfolio. What is fascinating about all these stages is that they create a context in which old routines can be busted and transformation capabilities can be strengthened.

5

Scenarios

Possible selves

A long life has so many exciting possibilities: more hours to be spent, more opportunities to be grasped, and more identities to be explored. You are likely to live for longer and witness greater labour market churn. That means you can no longer rely on an extended three-stage life as a route to a good life. So what comes in its place? To provide a point of comparison and discussion, we have developed various ways in which Jimmy and Jane can structure a balanced life that both solves the financial challenges outlined earlier and supports their intangible assets.

These descriptions of their possible future selves are not prescriptive, nor are they paths you should necessarily follow. In fact, one of the major conclusions about the 100-year life is that there will be considerable diversity in the lifestyle and life path that people will choose and this will reflect both their personal preferences and their circumstances. This diversity makes prescriptive approaches unhelpful. Instead, we outline these possible selves to show that there are workable alternatives to the three-stage life that make a long life a gift rather than a curse.

The traditional three-stage life required only the lightest planning touch and little in the way of reflection, since it had certainty and predictability baked into it. In its place comes variety and choice. Over a long life there will be significant uncertainty: what jobs will there be, what education will be needed, what sort of person will you be, and what will be your goals? There is much that cannot be known and that makes the creation of a single linear route into the future both impossible and misleadingly simplistic. That's why we tend to construct possible future selves that can be both symbols of hope or harbingers of doom. It is this bleak view that captures the anxiety we all have about making the right choices. Most people tend to make poor choices about what our future self could need – we prefer the status quo and have a strong preference for the familiar – and most of us have difficulty imagining ways of life that we have never experienced.

That is why possible selves can be such a motivator of behaviour, particularly, as we described earlier, if they are connected with feelings of efficacy and agency. Here we operationalize the concept of possible selves by building a series of scenarios for Jimmy and Jane. These scenarios create an opportunity to play through alternative sequencing or different transitions and to track the long-term balance between tangible and intangible assets. These different scenarios are a very concrete way to surface some of the key issues we all face, creating a base for you to evaluate possible paths to get where you want to be and avoid where you don't want to be.

When we do this with our MBA students at London Business School, the scenarios they create forcefully reveal implicit biases and conflicts that require debate and resolution. Questions rapidly arise, such as: Do you want to be a high earner all your life? How can you sustain a partnership with one person? How much risk are you prepared to take? What sort of work will be meaningful to you? What is the contribution you want to make to society? Are you making the most of the possibilities? Are you being too traditional?

Ultimately, the scenarios you think about for yourself will be moulded around your own unique needs, aspirations, wishes and desires. This integration is for you to make, but we hope the examples of Jimmy and Jane trigger useful issues for your own thinking and planning, and help set the scene for the themes of leisure, financing and partnership that we will analyse later.

Jimmy: The audit

Born in 1971, Jimmy began his working life imagining that he could follow Jack's three-stage life. If at 20 he had been asked to build a life plan, he might well have sketched a three-stage life with retirement around 60 to 65. Ask him to do so now and he would find it much more difficult to have this clarity. So, in his 40s, Jimmy's scenarios are about the choices he has today as he contemplates the next phase of his life.

We first audit Jimmy's current tangible and intangible assets to gain an idea of the options and challenges he faces. Then we look forward to what his life could be and develop three scenarios, each of which brings a central question to the fore.

Jimmy's working life up to his mid-40s can be categorized into four distinct phases, described in Figure 5.1, which shows his asset balances rising when he invests in them and declining through depreciation and lack of attention at other times.

Now 45, Jimmy has been working since the age of 21 when he left college with a degree in computing. From a financial perspective, like many others, he left with debts accumulated by tuition fees and living expenses. After college, it was relatively easy to find a job and he joined a medium-sized IT company, 'TransEx', in his local town (first phase). Over the next five years, Jimmy works in a team advising a range of clients on their back-office IT needs. He is beginning to pay off his debts, but is not buying a house, and his assets are still negative.

At the age of 26 Jimmy moves to work with one of his clients, in the IT department of a larger retail company, 'Smartbuy', which employs 850 people (second phase). He is now working with a

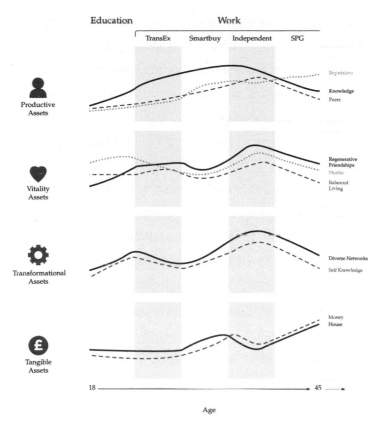

FIGURE 5.1 *Jimmy's asset flow.*

team of around twelve people, some of whom work in another branch of the company. He is coached by his team leader, who supports him to develop his collaborative skills. That's why at the age of 30 he is promoted to a team leader role responsible for an IT team across four locations. So every two weeks he travels to these locations to catch up with the team and talk to the outlet managers. The impact on his family is that he is away from home for two or three days a week. As he moves up the managerial ladder in Smartbuy, Jimmy is able to begin to save and to put down a deposit on a house. During the early stages of his managerial work, the company decides to outsource half of the IT back-office to Mumbai in India. Jimmy is responsible for the negotiations with the Indian IT supplier and also visits the outsourcing company in Mumbai on two occasions.

It is going well, but by the age of 39 Jimmy is without a job. The outsourcing has been so successful that the executive team decides to move the whole IT back-office to India. This catches Jimmy by surprise and it takes him time to find another job. The date is 2010 and the world is still under the stress of the banking crash of 2008. Many companies have decided to freeze their recruitment and Jimmy really struggles to find the right level of responsibility.

That is why he decides to work as a freelancer and for the next two years he works as an independent IT specialist, selling his time by the hour and building a website to advertise his skills (third phase). Financially, this is a tough time. He and his wife Jenny have stopped saving and have had to remortgage their house to pay for their household expenses.

By 2012 things are looking brighter; companies are beginning to hire again and Jimmy sends his CV to more than thirty of them. Eventually, after a long selection process, he gets a job with an IT consultancy company, 'SPG', in a city about 400 miles away (fourth phase). He is excited about the job – it's a big jump in salary and he can begin to pay off his mortgage and save again. However, he has to uproot the family and relocate them. Jimmy is now 41. Once in the company he quickly becomes a team leader, this time managing a team of fifteen IT consultants. Jimmy finds this a tough company to work with. The members of the senior team are highly competitive with each other, revenues are calculated and communicated on a weekly basis, and the teams across the company actively compete with each other for client work.

Current account

If we were to evaluate Jimmy's intangible and tangibles assets at this time, what would be the results of this audit? In Figure 5.1 we map the asset rises and depreciations.

Productive assets: Jimmy made an initial investment in his general knowledge and skills when he took a technical degree and then deepened his mastery of IT systems and began to develop his managerial capabilities at TransEx (first phase). His stint at Smartbuy (second phase) added another important dimension to his repertoire as he learnt about the Indian IT outsourcing market and how to manage a complex alliance. This period of asset appreciation came to an end at SPG (fourth phase) where he no longer used his alliance skills, instead focusing on day-to-day delivery with very little time to develop or to learn. As a consequence, this was a period when his knowledge and skills had begun to deplete.

Jimmy developed two important groups to support his productive assets: the group at Smartbuy (second phase), and during his stint as an IT independent with knowledge of his specialist IT interests (third phase). However, with the sheer weight of work at SPG (fourth phase), Jimmy began to inadvertently let both of these networks atrophy and failed to build any others. That's why we show the deterioration of Jimmy's productive assets as he reaches 45.

Vitality assets: College was for Jimmy, as for many, a time when the foundation for regenerative friendships was created. He marries soon after leaving college and within a couple of years the first of their three children is born. These are the TransEx years (first phase) and very quickly they develop a good neighbourhood group with the parents of their children's friends. Jenny works part-time while bringing up the children, with her retired parents helping out in the morning and some evenings. These were good years for Jimmy's vitality assets. The Smartbuy years (second phase) are harder: the children are growing up and demanding more of Jimmy's attention, and his weekly absence from home is tough on the family. Jenny's parents are travelling more and are therefore less able to support her with the children, so she is finding part-time work more demanding. The marriage is still strong, but there are many days when Jimmy leaves the house feeling guilty about not spending more time with the children. After a positive start, his vitality is beginning to deteriorate.

But the balance shifts in the two years he spends as an independent freelancer (third phase). He devotes more time to the children, reconnects with old friends and takes a couple of holidays with Jenny. This may have not been a good time for his tangible assets, but it is a time of significant investment in his intangibles.

After this boost, in the SPG years (fourth phase), his vitality assets start to erode. He is working long hours, often coming home feeling frustrated and annoyed. Jenny is upset with his bad temper and feels that he is constantly under work pressure and taking it out on the family. His mobile phone is never switched off and he often takes calls in the evening and at weekends. Jimmy has little time outside of work and he has to put his friendships on hold. Jenny wants his attention; she is keen to start her working life again and irritated with Jimmy that he cannot support her more.

Transformational assets: There are two periods of life when Jimmy extends his networks: when he begins with Smartbuy (second phase) and links to Mumbai on the outsourcing deal, and when he becomes an independent IT specialist (third phase). These are times when he starts to build the capability to make transitions, expands his self-knowledge, and is open to new experiences. During his time at SPG (fourth phase) he neither invests in building more diverse networks nor takes time to really think about himself or his life.

Tangible assets: Jimmy, like many people, enters his working life with debt accumulated from education. It is really not until Smartbuy (second phase) that he can begin to put down a mortgage for a house and save around 15 per cent of his income. The years of being an independent IT specialist boost his intangible assets as he reconnects with friends and becomes healthier, but his tangible assets depreciate as he has to remortgage the house. His major tangible investments come at SPG, where his salary climbs and the family is able to return to their previous savings rate.

So now, in his 40s, Jimmy is in a phase where he is finally rebuilding his tangible assets but where his intangible assets are beginning to be depleted. He is now facing the second half of his life. What options does he have?

The 3.0 scenario

One possibility is that Jimmy follows in the footsteps of Jack, relies on his initial educational investment and aims to retire at 65 after completing a three-stage life.

Jimmy in 2021: Jimmy is 50 years old and finding that, in a fast-changing technological world, his skills are becoming ever more obsolete. As a consequence, he is beginning to notice that at work he is being increasingly sidelined. He reviews his tangible assets: while he has begun to save in the last five years, prior to that he was struggling. As he makes a rough calculation, he realizes that he does not have the savings to enable him to retire at 65.

Jimmy in 2031: Jimmy is now 60 and insufficient financial investment and inadequate intangibles make him increasingly worried about his future. Although recent savings have improved his financial assets, he still doesn't have enough to achieve a 50 per cent pension. Further, he has found that his state pension has been reduced, and in 2034 the state retirement age will increase to the age of 70. The first company he worked for provided him with a company pension, but in subsequent companies the provision has been reduced. His intangible assets are also depleted. With no significant investment in learning and education, his skills have atrophied and he finds he has to move down the skill level and take a lower-paid job. He had hoped to create a 'portfolio' life after he retires, but finds in reality that he does not have the specialist skills, the knowledge or the networks of associates and clients to make this work.

Jimmy in 2041: Now 70, Jimmy is finding it more difficult to get well-paid work and decides to leave full-time employment.

He finds himself on a low income, living a life that is a great deal more austere than the one he had imagined.

We based the above scenario firmly on the past. In this scenario Jimmy keeps his eyes shut to the reality of changes going on around him. He does not pause to reflect on what might happen, nor does he actively plan for his future. There are, of course, different versions of how this three-stage life can play out for Jimmy, and some will have less of the curse of Ondine about them.

The 3.0 scenario captures two factors that we think will catch out millions of people like Jimmy who are currently following this path. The first is inadequate savings history: Jimmy is reaching his 50s and 60s inadequately prepared financially. The second is a lack of investment in intangibles: relying too much on initial education and a posse established early in his career leaves Jimmy struggling to maintain his career and earnings into later years.

The 3.5 scenarios

We don't think it is too late for Jimmy to avoid this fate. But if he wants to engage with a more productive long life he has to face up to his choices, make decisions, and engage both his *efficacy* ('I am competent to do this') and his *agency* ('I have the self-control and will to make this happen'). In other words, he needs to be less passive. We can think of the stretch of these possible selves from the most ambitious to the less ambitious. We begin with a less ambitious future path and simply add a half stage to his career. The half stage requires some renewal or change but does not require a major investment in intangibles or an extensive use of transformational assets. We see this 3.5 stage as most likely for those who are more risk-averse and who do not want to embark on substantial and potentially risky change in their mid-40s. Alternatively this scenario could work for older individuals – those closer to retirement, with not enough time to embark on more substantial transitions.

Imagine Jimmy in 2026 at the age of 55. The announcement that the state retirement age will now be 70 spurs him into action. He realizes that his current technical skills are becoming less valuable at SPG and are not strong enough to secure him a well-paid job in a rival firm. Yet he calculates he has at least another fifteen years of work ahead of him. Just a few streets from his house is a college of further education and an old friend from Smartbuy is head of department there. He offers Jimmy the chance to teach IT and Management one evening a week. The pay isn't great and Jimmy can't teach the hot topics that the students are desperate for to secure jobs with the fastest growing new firms. And there are plenty of other Jimmys offering their services. But Jimmy is conscientious and appreciated by the students, so by 2030 he is offered a post which enables him to resign from SPG and go full-time at the college. The pay is less, but Jimmy feels better utilized and certainly more appreciated, and the better hours help him balance time spent at work and at home with Jenny and his first grandchild, Julie.

Financially speaking, the real advantage of the job is that even though the salary only pays his living expenses, every year Jimmy works is another year when he does not draw down his pension. Importantly these years of a lower salary help Jimmy and Jenny adjust to a reduced standard of living, which will also ensure that Jimmy's pension pot lasts longer. Of course their house is looking a little shabby, and his college commitments and finances mean that he and Jenny can't travel as much as many of their friends, but there are plenty of others worse off.

There are no major differences between the 3.0 scenario and the 3.5 version, but 3.5 works better for Jimmy because he has found a job that he can continue into his 70s. Getting the job is characterized by a piece of luck (his old friend from Smartbuy works at the local college), as well as a conscious effort by Jimmy to take control of his life and open up a new opportunity. He takes early action to avoid the failed 3.0 stage life and so sustains his financial assets for longer.

But this 3.5 stage does not involve a major change for Jimmy. There is no major transformation, just a quiet transition into the college down the road. He is still working in the same sector, still talking about the same things. This becomes a problem for Jimmy. Although he is appreciated as a good colleague in the department, it is clear as each year goes by that his experience and knowledge are becoming increasingly dated. When he finally retires in 2042 aged 71 he doesn't even have a farewell party, as many of the faculty assumed he had already left. To paraphrase Dylan Thomas, Jimmy goes very gently into that good night.

There are, of course, other 3.5 scenarios. Jimmy could work until the age of 65 and then secure some part-time consultancy, either with SPG or through his contacts in the industry. However, achieving this isn't straightforward. Jimmy needs skills that are useful and relevant, and his age coupled with the period of time since leaving SPG will make it harder and harder. There are always times when SPG needs another body they know and trust to help out at busy moments and Jimmy is happy to oblige. The occasional consultancy keeps his mind engaged and every year in which he makes some money is a year he does not have to draw his pension. Jimmy is only too conscious that his expenditure can't be supported long-term by his pension.

Other versions of the 3.5 scenario involve Jimmy leaving the IT sector but still not really going through any form of transition. For instance, Jimmy and Jenny's long-time friends run a shop in the next town and are only too pleased to offer Jimmy a regular job helping behind the counter and keeping an eye on the other staff. Jimmy has plenty of management experience and they trust him totally. They know it's not a lot of money, but as Jimmy would say, 'hey, every little bit helps, doesn't it?' and he is a social creature who enjoys the interaction with the public.

All of these 3.5 scenarios work at one level. While they don't help build up tangible assets, they do shorten the period over which Jimmy will run down his assets so they help achieve tangible balance. In all these scenarios Jimmy has more time for his vitality assets: his friends and family, personal fitness as well as mental happiness. However, they do very little for his productive assets and make little use of transformational assets. These 3.5 scenarios all lack investment – in either tangibles or intangibles – and all lack major changes. They do, however, possess sufficient change, however modest, to make the three-stage life more palatable. However, the lack of significant asset investment and transformational change means that this extra stage is more of an addendum to a three-stage life. The longer it is stretched out, the more this lack of investment becomes a problem.

The 4.0 scenarios

There are more active scenarios available to Jimmy. These could be possible selves that choose to invest more, take more risks and undergo more change and transformation. We consider two such scenarios. Each is based on a conscious and determined effort to change and transform, and so we term them 4.0 scenarios, reflecting a fourth new stage. In the first scenario, Jimmy continues to work in the IT sector but undergoes a personal transformation and creates a portfolio career. In the second, Jimmy takes a major risk and starts his own company. What distinguishes these from the 3.5 scenario is that, early on, Jimmy is aware of the need for change and the length of working career ahead gives him time to make that change.

The portfolio fourth stage

Jimmy in 2016: This marks the year when Jimmy, now aged 45, really develops and uses his transformational assets. He strengthens his self-knowledge by standing back and reflecting on his own life and the world around him. He begins to comprehend the scale of the change he faces and as he performs some financial calculations, he realizes that an early retirement will leave him with very limited financial assets. He accepts he will have to work longer. As he thinks more deeply about his work in the IT sector and its rapid technological developments, he figures out that with some re-skilling he could increase the probability of being able to move into a high-growth area. He is bringing to bear his efficacy and, as he talks to Jenny, he is sure that he can stretch his skills.

Jimmy knows he has to make some short-term changes and ramp up his skills. But how will he do this? This is where his posse of professional friends are really useful. They point him to a programme of training designed to boost skills in some of the hot IT areas. He speaks to his line manager and it is clear that his current company, SPG is not prepared to fund his development. So he makes a big leap of faith. He decides to work two evenings a week and every other weekend for the next year in order to go through the programme. Part of his course is online with peer-based coaching, and every other Saturday he meets with others who are following the same course. Simply put, Jimmy has decided to convert his *recreation* time into *re-creation*. Though it is tough, what the course does is provide him with enhanced skills and introduce him to a whole new motivated work group. More importantly, at the end he is awarded a certificate that is well known in the industry. Once Jimmy has made the investment and has the course under his belt, he begins to look for a new job. This is not straightforward. Jimmy regrets joining SPG and he doesn't want to make the same mistake again. So he begins engaging in a detailed search; he is adamant he will not join another company with a poor record in developing employees. After a long search he eventually gets a job with a large global IT company based out of Mumbai. His research has convinced him that they take a developmental approach and really value his capacity to manage virtual teams and support complex partnerships.

Jimmy also thinks hard about the way he has been managing his vitality assets – he feels the home/work balance is not working for him. He has grown used to being the major breadwinner and the traditional role that Jenny, his wife has taken. But as he listens carefully to what Jenny has to say, he realizes that the dynamics of their partnership have to transform. Jenny wants to return to full-time work, but to do so they have to make some changes in the household rules. So he and Jenny sit down and begin the (often painful) process of renegotiating their partnership and their roles and responsibilities. From this they create a number of commitments that allow both of them to work.

Together they also look carefully at their health and well-being. It is clear to them that the years of hard work have taken their toll on their health. Both of them are overweight and under-exercised. They know that this will impact on their ability to make some of the desired changes in their lives. So they decide to focus on their health and do something about this. They join the local gym and watch what they eat. The company Jimmy works with also has a corporate marathon programme to support a cancer charity, and he and Jenny sign up for a half-marathon.

Jimmy in 2021: Jimmy celebrates his fiftieth birthday in New York by running the marathon. It's been a good decade for him. The company he joined is dedicated to supporting his development and they provide ten days a year when he can choose what development activities he wants to pursue. So every year over the last decade he has made a continuous and annual investment in his development. In the first year he strengthened his skills of managing a virtual team; in the second he learnt more about augmentation; in the third he took a course in advanced robotics. These continuous investments paid off for Jimmy and he loves his work.

In 2021 he takes time, as he did before, to consider his next ten-year plan. As he looks ahead, he knows that the idea of building a wide portfolio of work will be important to him and he also realizes that he needs to start now to prepare for this. He does not want to leave full-time corporate work, but he does want to make some bets and some investments. One of the investments he makes is to embark on a high-level project management development programme. His company is prepared to give him two weeks off to go on the course and he also spends ten weekends a year on a residential course with fellow project managers. He begins to build a wider network of project managers from across the world. His research shows there are three active global communities of practice in this areas and he joins all of them. He becomes registered as a global project manager and seeks certification in a couple of related skills.

Jimmy in 2036: By the age of 65, the thought of retirement has not crossed Jimmy's and Jenny's minds. Jimmy left the Indian IT company two years earlier and now works as a certified project manager. The ten years of investment in building contacts within the three global communities he identified previously are paying off and his skills are now in demand. By now his children are financially independent, and he has begun to specialize in running large-scale IT projects in sub-Saharan Africa. Jenny is continuing to work in her job and is happy to build a more independent life when Jimmy is away. Jimmy is living the portfolio life he wanted: with valuable skills he is able to find interesting work, and even in his late 70s he is still in demand.

With regard to the finances of the 4.0 scenario, if Jimmy works until the age of 77 and his portfolio salary amounts to the same as his earnings in his final job, then he only needs a constant savings rate of about 8.5 per cent. He is able to retire later because he made earlier investments in both his productive and vitality assets. It is this balance that changes Jimmy's finances. In the earlier financial calculation of Jimmy's three-stage working life, we showed that to achieve forty-four years of work and twenty years of retirement he would need a constant (and probably impossible) savings rate of 17 per cent. In this scenario he works for fifty-six years and retires for eight.

The entrepreneur fourth stage

In the previous scenario, Jimmy made some important investment decisions in his productivity and vitality assets, and really boosted his transformational assets. He added a stage to his life by shaping a portfolio in his 60s. But what if Jimmy decided at the age of 45 to really take a risk and to jump – how might that play out? In this scenario, Jimmy makes a much bigger decision about his life and decides to take a risk and become an entrepreneur – or what we later call an 'independent producer'. How might this look?

Jimmy in 2016: We begin with Jimmy reflecting on his life and feeling stuck. Working with SPG has been tough and has placed a great deal of pressure on the family. He thinks back wistfully to the time when he was self-employed – would it be possible for him to recreate those times? The challenge is that he has a family and a mortgage and calculates that his tangible assets are not sufficient to provide a retirement income before he is 70.

So, as in the portfolio scenario, he becomes volitional and decides to convert some of his recreation time to re-creation. What he does with this extra time is rather different. Over the next two years he spends his weekends and holidays preparing to take the leap. He focuses his energy in three directions. First, he builds self-knowledge by looking closely at the market for IT. He concludes that many start-up companies want a low cost back-office and so he reactivates his old networks by connecting with his former colleagues in India. It takes him time to track some of them down, but most are delighted to reignite their association. As he reaches out to them, they tell him about the developments that they have been working on in India. A couple of these old associates are now at the forefront of cloud technology. Jimmy decides to take a week off as holiday from SPG and goes out to India to see what they are doing and visit their offices.

The more Jimmy investigates, the more he can see the commercial value in his plan. So he decides to take action and begins to learn more about these technologies. He develops a series of side projects that give him a taster of what he could become. For example, he joins a local entrepreneurs' club that meets every month. He also signs up for an online course in accounting and marketing. In the entrepreneurs' club, he meets a whole bunch of new people, some of whom are already running their own business. His dream becomes more concrete and as he thinks about possible new ventures, he comes to a big decision. He realizes that the town he lives in is simply not large enough to support a cluster of the type of start-up companies he imagines will be his new clients. So he takes his strategy a little bit further and persuades his boss at SPG to move him to a larger city with a thriving cluster of small companies. Within weeks of arriving, Jimmy is networking with small business owners. Over coffee he hears about their frustration and stress of running their own businesses. In his earlier travels to India he met Bob, who has a close working relationship with two Indian outsourcing companies. As Jimmy thinks more about the options he faces, he begins to realize that Bob would be a great partner to work with him. Bob knows the industry and the location well, and points him in the direction of government-sponsored schemes that train start-ups and also provide seed funding.

Jimmy in 2019: Three years later and Jimmy is ready to make the leap. All the side projects he has been involved with while he has been at SPG are beginning to pay off. He feels he knows enough about the cloud technologies, has strong links to providers in India, has positioned himself in the heart of a cluster of high-growth small companies, and has good links with government schemes. Over the last couple of years he and Jenny have also taken the opportunity to look carefully at their expenses and decided to change some of their lifestyle choices so as to reduce their general outgoings. They have stopped taking overseas holidays, cancelled the subscription to the golf club, and tried to live more modestly. This has given them a small cushion of savings while also ensuring that the family becomes used to living in more modest ways.

In early 2020 Jimmy launches his own company with Bob. They name it 'YourIT' and while his aspirations are not to build a multinational, he and Bob do want to build a viable company. Their contacts in the cluster they live in bring them their first two clients, and they work closely with their Indian partners to provide a low-cost efficient service.

How will Jimmy's life proceed in this scenario? Many other people over the age of 50 are already making the same decision as Jimmy to start their own company – some, of course, because they have no other option. What is interesting about Jimmy is that this is a decision he planned and prepared for. He began four years earlier to get his tangible and intangible assets in better shape, and the experiments and side projects gave him ample opportunity to learn more about himself and the market. Of course this planning period is rarely available to people who have lost their jobs and are now self-employed. Nevertheless, many small businesses fail and we can assume that there is a high change that Jimmy's will fail too. But because he has developed his tangible and intangible assets, and in particular strengthened his transformational assets, we imagine that he continues to have options. Even if he fails, he still has the skills to move back to the portfolio stage we described earlier.

In both this scenario and the portfolio fourth stage scenario, Jimmy must open his eyes to his present circumstances and take a thoughtful view of the terrain that lies ahead. Once he steps into this mode of self-knowledge and opens himself up to new experiences, he is able to begin to work out the consequences of the choices he makes. It is this that helps him realize that he has to make significant investment in new skills. In both these scenarios, Jimmy has the courage to commit to major transformation and re-creation. We do not imagine this to be an easy commitment. In the way we described these two scenarios, we made them sound relatively straightforward and both were successful. Of course, not everyone who tries to create a portfolio or become a late stage entrepreneur will succeed. Some will not have luck on their side; some will fail to really develop the skills or contacts they need; others will not be prepared to put in the time or effort. We imagine that even those who succeed will find the change stressful and challenging. This is, of course, precisely where transformational assets become so important. Being able to invest in self-knowledge, in building new and dynamic networks, and staying open to experience are precisely what it takes for these later scenarios to succeed.

Given the amount of hard work and focus they require, what are the advantages of these 4.0 scenarios? Both scenarios build and strengthen tangible and intangible assets; both lead to longer periods of high income and so help support a larger pension; both involve stronger productive assets and also vitality assets. There are, of course, important differences between the two 4.0 scenarios we paint. The fourth-stage entrepreneur is risky and more stressful – both in terms of financial assets and intangibles. The portfolio career offers more time for Jimmy and Jenny to be together. Which Jimmy would prefer will depend on his preferences and on his starting point.

Scenarios for Jane

If you are younger than Jimmy, you probably feel, rightly, that you are less constrained and have more options. In the Jimmy scenarios he is already mid-stream, so his starting point in his mid-40s will limit him. Jane, by contrast, is setting out in her adult life and has much greater flexibility. Born in 1998, she has her whole life ahead of her. So what does this mean for her possible scenarios?

The 3.0 scenario that looks uncomfortable for Jimmy would totally fail for Jane. The long second stage of continuous work needed to finance retirement fails to support the development of Jane's intangible assets. We articulated a 3.5 scenario for Jimmy (teaching at a local college, working as a consultant for SPG, working in a friend's shop) that managed to provide the finances for a long life and just maintained intangible assets through focused and minor reinvestment. It is possible that Jane could also try and use a similar 3.5 approach, but we cannot help thinking that it is unlikely to succeed, given Jane's long life. The problems with a 3.5 approach are both tangible and intangible assets. As far as her finances go, the 3.5 scenario involves fairly modest income, and stretched over a long period of time would not help her accumulate sufficient funds for a pension. As for intangible assets, even for Jimmy this approach was stretching his productive assets – whether as a teacher or a consultant, his knowledge and experience were becoming increasingly dated.

It is clear to us that, for Jane, the structure has to be a 4.0 or even 5.0 scenario. The length of Jane's working career requires significant reinvestment in her intangible assets and a serious effort at re-creation and transformation. The more modest efforts at investment and transformation that Jimmy used in the 3.5 scenario are simply not enough.

The 4.0 scenario for Jane

So if Jane does follow Jimmy and pursues a 4.0 stage life, how would this work for her, given her greater longevity? Could she work continuously through her life and then build a portfolio in the final decades of her productive life? If she manages to save 14 per cent of her salary, then the analysis in Figure 2.7 suggests that if she wants to retire on 50 per cent of her final salary, she will have to work until the age of 80. With this sixty years of work in mind, is a scenario based on the 4.0 portfolio model (education/work/portfolio/retirement) viable?

Jane will be entering the job market around 2019. Over the following decades, numerous high-skill and low-skill routine jobs will continually disappear. As a consequence, Jane will have to devote considerable amounts of time to developing new skills and foresight about market developments. She can preserve her *productive assets* by on-the-job coaching and training and by taking time out to retrain. If she wants to develop new portable skills on the job, she will have to find a company that supports her to do this. As Jimmy found in his career, companies differ in their capacity and enthusiasm to support the development of portable skills in their employees. But even if this is possible, will on-the-job development be sufficient to keep her updated? Probably not. Our guess is that she will also have to reassign some of her discretionary time from recreation to re-creation. In other words, like Jimmy in the 4.0 scenario, for some periods of her life Jane's weekends and holidays will be devoted to development and learning. If Jane is not prepared to make this continuous investment in her productive assets, then it's unlikely she will be able to keep her skills at the required level.

Could she sustain her *vitality assets* over such a long period of non-stop work? Surely they will become depleted if she works for sixty years without a significant break? This will be the case if she is employed in a traditional company where she works from 9.00 a.m. to 6.00 p.m. and has three or four weeks holiday a year. So would it be possible for Jane to actively find a company where she works fewer than five days a week? Taken on a regular basis, a shorter working week could give her a much-needed opportunity to either beef up her skills or indeed relax and re-invigorate. This is certainly not currently the norm in most corporate workplaces, but we think that by the time Jane is moving into her 30s, this will have changed in some companies. As we suggest in Chapter 8 on leisure, the three-day weekend or the four-day working week could well emerge as strong alternatives and thus help to preserve vitality across longer working lives.

The 5.0 scenarios

So a 4.0 stage life could work for Jane if she continually reinvests and re-energizes her vitality and productive assets. However, she has more options than Jimmy and could therefore possibly construct a wider range of scenarios. If Jane becomes skilled in transformation then she can go beyond the 4.0 stage life and structure her life around 5.0 stages.

Jane in 2019: Jane enters her 20s knowing that there is a good chance she will live for 100 years and it is this probability on which she bases her decisions. She decides to put off making any immediate major commitments and instead to explore her options. So after graduating from university with a degree in Modern History, she decides to travel. At this stage in her life she is asset-light and happy to engage in casual work. This is an exploration phase. As she travels across the continents, she meets many different people and begins to establish the broad network of friends and acquaintances that will create such a strong foundation for her transformational assets (first phase). Let's imagine that she travels through Argentina and Chile; as she does so, she learns about Latin America culture. To build her languages skills, she stops in Buenos Aires and spends three months on an intensive language course, passing the qualifying exam. Jane has always loved cooking and is fascinated by the way street food is prepared in Latin American cities. She has seen 'pop-ups' work and is excited to think that she could use the same ideas for 'pop-up' fiestas. With her good Spanish, she reaches out to fiesta organizers around a couple of cities and begins to really understand the trade. She earns little money, but enough to help finance her stay. In this early period of her life, Jane is beginning to hone her organizing skills, learn the basics of budgeting, and build a network with festival organizers in Latin America while also having a lot of fun and enjoying what she does. When she returns home she keeps in touch with her contacts and begins to import some of the fiesta paraphernalia, organizing fiestas for some friends' birthday parties.

Jane in 2026: Now in her late 20s, Jane is really excited about building this business. So she persuades a couple of friends to come along with her and start their own company. This is the second phase, where she is an independent producer. Her first big venture is organizing a few street feasts. But like many people running their own business, she struggles to get the finances right. It is at this point that she meets Sam, who has experience of making events profitable. She introduces Jane to others who are trying to make pop-up events work and persuades her to widen her ideas about financing. By 2026, the crowd-sourcing market has really taken off and Jane takes the plunge to see who will support her venture. She needs to actively build her reputation and over the next couple of years this is a real focus of her attention. Sam shows her how to create a really vibrant and exciting virtual online presence and her weekly blog attracts a steady stream of enthusiasts. Over time, thousands of people begin to follow her fiestas and she starts to build a thriving online community. This community of people running pop-up fiestas grows into other cities and other countries. Jane finds she has a significant following in Finland and Korea, and has wonderful times visiting these places and talking to other fiesta enthusiasts.

These are Jane's years of self-knowledge and discovery. She is learning more about herself and what she likes doing. She is wary about making choices now that she could regret for many years. So she is throwing herself into experiences that broaden her view of the world. We don't expect Jane to invest in her tangible assets at this time. This is a period of heavy investment in intangible assets: creating options, building skills, establishing networks, and building the reputation and the behavioural currencies she will need to navigate the long years ahead. She funds this stage of her life by using her nascent skills to create sufficient money to live modestly and without getting into debt.

What separates this approach from simply hanging about is the focus Jane is placing on actively building intangible assets and options. Her *productive assets* are forming as she learns some basic working skills and how to build an online reputation. And unlike Jack, by travelling widely and purposefully and meeting a wide array of people, she is beginning to build her *transformational assets* and, in particular, the diverse network that will be so crucial as she flexes her sense of identity. She is innovating and experimenting, learning skills and knowledge, understanding what she is good at and what she likes doing in an environment that is under her own control and not governed by the inevitable rules and procedures of an established organization.

It is during these years that Jane really builds her *vitality assets*. As she dashes around the world she is working extremely hard and certainly not creating a particularly balanced life. But in her travels she has made some incredible friends who she has worked with and got to know really well. These regenerative friendships will turn out to be a crucial investment later in her life.

During this early stage of her working life, Jane uses technology to curate her own experiences and her reputation. Her online persona, the broader networks she establishes and her achievements in terms of innovation all advertise who she is, and will act as an effective launch pad for her future career. For Jane and her peers, her online presence and network will be just as important as her academic qualifications. During this time Jane has a number of boyfriends, but does not commit to any of them – she wants to be sure that she will make the right choice.

Jane in 2033: We now find Jane in her mid-30s. What are her options now? One would be to continue to build the business and to take it into something that is more sustainable. If Jane sees herself as a long-term entrepreneur, then this would be a good path for her. Let's imagine that Jane decides that this is not what she wants. What, then, are her alternatives?

Jane knows that over the next decade she really needs to consolidate her finances. To date she has focused on building her intangible assets and enjoying herself, but now she needs to prepare financially for a long life. Her phases of exploring and building a small business have been fun and enlightening. They have given her a strong sense of what she is good at and the beginnings of a track record of innovation and change. Her reputation and online presence have begun to attract the attention of executives in larger organizations and she is approached by a couple to join them. They see her as someone with deep experience in the food and entertainment industry, a fantastic network of contacts, and a track record of innovation and understanding customer needs. So a well-known food company – let's call it 'EatWell' – reaches out to her. A marketing executive has seen Jane's website and is intrigued by the way she has brought fun and food together. They are keen to build an online capability and to curate food events around the world, and want Jane to build this capability for them.

With her experience in innovation and direct customer knowledge, Jane is able to negotiate a good starting salary and take a reasonably high-level position – unlike Jack, who joined his company straight from college. For this to be an option for Jane, we are assuming that, by now, corporations will have changed and become adept at knowing who is in their 'ecosystem' and reaching out to the most talented. Rather than relying on internal fast-track talent, more and more companies will see broad external networks as a place where talented and innovative people can be found.

Now in her mid-30s Jane struggles to adapt to the corporate culture. Like many people who join a large company from a start-up, she finds it annoyingly slow in decision-making and bureaucratic in approach. But she is prepared to make it work and takes on several international postings that come with substantial pay increases.

This is a time when Jane continues to build her *productive assets*. Her professional identity really begins to be reshaped from a reputation as a start-up person to someone who is able to work in the corporate world. This is a time when she is also building and broadening her knowledge and expertise in the corporate world. She realizes that her experiences in Latin America have given her real insight into the challenges of creating sustainable supply chains, so she takes time out to spend three days on a seminar on the topic. She meets a completely different group of people from other large corporates and NGOs. So in her second year at EatWell she is able to make a proposal. She will work with teams in the Amazon and the forests of Rwanda to source new food flavours. This is an incredibly busy time for Jane, as she gets to know what's really happening on the ground. She also

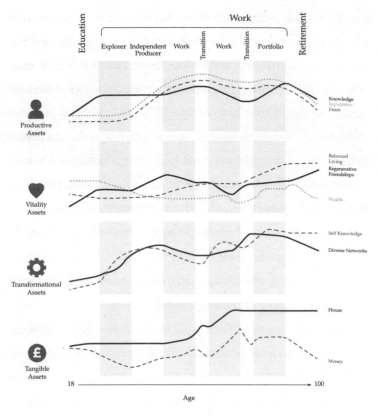

FIGURE 5.2 *The 5.0 scenario asset flow.*

deepens her links to local NGOs who are working with farmers on sustainability and transport issues. Jane continues to actively build her professional reputation: she blogs, writes articles about sustainable supply chains and speaks at conferences.

This is also a time when she is building her *vitality assets*. She continues to maintain her strong friendships, making sure she keeps in touch with people from her childhood and her early travelling years. Like many other women of her age, Jane has postponed partnership and motherhood. But now in her mid-30s she can feel the biological clock ticking. As we described earlier, although lives have elongated, there is no evidence that motherhood can be delayed. Some of Jane's friends had frozen their eggs in their mid-20s. Jane had not done this and is now confronting the question of her personal life. In her travels in Brazil, she meets Jorge, who works with a local NGO. He is passionate about sustainability and their romance blossoms. At the age of 37, Jane gives birth to her daughter, Lily, and two years later her son, Carlos. She and Jorge share the family duties with the help of a young Brazilian nanny.

Jane in 2041: After fifteen years of hard but successful work, Jane begins to feel frustrated at her firm. She has already risen high and is in senior management. But with the arrival of a new CEO and a new team, she senses that she may have risen as far as she can. So she is keen to explore new options. After twenty years in international food, Jane is looking for something different.

Now aged 45, Jane resigns her position. This is a tough decision. She doesn't have a job to go to and it represents a significant drop in the family's income. Her partner Jorge is still earning, so financially things are tight but manageable. Jane uses this period to help her children through their education and to spend time that she hasn't been able to do before with her elderly parents. However, it only takes six months for Jane to realize that in a few years she will have to return to work – she misses work and she will need the money. But as she thinks about her possible selves she realizes she wants a change. So begins her first transition. Just as the initial exploration phase was a time to understand her identity, so this phase allows her to reassess who she is and to think about her future. She spends time talking with friends and acquaintances about what is possible and investigates various options. This is a time when she is really strengthening her *transformational assets*.

This is another decision point in Jane's life when her path could take a number of directions. She could decide to go back to building a company, she could begin to build a portfolio career, or she could stay in the corporate world. How will Jane make a decision? In her mid-40s it could be that she figures that ahead of her are key earning years and she may decide to invest her time in building up her savings, paying off the mortgage and supporting Jorge, who will leave his job and take a similar break for the same purpose when she returns to work. To really maximize her earnings she decides to become a search consultant. When she reaches out to others in this field she realizes she has the commercial experience but not enough insight into human nature. So her decision is to re-skill and to strengthen her *productive assets*. Over the next two years she takes a series of online courses and another university degree (in Occupational Psychology). These prepare her for a role in a search firm and she joins a company – let's call it 'TalentFind' – that specializes in the hotel, travel and food sectors.

Jane in 2046: Jane's career as a search consultant – the fifth phase – starts at age 48 and she works hard to make this a success. This is a phase when she is really focused on accumulating her *tangible assets.* Over the next fifteen years she changes jobs within the search sector several times and by the age of 60 is headhunted to become an executive director of one of the major search companies. This is a time when the focus of Jane's *productive assets* is beginning to change. She mentors and coaches others and plays a stronger role in their professional network. However, she is aware that she is drawing down her *vitality assets* and doing little to replenish them. Work is hard, she travels a great deal and finds little time for her partner or children.

Jane in 2068: Financially successful and with accumulated assets, Jane faces a choice. She could carry on in her role accumulating tangible assets. But over the last twenty years of hard work she is seeing less of her friends, the relationship with her partner is strained and her health is beginning to deteriorate. It feels like a good moment to take a break and make some time for herself. Here her real emphasis is on replenishing her *vitality assets.* With her children now growing up (they are in their own explorer phase) this is a perfect time to spend with Jorge, so aged 70 they go off travelling again.

Jane in 2070: Jane is refreshed and excited about entering the next phase of her working life. Like many around her, she wants to work but does not want a working life with heavy responsibilities and substantial time commitments. This is when her *transformational assets* are really coming to the fore. With her diverse network of friends and acquaintances, it does not take her long to put together four projects that produce sufficient money to maintain the family's lifestyle and also bring Jane the interest and excitement she craves. It's also time for her to focus her *productive assets* on the community and wider world. She develops a portfolio with a number of elements. She takes on a one-day-a-week (but only thirty weeks a year) role at an international charity that helps street kids in Latin America and a one-day-a-week role as a non-executive director of a mid-size regional retail company, and agrees to serve one day every two weeks as a local magistrate.

Over time Jane's portfolio changes – sometimes with less commitments, sometimes with more – but the balance is always around the same mix of charity, social and commercial commitments. Aged 85, Jane feels that it is time to truly retire. It is time for her to take time out with her grandchildren and great-grandchildren, and ever year she takes a group of them to the Amazon to visit the places that are so important to her.

Do Jane's finances stack up over this long working career? One question we can ask is what her lifetime savings rate will have to be.

In this scenario Jane's savings are more complicated to calculate. She has a shorter pension stage to finance because she does not stop work until the age of 85. But she has two distinct periods of transition to finance and also a lengthy early period as an explorer when she is not saving. In fact she does not start commercial work until her mid-30s. So as well as saving for a pension, Jane also needs to save to finance these periods. Therefore we have to make a number of assumptions. Our first is that, while she is travelling and exploring in her 20s and early 30s, she does not save. But during these periods she is able to earn enough to pay for her living expenses and so she is not accumulating debt during these low-income periods of her life. Taking these assumptions into consideration, we calculate that she will need a savings rate of 10.9 per cent for every year she works (at EatWell, the search firm, and her final portfolio stage) in order to finance both a 50 per cent pension and the periods of transition.[1]

In this scenario, we have drawn a fairly linear arc through Jane's career. Of course it could take so many other paths. She may prefer to zigzag far more across different sectors or different positions in the corporate hierarchy. In her fifth phase, instead of a portfolio career she might decide to build on her love of food – for example, she could set up a restaurant with her partner Jorge. Or she might return to her earlier career within the food sector, but this time in a more junior and less stressed position.

All of these changes would demand a different set of transitions, and each would bring their own challenges and issues to be confronted. Some would be about preserving reputation in a career that moves across sectors. Others will be concerned with the challenges of setting up a business. But in many senses it is the final possibility that is the most interesting. Corporate careers are described as 'ladders' where people ascend upwards with age. In deciding to return to the food sector in a more junior position, Jane will be breaking the norm, which of course also poses some interesting questions about her own sense of identity and indeed for her employer. There is much Jane could offer in a more junior role. She would be mixing with younger people for whom she would have a lot to offer, both as a coach and as a role model; she would also learn much from them. Indeed she could benefit from juvenescence, boosting her vital assets and her outlook on life and keeping herself younger for longer. But her line manager might find this complicated – having a junior who used to be more senior and is more experienced can either be exploited to their benefit or become a source of distrust and concern. We imagine that more and more people will decide to both rise and descend the corporate ladder; there is no doubt that this will become a major agenda in future as people make the many adjustments demanded by a 100-year life.

Why Jane is different

As with Jimmy, we have painted scenarios that work for Jane. But of course there are also clear risks in the path Jane pursues. For instance, after years of travel and being a sole trader, can she really adapt to corporate life? Will she have the drive and motivation not just to focus on fun during her travels but also to build up sufficient skills to launch her own company?

When we teach our students, we recommend that they stand back and assess the risks of their view of their possible selves and the scenarios they create. We ask them to do a risk assessment and then consider how they can recover from setbacks. For Jimmy and Jane we have written positive scenarios. We have not considered unpleasant and unwelcome shocks such as losing their jobs, divorce or ill health. Stress testing different scenarios to these outcomes is an important part of life planning.

What is clear, however, is that even if Jane is successful in this 5.0 scenario and doesn't experience adverse shocks, she will still go through a number of major transitions and changes. Jimmy in his mid-40s is realizing the importance of transformational assets – that's the real shift from the 3.0 scenario he thought he was embarking on. From the very beginning Jane is basing her future life on the concept of transformation.

Another sharp distinction for Jane is that the 5.0 scenario reveals the challenge of maintaining vitality over such a long life. That is why we created two periods when Jane was able to jump out of her current life and spend time refreshing and transforming. These were also times when she was able to build her transformational assets as she widened her networks and thought more about her identity. With a longer life we feel that these blocks of time aimed at re-creation will become a common way of achieving the replenishment of intangibles and the scale of transition required. Jane will have to use substantial amounts of her leisure as a form of investment rather than consumption and these transitions will require more savings to finance them.

The other feature we have tried to emphasize in this scenario is identity. With more stages and different careers, there has to be a stronger thread that ties activities together and turns the scenario into 'your scenario'. This is why Jane's initial phase of exploring and travelling is so important. As Jane builds up a stronger sense of who she is and what she values, it is this that will bring continuity to the many transitions she makes. By creating some continuity to her narrative about her past and her future, Jane is reducing the risks involved in switching from stage to stage.

A further issue that emerges from both the 4.0 and 5.0 scenarios is the household relationships needed to support these multi-stage careers and transitions. In the archetypal stereotype of the three stage life, Jack works and his wife Jill looks after the home and family. This is how tangible and intangible assets are balanced, especially when viewed from Jack's perspective. With a longer life, dual income households become more attractive as they can help finance retirement and create the savings for transitions and re-creation. Jack and Jill did not have to coordinate their life plans, as following the tradition of role specialization made this a great deal easier. In dual income households, the need to closely coordinate across the development of intangible assets and the sequencing of stages and transitions becomes a lot more complex and challenging. Managing transitions and change in a family requires mutual support and commitment, as partners plan and balance the ebb and flow of their lives.

Finally, compared to Jack, Jane's finances show a highly oscillatory pattern. In a 3.0 scenario Jack's wealth at first slowly descends and then gradually increases until it reaches a peak at retirement, whereupon it is then run down: a single trough and a single high peak. So for Jack his peak income came near the end of his working life. By contrast, Jane's finances look like a series of hills with many troughs and peaks and with a gradient that varies markedly from stage to stage. So for Jane her peak income comes well before she finishes work. That means that she has to build up her assets not just to finance a pension and pay off a mortgage, but also to provide a buffer for these periods of low-income transition. Consequently her income, savings and wealth will go through multiple periods of increase and decline.

It is not just the oscillatory pattern of her assets that makes Jane's financial planning so complicated. Jane has many decisions to make and a number of variables to track over her life. With her three distinct phases of employment, she has to forecast the relative earnings she gets from each and calculate how long each of her transitions are; then there is the question of her 50 per cent pension. But of course we are assuming that this is 50 per cent of her salary in her last job. Is that a reasonable assumption, as in effect it is likely to be 50 per cent of her highest-ever salary? As we showed in Figure 2.7, decisions about what percentage of final salary to retire on can make a big difference to financial planning. In making the financial calculations for these scenarios, we have attempted to keep the financial simulations as simple as possible. However, there is no doubt that as we reach the multiple-stage life that Jane followed, even the simplest scenario has many possible choices. This makes financial planning more complex both to implement and to monitor; indeed that is why in Chapter 7 we return to the issue of how to finance a long life.

We did not design these scenarios to be prescriptive – they are not descriptions of what you *should* do. Neither are they intended to be exhaustive; there are many other ways of sequencing a multi-staged life. The 5.0 scenario presents more stages to chose from, more ways of sequencing any given set of stages, and of course with each stage there will be risks and outcomes which may push your life along a different path.

By looking more closely at possible lives, we wanted to dispel the doom created by our analysis of the three-stage life. Over a long life, the three-stage model certainly doesn't hold up. But in its place are many opportunities, and in sketching some possible scenarios we hope to show that it is possible to balance tangible and intangible assets. Of course these are simply illustrations. Each one of us has to reflect on the possible lives we find attractive and what these look like in the details of a scenario. In the end it's up to each of us to let our imagination roam and to be creative about what is possible. We now take a closer look at the new stages we have sketched for Jimmy and Jane.

6

Stages

New building blocks

The gift of a longer life is ultimately the gift of time. In this long sweep of time there is a chance to craft a purposeful and meaningful life. The violinist Stephen Nachmanovitch captured this in his discussion of creativity:

> If we operate with a belief in long sweeps of time, we build cathedrals; if we operate from fiscal quarter to fiscal quarter, we build ugly shopping malls.[1]

Freed from the straitjacket of the three-stage life, we see new stages already emerging that create opportunities to craft a life that balances tangible and intangible assets, depreciation and accumulation. In a long life, you have the potential to build a cathedral rather than a shopping mall.

We experience this potential whenever we discuss these new stages with our students on the Masters in Management course at London Business School. This is a group of young people from around the world who, fresh from their undergraduate degree, are spending a year at the business school to learn the basics of management. We are struck by their insight. Many implicitly understand these new stages and are either already embarking on them or planning to do so. In fact, some hope they could encourage their parents to read this book so they would understand what they are doing and why it makes sense. They felt their parents saw their career aspirations as subversive, when in fact all they were planning was to subvert the dominant model of the three-stage working life.

When we outlined possible lives for Jimmy and Jane, both subjects made use of stages that we think are emerging strongly as popular options as life is restructured in response to longevity. In this chapter, we articulate in more detail the purpose and features of these new stages: the Explorer, the Independent Producer and the Portfolio. We also examine the different types of transition that emerge in this multi-stage life.

It may sound momentous to talk about new stages of life, but this has happened before and often for reasons connected with longevity. For most of human history there were just two stages: being a child and being an adult. Over time the boundary between childhood and adulthood shifted,[2] and in the twentieth century two new stages emerged: *teenagers*[3] and *retirees*[4]. These two distinct and now standard stages of life originated at the end of the nineteenth century and became fully established with Jack and his cohort of Baby Boomers after the Second World War. The emergence of these two stages took a surprising amount of social experimentation, and required substantial shifts in government regulation, corporate policy and social behaviour. We suspect that the twenty-first century will see the same amount of social experimentation and change before these new stages become as embedded as the traditional three stages.

That is why we are all participating in a gigantic social experiment. Sometimes as individuals, sometimes in groups, perhaps in family units or communities of friends, we are crafting new ways of living and taking many paths. This diversity is intrinsic to the 100-year life rather than just a feature of experimentation. Once people move away from three to multiple stages, there are many possible sequences and not everyone will select each stage. Earlier we sketched some of the possible scenarios that Jimmy and Jane could navigate. Of course there are many other options and some stages will appeal more, resulting in much variety in the combinations and sequencing.

Viewed within the framework of the three-stage life, experimentation is dangerous. Unconventional paths are invariably seen as suspicious by firms and can have long-lasting implications for your career. Given the need for experimentation that the 100-year life creates, the end of lockstep will require a much less judgemental corporate response. In *The Wild Palms*, William Faulkner suggests that those slipping out of 'anonymous lockstep' risk being trampled to death. The end of the three-stage life, the end of lockstep and the rise of experimentation in structures and sequences has to lead to a more broad-minded attitude.

This experimentation and variety of life sequences is at the heart of the breakdown of the simple classification that equates stage with age. The last time stages emerged – teenagers and retirees – these were age-located stages. You have to be young to be a teenager and old to be a retiree. What is fascinating about these new emerging stages is that they contain many features that are age-agnostic.

Although the focus here is on the new emerging stages, we don't see these new stages replacing the elements of the traditional three stages. The traditional stages (education, work, retirement) will not become redundant and disappear from an individual's choice set. There will still be periods when focusing on generating financial assets through hard work will be crucial. Indeed, given that other less lucrative stages will also be present across a long life, it may even be that this maximization stage becomes even more intense. Currently during an uninterrupted second stage of work, most people strive to keep some focus on valuable intangible assets such as rest, fitness, family and friends.

Perhaps in a multi-stage life these intangible assets become less important and the focus will be on an even more intensive financial accumulation stage.

We have not designed each of these new stages in the abstract. Rather they are the result of deductions sketched from what we see happening around us and from observations of emerging trends. In outlining these new stages, we don't imagine we have captured all the ways individuals and society will respond to greater longevity. We do, however, think these new stages are likely to be much utilized, because they respond to some of the major flaws that are emerging in the concept of the traditional three-stage life and create more opportunities for people to grasp the gift of a long life.

Juvenesence

One of the most exciting aspects of the emergence of these new stages is that they are age-agnostic. In a three-stage life, age is a straightforward indicator of stage and this conflation of age and stage makes for a simple linear progression in terms of life. As the riddle of the sphinx tells us, we walk on four legs in the morning, two at noon and three in the evening. With the multi-stage life and the variety of ways of arranging activities, age and stage are no longer conflated. So the explorer, independent producer and portfolio stages that we describe in this chapter are relevant in different ways at many ages.

With this decoupling of age and stage, we will see characteristics previously associated with a specific age becoming more widespread. In particular the multi-stage life requires all ages to retain features previously associated with the young: youthfulness and plasticity; playfulness and improvisation; and the capacity to support novel action taking.

Youthfulness and plasticity

The phenomenon of increasing longevity is often referred to as ageing, and the usual focus is on people being older for longer. We think that there are powerful forces that instead will make us younger for longer – what Robert Pogue Harrison[5] terms *juvenescence,* or the state of being youthful or growing young.

This youthfulness in part reflects the elongation of adolescence. Humans are unique in the length of time they are socially and economically dependent. The evolutionary advantage of an elongated juvenile stage is the fact that there is more time for education, ensuring that the adult is operating on the basis of learning from past generations rather than simply instinctively. It makes sense with a longer life to further increase this investment in education. Adolescence is a time of flexibility – a time for discovering options and keeping them open rather than making commitments. With the lengthening of life, options become more valuable and so the period over which we explore and create options also lengthens.

Take a look back to the pictures of 16- and 17-year-olds from your grandparents' generation. In these pictures you will see serious faces that look full of life experiences and dressed in a way indistinguishable from their parents. Now look at pictures from the mid-1950s and already people of the same age are looking and dressing in a more youthful manner. Their style marks the emergence of the teenager – a new social phenomenon of that time. Now look at current photos of people in their 20s and 30s. A similar phenomenon is occurring – but at a different age. These people have the same youthful experience and responsibility-free look of those 1950s teenagers.

However, juvenescence is more than the elongation of adolescence. It is possible that all ages will act in a younger way and that these new stages can serve as a vehicle for this. A 100-year life with its multiple stages and several transitions requires flexibility and plasticity, so retaining adolescent features into adulthood will become more useful. In evolutionary biology this retention into adulthood of adolescent features is termed *neoteny*. From an evolutionary perspective, juveniles tend to be more adaptive and more flexible than adults. They have not yet developed the conservative perspective and fixed habits and routines of adults, and instead have the adaptability and plasticity of adolescence. Rigidity and fixed habits can work well in a linear, three-stage life in which there is limited need or opportunity for change. In a longer life with multiple stages, rigidity could become counterproductive and juvenescence a more valuable trait. Indeed it isn't just pictures of 20-year-olds that show greater youthfulness. People in their 50s and 60s tend also to look more youthful than pictures of your grandparents at that same age – both physically but also increasingly in how they dress and act.

There is also another aspect of the 100-year life that will lead to greater plasticity. As the disconnect of age and stage continues, this will create incredible opportunities for the ages to mix. Historically, age equalled stage and so those of the same age tended to go through the same experience and routines. Moreover, as the three stages became clearer, so age separation became firmer. In fact there is a view, held by the sociologists Gunhild Hagestad and Peter Uhlenberg,[6] that modern Western societies institutionally segregate the young, adults and the old through the mechanism of the three-stage life. This reinforces the link between age and stage that is in turn reinforced in educational institutions, work settings and retirement, all of which cater for distinct age groups.

Hagestad and Uhlenberg decry this age segregation. It leads, they argue, to a fall in respect for the old, denial of a traditional mentorship role for the old, and a lack of social embeddedness in the young. So perhaps one of the most exciting impacts of the multi-stage life is that the disconnection between age and stage will shake up this institutionalized age segregation. As different ages begin to engage in shared activities and mix with ease, so some of the stereotypes of age melt away. This creates the opportunity for everyone to grasp the flexibility and inquisitiveness of youth and the wisdom and insight of age.

Play and improvisation

What distinguishes humans from robots and machine learning is their capacity to be innovative and creative, to play and to improvise. Intense periods of full-on work are rarely times of play, although corporate leaders would very much appreciate it if they were and many worry that the design of work pushes out time for creativity. We wonder whether these new stages, freed from the institutionalization of work, could provide a place for play and improvisation.

We saw some of this in Jimmy's and Jane's lives. What distinguishes Jimmy's portfolio scenario is the excitement of making a transition into something he can be really excited about: building a working life with many elements that he finds meaningful. Or think of the young Jane exploring Argentina and Chile and walking the street markets of Buenos Aires;

working with Sam to build the business they really cared about; taking that short transition at the age of 45 to reconnect with her children and parents; or the 60-year-old Jane returning to her youthful haunts in South America; or the 70-year-old Jane bringing together her young and old self to construct a portfolio of interesting ideas and work.

These are moments where our characters are playing and improvising. Freed from the bonds of full-time, relentless work, they are letting their spirit soar.[7] They are discovering that play is not what you do, it is how you do it. Some of their time is spent in that marvellous term that anthropologists use: *galumphing* – the 'seemingly useless elaboration and ornamentation of activity'.[8] Stephen Nachmanovitch describes it thus:

> We galumph when we hop instead of walk, when we take the scenic route rather than the efficient one, when we are interested in means rather than ends. It is profligate, excessive, exaggerated, uneconomical.

In some of her life Jane is galumphing, experimenting with all sorts of combinations, engaging with the pleasure of doing. When she is at her most playful, there is no question of 'why' or what she will immediately gain. Indeed, once you put a price on it, it is no longer play. In her travels and her actions she is finding her authentic voice, giving herself space to hear her intuition and then improvising by putting this intuition into action.

Novel action taking

These new stages create opportunities to take novel actions and in these actions there is an opportunity to learn experientially. We fundamentally learn through doing, and these new stages are a wonderful opportunity to do, to take action and then reflect on how it felt. When Jane went onto the streets of Rio, how did she feel? Was she anxious, frightened, intrigued? If she can keep her awareness of the present then she can engage in what the therapist Janette Rainwater called the 'routine art of self-observation.'[9] This is a process of self-questioning of how an individual handles the time of her lifespan. It is about thinking about time in a positive way, allowing for life to be lived, rather than consisting of a finite quantity that is running out. As the sociologist Anthony Giddens puts it:

> Taking charge of one's life involves risk, because it means confronting a diversity of open possibilities. The individual must be prepared to make a more or less complete break with the past, if necessary, and to contemplate novel courses of action that cannot be guided by established habits.[10]

These new stages provide many opportunities for these novel actions and the experiential learning that comes with them: opportunities to question old habits and routines, to challenge stereotypes, and to experiment with new models for integrating the different parts of life.

Becoming an Explorer

When we think about the exploration stage, we imagine excitement, curiosity, adventure, investigation and anxiety. Not settling down but staying agile and light, and keeping financial commitments to a minimum so as to move easily. This is a period of discovery: journeying to discover something about the world and also finding out about oneself.

There have always been explorers – people who have spent their life exploring and travelling, seeking new experiences and opting out of the three-stage life. The concept of a gap year before university in some countries has become a well-established life stage and can fit into this explorer pattern of behaviour. However, what we think of as an explorer is a radical development of these behaviours.

This exploration is not a predetermined gap year, but rather a more extended new stage. Explorers are investigating the world around them, discovering what is out there, how it works, what they like and what they are good at. The exploration stage begins with the uprooting from everyday life and everyday experiences: moving to a new city to meet others, or journeying around a new country to explore their way of living. Exploration works best when it is not simply observation, in the sense that a tourist would observe a new city. It is a process of engagement, in the way that Jane engaged with the street food vendors in South

America and actively tried to figure out how they worked. Not all explorers have the same purpose.

Some will be *searchers* – setting out on the journey to explicitly answer a question. They are on a quest where they have an idea of the destination. An analogy would be Stanley's quest to find the source of the Nile. He and his party did not know the path they would take, but they knew what their destination would be. Right now we see explorers setting out with questions: what is really important to me, what do I care about, who am I? The journey they embark on is designed to help them answer these questions.

For other explorers there is no single question that guides them. They are the *adventurers* with no goal other than the everyday joy of discovery – they are galumphing. In these adventures they create the stories that will narrate their future lives: what they saw, who they met, what they learnt. In a sense it is the real essence of being a human – the marvelous freedom to stretch out to discover the world. Within 100 years, we can imagine that many people will want to embark on their own adventure.

Exploring works best when it is a period of genuine experimentation, with as much variety as possible. When Jane explored South America, she was confronted by the lives of others and pushed to think hard about her own values and priorities. It was also during this period of exploration that she had the time and inclination to widen her networks and make them more diverse. As her networks embraced a greater diversity of people, she was able to create more variety as she thought about her future possible self.

The psychology of the explorer stage is interesting. Explorers are pushing the boundaries of their existence, taking themselves out of the norm, confronting themselves with how others behave. They are standing at what MIT professor Otto Scharmer calls 'the edge of the system',[11] and by doing so they are shining a light on their own assumptions and values.

Crucible experiences

The very best periods of exploration have crucible experiences embedded within them. When leadership scholars Warren Bennis and R. Thomas interviewed leaders about their lives, they discovered that one of the common links shared by those leaders who had a strong sense of themselves and a strong moral anchor was their crucible experiences.[12] These were episodes in their life when they viscerally experienced the lives of others: the pain and the anguish, the exhilaration and the joy. They were, in a sense, walking in the shoes of others. These crucible experiences took many forms, from simply living in another city to spending time in a completely different context, such as a refugee camp. Philip Mirvis, who has looked deeply at the impact of these crucible experiences, believes that while the experience itself is vital, it takes inner questioning to create an opportunity to transform how one sees the world and then share this personal narrative.[13] That means asking questions, observing carefully and listening intently. With this depth of questioning, these experiences become times when people confront their own values and think more deeply about their identity and the roles they are playing. It can be a time when an individual's own narrative is confronted by the narrative of another.

Long lives mean change and transformation – that is why transformational assets are such an important new asset category. These assets are really brought to the fore in situations that involve crucible experiences. What is important is that rather than simply reading a book or visiting a website, these are real, face-to-face, visceral events. At such times, people are able to glimpse the totality of human existence: the life that got these people to this place, the pressures they are under, and the opportunities they face.

Exploring at any age

Anyone can be an explorer at any time or any age, but there are three periods of life – from 18 to 30, during the mid-40s, and around 70 and 80 – when, for many people, the fit will be perfect. These are often periods that mark natural life transitions and at these times such periods of exploration could serve a more directed role: a time to take stock, to understand options more deeply, and to reflect more on belief and values.

Becoming an explorer could be an incredibly rejuvenating experience later in life. For those in their 70s, the danger of facing a long life is becoming stuck in a rut. So casting everyday life aside and becoming an adventurer could well play a vital role in revitalization, as people question their current lifestyle and identify which other options are out there. That is what we saw Jane doing in her life.

For Jimmy in his mid-40s, this period of exploration may well have to be more focused. This is a time in his life when there is a growing realization that his current plan and the depleted state of his intangible assets are insufficient to support him in later life. So in one scenario Jimmy takes time out to explore possible new ways of living and begins to move out of his current well-trodden path. He is in the searching mode of exploration as he wakes up in his 40s to the reality that he faces a potentially very long three-stage life. At this point in time he has an idea of what he does not want, but a much less formed notion of what he does want. He needs time to experiment, to reflect and to begin to free himself from the habits of his existing role. So for Jimmy – and perhaps others of a similar age who decide to take time out to explore – this will be a period when activities such as education and re-skilling will be slotted in.

The most obvious period of exploration is between the time people leave formal education until their early 30s. Often they are searchers, learning more about themselves, thinking more about who they are, what they like, and what they are good at. And because exploration is an external rather than an internal period of discovery, they are learning about who they are in a context which tests and confronts, and provokes anger but also sometimes joy.

Options, searching and matches

Those who, like Jack, dive straight into the corporate world in the first stage face the distinct possibility that the early decision they make about where to specialize turns out to be a dead end, as the landscape of work changes or they misunderstand their own skills and aspirations. For Jack this did not really matter; he was not faced with a great deal of choice, as his life course would not contain many transitions and he only worked for forty years. Those with the gift of a long life will be presented with many more options, more variety and more decisions to be taken, and taking time to choose the right ones is important: following an education course that mirrors your interests and enthusiasms with an eye on the future; finding a job that matches your values and is meaningful to you, that reflects your skills and interests yet does not lead to a dead end; choosing a company that espouses your own values and will provide a context to develop your skills and knowledge; meeting a partner with whom you believe you can spend a long period of time and who is a good match for you; indeed possibly encountering a business partner with whom you can work and who matches and perhaps complements your own skills and ways of working.

Making a good match becomes a crucial attribute in a long life, in part because the consequences of the match are felt for longer. It's also because many matches are taking place in what Giddens calls a 'post-traditional' society, where many of the traditional match-making practices are waning.

Some of the choices made will turn out to be good decisions. Others will not, and over a longer life the costs of making bad decisions and mistakes increase. That's why it is not surprising that Jane will spend time exploring her options. The value of finding an optimal match – either over lifestyle, career or marriage – is greater with a long life and, of course, the costs of a bad match or a wrong early commitment are also greater. The old maxim 'decide in haste, repent at leisure' becomes a powerful motto over the course of a 100-year life.

We think it is the enhanced focus on options, finding the right match and crafting her own identity that makes Jane and her generation so distinct. There has been much talk of the generational cohort that Jane has entered, variously termed *Millennials* or *Generation Y*. Much of this is stereotypical and an overgencralization of what Gen Y wants or needs.[14] For us, what really distinguishes this generation is not the particular milieu into which its members were born, but rather that this is the first generation that is really aware of the 100-year life and is planning accordingly. Options, matching and personal identity are different issues for this generation than for Jack's, and their response is not a generational one but that of social pioneers whose actions will be copied by subsequent generations.

We see periods of exploration as being crucial to understanding options and trying to create the optimal match. However, it is undeniable that exploration is fraught with danger and the risk of failure. John Franklin and his crew never found their way through the North West Passage and Scott's expedition never reached the South Pole. For that reason, we don't expect everyone to embark on an exploration stage. Some people may well have a strong sense of their own identity and a deep awareness of their strengths and preferences. For them, channelling their passion to pursue their goal may be the best option and they would view a period of exploration as a distraction. Others may be risk-averse and keen to commit and achieve some financial goals and pursue a conventional career straight after their education. For others still, it could be a life-changing stage. But it can only be so if it is a period of activity and discovery. The explorer stage is not a time for sitting around and doing nothing, nor is it an elongated version of the student gap year. It is a period that really gains from thought and planning, and without this momentum there is a risk of decay and depreciation of assets rather than investment and renewal.

Being an Independent Producer

A new stage of economic activity is emerging that involves creating novel forms of entrepreneurship or building new patterns of partnerships and firms. It happens when a person forsakes a conventional career path to start up their own entrepreneurial activities. Just like the explorer stage, this will not be limited to any particular age group. People can and will become independent producers at many different points in their lives. These are job creators rather than job seekers.

Pop-ups and prototypes

Of course there have always been entrepreneurs. The reason we refer to independent producers rather than entrepreneurs is a reflection of the scale and aspiration. Independent producers are not, in the main, aiming at building a lasting company that is intended to grow and prosper and then be sold on. These are more transient structures; some will be pop-ups aimed at grabbing the moment. With pop-ups, the emphasis is all on the activity itself rather than the outcome – the start-up, not the sell-out. There is a playfulness and experiential quality about them that goes right back to our youthfulness discussion earlier. So it is less about building a corporate entity and accumulating financial assets, and more about spending a block of time, at any stage in a working life, engaged in independent self-supporting productive work: making a product, creating a service, building an idea. These periods of independent production played an important role in both Jimmy and Jane's life, and although this time can be short on tangible assets, it is rich in the development of intangible assets.

For many independent producers, this is a time of fast experimentation as they learn what works and what doesn't. Otto Scharmer uses the term *prototyping* to describe this activity.[15] His observations suggest that it works best when it's associated with a heightened sense of mindfulness and rapid cycles of prototyping to learn more and more deeply. Often the independent producer stage begins with prototype activities that are not yet fully blown pilots. For those people already in work, these prototyping activities often take place in parallel with their day work, in a sense giving them permission to move into something much earlier than if they first had to completely figure out what to do. During these cycles of prototyping, intuition comes to the fore and the independent producer has a wider sense of possibilities. These rapid cycles of prototyping generate constant feedback that helps people to evolve their ideas about how they could make a project work.

Learning by producing

The independent producer stage marks a period of building expertise, learning and producing. While earning money to fund this life stage is important and a sign of validation, this will rarely be a stage of significant accumulation of financial assets. It is a time when learning by producing really comes to the fore.

Critically, this is a stage that can provide a platform for failing. Because this is a period of relatively low commitments, it's a great time to fail without the anxiety of serious consequences. The entrepreneurial nature of the independent producer stage also provides plenty of useful learning by doing: Can you raise the finances required? Can you obtain the resources you need to operate? Do you have a wide enough circle of contacts to borrow, get support and advice to make your initiative fly? All these are great intangible assets to invest in from a working perspective. Often these are grounded, practical and general skills that are portable across many sectors and future jobs. So while these assets can build on the academic knowledge acquired through study, they also bring deeper insight because they are experiential.

When someone becomes an independent producer at the beginning of a career, we can think of this situation as having two faces. Like the Roman god Janus, it looks both backward and forward: backward in the sense that this is still a form of education and practical learning; forward because it can be a crucial time when credentials are earned before embarking on job seeking in the more conventional sphere. In this case this puts a significant emphasis on building credentials and creating a good reputation. This is sure to be more than a traditional linear autobiographical record of institutions attended or qualifications gained. Instead it is a period of curating a reputation that is made up of many different forms: what has been achieved, what has been experienced, networks that have been created, and evidence of co-creation and working collaboratively with others.[16]

Being an independent producer could also be a lifestyle choice and the means of preservation of financial assets later in life. For example, in those over 55 there is already a sharp increase in entrepreneurship, with this age group now accounting for 26 per cent of entrepreneurs in 2014 compared to 15 per cent in 1996.[17] We would expect those in their 70s and 80s to also engage in this. Some will choose to continue to work full-time, others will build a portfolio, but some will choose to put their time and energy into creating something that has the potential to excite and interest them and possibly to be a legacy for others. Working actively under their own self-management is a wonderful way to preserve their lifestyle while also supporting their vitality and productive assets. Most independent producers will want this to be a period of minimum depletion of tangible assets; their income, net of expenditure, will provide just enough to live on.

Creative clusters

Independent producers are already emerging as a stage for those aged 18–30. What is interesting is that most are clustering together to learn from each other, often at the margins of smart cities. When teenagers emerged as a separate age cohort, they were spotted first by marketers: this was a group with a unique consumption pattern. For this age group, the crucial addition is that their interaction is based around production as well as consumption, and as they cluster together in towns or cities they begin to define a lifestyle and a distinct way of blending living and working.

While entrepreneurs of an older vintage may have jealously guarded their intellectual copyright, among independent producers there is a much greater emphasis on sharing in this productive phase. Copying and replicating are high forms of praise and indeed can raise their profile. They are proof of concept but also blur the concept of an idea, a product and a firm. The ethos is 'everyone joins in' – the very essence of a collaborative, high-value network. Being at the hub of one of these networks, being well connected or being seen as a creator of new ideas is the intangible asset that can really boost reputation and provide the possibility of financial benefit at later stages.

This focus on connectivity as both an input and a measure of success explains why smart cities are growing and attracting clusters of independent producers.[18] Although the popular focus is on independent producers in the technology clusters such as Silicon Valley in California, Silicon Roundabout in London, Bangalore in India and Chengdu in China, it is clear that the independent producer stage can be a great deal farther-reaching and many more clusters will form. These clusters will become ever more important and pervasive because the independent producer stage is essentially experiential; for most, it cannot be easily achieved by living remotely and digitally. Urban concentration is important and because this is a stage of low income, the focus will be on finding places in cities that are cheap but central. Of course, as a result, the area will take on the lifestyle of its distinctive inhabitants. As befits the independent producer, the separation between work and play will be vague as home, office and social life could occupy the same location. Also as befits a stage not focused on asset accumulation, you can expect to see more bikes than cars, and more coffee shops than offices.

These physical clusters of independent producers attract people who are looking for learning experience, a place to experiment, perhaps to meet partners both in terms of marriage and in terms of business, with a focus on experimentation and investing in intangible assets. They see that it is plausible to work in the informal rather than formal economy and are making use of fast-developing technology that enables rapid prototyping and scaling of ideas. Their work is characterized by brevity; it is transient, deliberately short-lived and episodic.

Reputation and curating

The focus for the independent producer is on making things happen and, through this, gaining a reputation for being action-orientated and able to overcome obstacles. The reputation won during this period could become a crucial intangible asset for the next stages of life. The website that describes their work, the hackathon they won, the Twitter stream of their activities, or the YouTube channel they create, all serve to advertise and broadcast ideas and competence to the world. As firms look into their ecosystem for ideas, these are the broadcasts of reputation that are most likely to catch their eye.

Building, curating and broadcasting their capabilities is crucial for independent producers. Much will be learnt experientially from peers and mentors, while other skills will be learnt more formally. In creating this combination of skills and knowledge, those who pursue this path will need to consider how they signal to future employees or acquaintances what they have learnt and established. Of course, their engagement with social media will leave a visible footprint of their economic activities, but there will doubtless be experiments about how to create a more formal way of narrating credentials. At the time of writing, LinkedIn is serving as a platform to broadcast skills, and we can imagine that this will be joined by other innovations.

We can also imagine that educational institutions will develop assessment formats that provide credentials for skills that are not tied to specific courses. So independent producers could go about their entrepreneurial activities, perhaps attend some course of study or take a MOOC (Massive Open Online Course) and then sit an exam to earn credentials that show their competence in specific areas. This will be crucial. Experiential learning is great and hugely effective, but precisely because it is experiential it is hard to document. Looking simply at the financial success of the business will not necessarily be the metric to measure the success of the independent producer, so it will be imperative to find ways to credentialize the attainment of intangible assets.

This will also be important in building a reputation with larger firms. We expect that corporations will become more willing and adept at spotting talented independent producers, and creating a personalized relationship with them that could range from full-time employment, to part-time work, right up to buying their IP or the business itself.

Travelling light

The major investment of the explorer and independent producer stage is in intangible assets – particularly *transformational assets*.

So during these periods, financing is always going to be tricky. That is why developments in the technologies of the sharing economy are so interesting.[19] The sharing economy is a great way of enabling people to remain asset-light or to bring income in to finance their asset accumulation. Sharing platforms such as Airbnb, Simplest, Lyft or even Dogvacay are all examples of an emerging economy where people share capacity of assets that they may have purchased or created. So not only is it possible to put off making big financial decisions, it is also possible to reduce the exposure to these financial decisions. Buying a house or a car is expensive, as it involves purchasing a capital stock and making a financial commitment. This needs evidence of a reliable salary in order to secure the credit or to purchase it outright. For a stage of life where options are important, this becomes very undesirable. Worse still, buying a capital good is not only expensive, it also creates problems of capacity. If you buy a car, you won't use it all the time, so there is money lying idle rather than being invested in a start-up; if you buy a house and then travel on your explorer stage, the money used to finance the purchase is doing nothing. The promise of the sharing economy either helps solve these capacity problems by providing income from a purchased good, or it enables a person to get the benefit of an asset without having to commit to a job or the financing of it.

Crafting a portfolio

There will be times when the focus is on one activity: taking a high-value corporate role, building a business, exploring, or going back to full-time education. There will be other times when people will want to pursue a combination of activities. This is a portfolio where a variety of different types of engagement are undertaken simultaneously. Like the other new stages, this is not age-dependent; you can build a portfolio at any point in your productive life. For some it will be an option that is actively pursued to explore and experiment; for others it will be a situation that is thrust upon them because securing a meaningful job has been so hard to achieve. However, while in theory creating a portfolio is possible at any age, we imagine it will be particularly attractive for people who have already built a well-established foundation. Indeed when we talk about the 100-year life to senior executives and then ask them to envisage their future lives, many of them see building a portfolio as central to their long-term strategy. They imagine themselves actively balancing different types of work, some focused on making money, others on building community relationships, helping their extended family or perfecting a hobby.

For those who are building from a well-established platform of skills and networks, this high-value portfolio is a good option.

At its centre is paid work, perhaps one or two days a week in an activity that links to the past. For CEOs, for example, this invariably includes being on a board; for other senior executives, it is some form of senior role in an organization that taps into their past experience and skills and provides some continuity with the past. But having worked hard throughout a conventional career, the desire is also to do more: to have fun, to contribute something back to society, to spend more time with friends. So the portfolio is balanced in three ways: earning enough money to match outgoings and boost savings; taking a part-time role that links to the past and maintains reputation, skills and mental stimulation; and developing additional and new roles that broaden learning and provide a sense of purpose. As a result, the portfolio stage inevitably has a range of motivations; in part it's about financial accumulation, in part about exploring, in part about vitality and stimulation, but also about learning and making a social contribution.

Leverage from the past

Portfolio living can be incredibly exciting. As we live longer, there is the possibility of boredom and repeating the past, and so our taste for variety increases. This is a genuinely attractive proposition, but we have some concerns, both about how easy it is to establish this stage as well as how hard it is to transit into it. We wonder how many of the people we have spoken to who envisage a portfolio stage in their life will actually achieve it?

The tension is that as we live longer, so habits become more entrenched. When someone makes a successful transition to the portfolio stage, they do so because they are able to change gear and see their working career as the development of competencies rather than the accumulation of job titles. Moving from full-time employment into a portfolio stage requires flexibility in mental agilities as well as working patterns for which a traditional second-stage career is not always a good preparation.

Those who make a successful shift into a portfolio stage do so because they make early preparations and begin to experiment with small-scale projects while they are still working full-time. They begin to experiment with projects that could be of interest to them, move towards role models of people who have the sort of portfolio lives they envisage, and begin to tip the balance from internal corporate networks towards more external and diverse networks. This is where their transformational assets are so important. As these networks expand, they are beginning to engage with people across a broad range of activities and are building reputation and skills that are transportable across sectors and easily communicated. This communication of skills and achievements across a broader spectrum is a crucial preparation for the portfolio stage. Without it, the move from full-time work can be a real disappointment.

Smoothing out inefficiencies

One of the challenges of the portfolio stage is that is has inefficiencies built into it. The variety of the portfolio brings excitement and interest, but the downside of this variety is that those who engage in this stage don't get increasing returns of scale. Picture a typical portfolio week: perhaps a couple of days of paid work, maybe one day working in the community, one day developing a hobby and one day on the board of a charity. As you move from one activity to another, there are big switching costs. One day you are engaged with a charity, the next working in the community, and another serving on a board. These all require different mental attitudes and could also involve physical switching, as you move from one location to another. We see these switching costs as a major challenge for this portfolio stage.

However, it is possible to reduce these switching costs. The most obvious way is to build synergies between the different pieces of the portfolio. This synergy could be created because all the activities have a span of capabilities and knowledge in common. For example, a high level of project management skills could be the foundation that unites a number of potentially disparate activities. The focus here is on ensuring that the skills and capabilities are associated with each other rather than orthogonal. The binding could be an interest in broad themes or core capabilities. Another way of reducing switching costs is by bunching up time rather than fragmenting it. That means, for example, working three full days a week rather than five half-days. Portfolio activities can also be stressful if past success was based around focus and concentration. While this seems to be a stage desired by many, it doesn't work for everyone, especially if there is a lack of congruence between the various activities of the portfolio.

The emergence of Yahoos

Although these new stages will be experienced by all ages, right now it is the 18–30-year-olds who are really embracing them. We shouldn't be surprised by this. After all, Jane's generation has the greatest need to adapt to longevity and also the greatest flexibility to do so. So it is they who will lead the way in experimentation and the adoption of new stages. Being an explorer, an independent producer and creating a portfolio (for this age group by utilizing the gig economy) will all be actively used and developed. This is an age group that, perhaps more than any other, realizes the value of options and is prepared to work hard to investigate and create them. In financial theory, an option is the right to buy an asset at a fixed price. The longer the period over which an option works, the greater its value. Moreover, the greater the uncertainty around the asset, the greater the value of the option. With their long lives and the greater uncertainty they face, this is a generation for whom options have the potential to be incredibly valuable. Their response has been to marry later, start a family later, buy houses and cars later and in general postpone commitments.

There are, of course, negative features that also drive this behaviour. In many developed countries this is an age group that feels betrayed by older generations. They find themselves saddled with higher levels of student debt, entering a labour force where getting their first job is increasingly competitive, and living in cities where house prices are beyond their reach. As a consequence, many have little choice but to be asset-light and imaginative about how they achieve economic self-sufficiency.

As this age group creates options, postpones commitments and remains flexible, they are displaying features traditionally associated with adolescence; they are, in other words, a great example of the juvenescence and neoteny we described earlier. Viewed from the perspective of a traditional three-stage life, this youthful behaviour seems wrong and is often described negatively in terms of lack of commitment. However, viewed from the perspective of a multi-stage life, the behaviour is not about lack of commitment but rather about relentless investment in intangibles – particularly those that create options. When those following traditional career paths fail to recognize this, it simply fuels cross-generational mistrust and leads to stereotyping of what people refer to as the 'Millennial', 'Generation Y', and so on.

When life lasts longer, it seems sensible to allocate some of those additional years to lengthening the period over which you develop as an adult. This is what lies behind the development of a distinct post-adolescent/post-teenage stage. The teenage years are a time of experimentation and establishing values through experiences and rites of passage. In terms of economics, however, it is mainly a period of consumption. With money from parents or limited part-time employment, this group can be seen as independent consumers where leisure and goods are ways of defining an emerging identity. For those aged 18–30, the economic context switches more towards production and learning productive skills and knowledge outside of education – hence the attraction of the explorer, independent producer or portfolio stages.

It took a while for society to coin a phrase to describe the increasingly standardized behaviour that was developing during adolescence over the twentieth century. Eventually the phrase 'teenager' became established. We think society will need to search for a similar phrase to cover those aged 18–30. We describe them (with apologies to Jonathan Swift) as 'Yahoos' – Young Adults Holding OptiOnS.

The nature of transitions

Three-stage lives have only two transitions: from education to employment, and from employment into retirement. Multi-stage lives have many more transitions. That is why we imagined that a new intangible asset based around transformation would become so crucial, and yet most people will have little in their repertoire of skills that prepares them for it.

We don't imagine transitions as distinctive stages. They mark the often indistinct boundary between stages and form part of the continuum of life often seen in retrospect rather than understood in the moment. Mathematicians have a way of thinking about continuums; they say that if summer follows winter, then spring must have occurred. It is the same with transitions. If you move from a corporate role into a portfolio, or an exploration stage into a portfolio, then a transition must have taken place. Many times, this transition will overlap with a stage. At other times the transition is marked by a separate preparation activity, which is often about investing in intangible assets: boosting vitality by investing in recharging, or honing productive assets through re-creating.

What transitions have in common is that they tend to unfold one step at a time. As Herminia Ibarra found, they begin with a feeling of being out of synch, that the possible selves we are constructing are beginning to look more attractive than the current self. This motivates action, and so there follows a time of exploration when ideas are tested and a cycle of learning occurs. It is at this point that diverse networks are so important to creating a sense of opportunity. So we begin to learn more by crafting experiments and side projects that allow us to get a better feeling for what is possible, and this is often when connections are shifted. Finally, as the transition comes to an end, there is a period of confirmation when commitments are escalated and more plans for the future are made.[20]

Recharging and re-creating transitions

We see two different types of transitions emerging, both of which involve heavy investment in intangibles and both of which we used in Jane's scenario.

One transition is based on the simple motivation to *recharge*. After periods of working intensively, working long hours and acquiring financial assets, it is inevitable that intangible assets such as vitality will be depleted. Health may be poor, family and friendships may need reinvigorating, and mental appetite and stimulation may need boosting. Taking time off to invest in these intangibles before recommencing the next stage of life is an appealing form of transition. A recharging transition is appealing but its reach and long-term impact is limited. At the end of a recharge transition, though vitality is boosted, productive assets such as skill sets, knowledge and networks may have diminished because of lack of use. So after a recharging transition, people will inevitably go back to their same sector and same type of role as before.

The alternative is a transition based on *re-creation*. Rather than investing in depleted intangibles, the focus is on positively investing in productive intangibles – be that new sets of skills and knowledge, new networks, or new perspectives. This may be as simple as attending college and taking courses; it may involve some part-time work; or it may involve more comprehensive shifts such as relocating and substantial changes in lifestyle. These re-creation transitions play a key role in shifting networks and skills in order to move into a new stage.

Financing transitions

Transitions can be crucial periods in which to reinvest in valuable intangible assets – both productive and vitality. But they are inevitably times when tangible financial assets are also depleted. The result is that this depletion has to be considered and planned for. In the scenarios we built for Jane, we dealt with this depletion through two devices. The first was that, in terms of the purpose of savings, Jane saved for her retirement but also accumulated financial assets in order to finance those periods of transition. The second way we financed Jane's transitions was that her partner Jorge was also working and saving. So within their partnership they were able to coordinate the timings of their transitions. While one member of the partnership was contributing to the financial assets, the other member could focus on building their intangible assets.

As social experiments proliferate, we can imagine that these new stages – the explorer, the independent producer, the portfolio stage and transitions, whether recharging or re-creating – will continue to grow in popularity. Rather than being seen as unique or unusual, they will drop into our everyday description of living, just as 'teenagers' and 'retirees' have done in the past. They will be viewed as common stages that people can utilize at different points in their life. And indeed, they may be joined by other stages as more experimentation takes place and more pathways are discovered.

7

Money

Financing a long life

It is no surprise that many people see the financing of a long life as a curse. There are many aspects of long-term financial planning that can be unpleasant and unrewarding. It is complicated, requires self-knowledge, involves tackling difficult questions, and needs some insight about future needs and aspirations. Without knowing what you want and having an idea of a life plan, it's hard to calculate long-term finances. Added to this, the terminology of financial planning is difficult, with concepts such as geometric progressions and compound interest.

There is also the question of reward. Basically, preparing for the future means transferring money from today to the future, and most people find it tough to create a close connection between their current and future selves.

So it's no surprise that financial planning causes great anxiety. But these issues have to be tackled head-on. Those who don't consider their future life, aren't able to make the complicated calculations, fail to understand the technical terms, or don't take full account of their future self run the risk of entering old age with insufficient resources. Alternatively they could find themselves in mid-life without the savings they need to take a career break to re-skill. It is no surprise that a recent survey of retirees found that 70 per cent wished they had saved more.[1]

Making the most of a 100-year life involves restructuring the decades by moving away from a three-stage life and shifting the way in which intangible assets are managed. However, while important, none of those changes will of themselves solve the financial problem we identified back in Chapter 2 – a long life simply requires everyone to work longer and save more.

Therefore, we return once more to the subject of finances and draw from both the economics and psychology literatures to focus on the rational and behavioural aspects of financing a long life. We revisit two concepts we discussed in relation to transformational assets: the importance of *efficacy* ('I believe I am competent to perform this behaviour') and *agency* ('I have the self-control and will to make this happen').

Appropriate financial planning depends on both. On *efficacy* in the sense of realism in creating financial plans, and self-knowledge in understanding aspects such as a general appetite for saving. Efficacy requires answering questions like: 'How much do I need to live on?', 'How long do I want to work for?', 'What is my knowledge of my financial situation?' and 'How financially literate am I?' Financial planning also depends on taking action that is determined by *agency* – having the self-control to act on this knowledge and thereby balancing current needs with future needs. The question is: 'Would my 70- or 80-year-old self approve of the decisions I am taking today?'

Making the numbers add up

In our analysis of Jimmy's finances, we calculated that he had to save 17 per cent of his income every year of his working life if he wanted to retire on a 50 per cent pension at the age of 65. We calculated that Jane needed to save 25 per cent to do the same. These are challenging, if not impossible, numbers. In Jimmy's 4.0 scenario, assuming he works until he is 77, then his required savings rate falls to 8 per cent; in Jane's 5.0 scenario, if she works until she is 85, then her savings rate falls to 11 per cent. For many people these remain challenging numbers to achieve every year, and they don't even factor in how Jimmy and Jane pay off their student loans or their mortgage, or finance their medical or old age care expenditures.

Given this difficult and painful problem, it is no surprise that many people grab at what appears superficially to be a simple solution. There are three common ways in which we typically try to deny the arithmetic logic of these calculations: we imagine it will be possible to survive on less than 50 per cent pension; we assume that the value of our home can be used to finance retirement; and we believe that if we are more aggressive in our investment behaviour then we will earn a higher rate of return. None of these lines of reasoning are likely to solve the challenge of financing a long life.

How much do I need?

Is it possible to survive on less than a 50 per cent pension and still look forward to a good retirement? In Figures 2.4 and 2.7 we showed alternative savings rates for different pension replacement rates. Could you live on less than your final salary? If so, how much less? The problem is complicated – you don't know how long you will live and you don't know how much it will cost to live when you retire.

Consider how much you currently spend and what you spend it on. In retirement, with more time and fewer work demands, how much money would you need? At first this may seem easy – you can think about what you do now during holidays. But that is a poor guide; a holiday is a temporary, not a permanent, break or change in lifestyle. Can you really imagine what you would want to do and what you would enjoy in retirement?

Perhaps, as you think about this, you have considered that a replacement rate of less than 100 per cent is reasonable. In retirement, there is less work-related expenditure (e.g. commuting, clothing) and more time to do the activities that were previously outsourced (e.g. cooking meals, DIY) as well as to be more efficient in shopping or searching the web for coupons and benefits. Indeed, people in their late 60s already do this – they make more use of retailer and manufacturer discount coupons and so pay 4 per cent less than people in their late 40s.[2] This may not sound a lot, but in the context of a 50 per cent replacement ratio that's a significant difference.

You may also imagine that when you retire there will be major shifts in your leisure activities. With more time, leisure becomes 'cheap', as people switch to activities that make greater use of this time by investing in things that 'money can't buy': spending more time with friends and family, taking longer and less intensive trips … watching the sun go down. Perhaps your image is that of the happy retiree who wrote to the *New York Times*: 'You can get by on a lot less when you're retired, without really depriving yourself of anything important … If I had known earlier how much "wealth" derives from such simple pleasure, I would have retired a lot sooner.'[3]

By the time you retire, your children will have grown up and left home. Indeed, when two children aged 16 or older leave home, the calculations are that the household can have the same standard of living for around 60 per cent of their past expenditure.

However, while these arguments sound convincing, they need to be tempered. First, there is the question of higher expenditures on health and care. There is no doubt that for many people longevity will be accompanied by a shortening of morbidity. However, as the economist Jonathan Skinner puts it, 'Saving for retirement may ultimately be less about the golf condo at Hilton Head and more about being able to afford a wheelchair lift, private nurse and high quality nursing home'.[4] It could also be that there will still be responsibilities towards others even when you retire: paying college or school fees for children or grandchildren, paying for their weddings, or providing them with a foot on the housing ladder or a car.

In our own calculations, we ultimately chose a 50 per cent replacement rate as a baseline. We believe this figure to be suitably conservative and broadly appropriate, especially for wealthier people. One study asked people directly (in the US and the Netherlands): 'What is the minimum level of monthly spending that you never want to fall below during retirement, at all costs?' While the poorest among those surveyed wanted replacement rates above 100 per cent, among the richest the average desired ratio was 54 per cent and in the Netherlands 63 per cent.[5] The UK Pension Commission of 2004 also used a 50 per cent replacement rate as their benchmark for high earners (those earning more than £40k).

While we believe this replacement rate to be reasonable, it is important to bear in mind that this is a conservative assumption. A recent survey of the actual replacement rates of 16,000 retired people found around a third of them had a replacement rate greater than 100 per cent, a quarter between 75–100 per cent and another quarter between 50–75 per cent. Only 21 per cent had a replacement rate of 50 per cent or less.[6] In other words, if you found the saving rates required for Jimmy and Jane uncomfortably high, it's unlikely that respite will come from you not needing so much money in retirement. In fact, if you are like most retirees, you will actually want to save more to support your lifestyle in retirement.

It is not only future pension and future consumption that have to be considered, it is also current consumption habits. The more a person is locked into high levels of consumption during any stage of their life, the harder it will be for them to adapt to lower consumption levels in retirement. There is plenty of evidence that shows that satisfaction derived from consumption depends not just on current levels, but also on past consumption. So restraining expenditure now doesn't just help boost savings, it also moderates consumption habits, which in turn makes it easier to feel satisfied in retirement when living on a lower income.

One further caveat about our assumption of a 50 per cent replacement rate: we have assumed in our calculations that you own your own house. If you don't, then you need to pay rent and in that case you need to think of a replacement rate of around 70–80 per cent.

Betting on the house

Tangible assets include pension, savings and a home – so what role should housing play in these calculations? The importance of housing varies around the world, but in most countries housing wealth is a significant part of most people's portfolio. In the UK, for example, housing accounts for around 25–30 per cent of the total wealth of the richest 50 per cent. That is why so many people believe they can use the value of their house as a means of financing their retirement.

Housing is, however, a very unusual type of tangible asset compared to money in the bank or investments in stocks and shares. That is because, as well as being a store of value, a house also provides a flow of consumption benefits. One benefit is known as 'imputed rent', which equates to the rent that would have been paid in order to live in the house.

Selling shares or running down a bank deposit helps fund a lifestyle without lowering the standard of living. By contrast, selling a house and downsizing in order to release funds immediately lowers the standard of living in terms of housing services. This, and the fact that homeowners have an emotional attachment to their house, helps explain why most people don't actually see housing as a way of funding their pension. In fact, one study found that 70 per cent of people aged 70 or under felt there was a minimal chance of selling their house to pay for retirement.[7] Another study found that when people retire they are equally as likely to move into a larger house as a smaller one.[8] It is generally only traumatic events, such as death of a partner or illness, that tends to trigger house sales as people age.

Given that owning a house provides imputed rent, and selling a house involves a fall in living standards, it is no surprise that equity release schemes have been growing in popularity with older home owners. Equity release helps provide financing without the loss of imputed rent. This clearly has a role to play in providing financing for old age, but while these schemes make a contribution, they cannot be relied upon to solve the problem. To use equity release, a person needs to have equity in their home. The savings calculations we made earlier focused only on funding pensions or transitions; we did not factor in caring for a mortgage. Equity release can help make a financial contribution to a pension, but the fact you need to purchase a house only raises the lifetime savings requirement we have calculated.

As you think about your financial planning, it would seem wise to consider housing wealth as a provision for precautionary financing such as medical or care issues; if that is not needed, then the house provides an inheritance.[9] Equity release provides an option for housing to make a contribution to your lifestyle, but it is unwise to rely on housing to solve the challenges of financing a 100-year life.

Investing like Warren Buffett

Our financial assumption for Jimmy and Jane was that they earned a long-run rate of return on their investments of 3 per cent above inflation. We explained why we settled on that number. But clearly a higher rate of return means less savings will be needed.

To see how important assumptions are about the return on investment, consider the 'Rule of 70'. This states that if you divide 70 by the return on investment, then that's approximately how many years it takes to double your wealth. In other words, if the return is 1 per cent then it will take 70 years, but if it were 2 per cent it would take only 35 years. Small differences in rates of return add up over time to big differences in saving requirements.

However, some investors do manage to outperform that 3 per cent average return, even over the long run.[10] One of the most famous is Warren Buffett, the Sage of Omaha. If you had invested $10,000 in his Berkshire Hathaway fund in 1965, then by 2005 it would have been worth $30 million – outperforming the aggregate stock market more than sixty-fold. Of course, pension planning becomes much easier with this level of investment performance.

In Figure 7.1 we show how the savings rate for Jimmy varies with changes in the average return on investments. With a 2 per cent rate of return, he needs to save 23 per cent of his income in

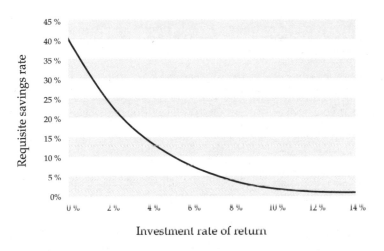

FIGURE 7.1 *Required savings for different investment returns.*

order to achieve a pension worth 50 per cent of his salary; with 10 per cent return, he need only save around 1 per cent.

However, before you phone your broker and shift your investments into an aggressive high return portfolio, it's worth remembering the most basic tenet in finance: the riskier a project, the higher its rate of return. Warren Buffett is a remarkable investor whose continual success marks him out as a financial legend. However, in general, high rates of return are a compensation for greater risk and so you may actually lose your money rather than make 10 per cent. As many investors found in the immediate aftermath of the 2007 crash, stocks can go down as well as up. For example, if you had retired in October 2007 with the S&P at 1550 you would have been looking forward to a very different retirement than if you had retired in March 2009 with the index at 680. Achieving the best return on your savings is an important aspect of financial planning, but relying on rates of return of significantly more than 3 per cent above inflation may not be the wisest move.

So here is our advice. You may get lucky as an investor and find a Warren Buffett to look after your money – but it's not a strategy you should rely upon. You can look to sell your house at retirement, but that will probably involve a drop in your standard of living and leave you with no precautionary funds for health problems or care homes. You could also say that you can get by with a much lower replacement ratio, but, as we showed, our calculations are reasonably conservative and any lower number would make you very much a minority among retirees. If you are going to resolve the financial challenges of a 100-year life by saving more, then we need to return to the dual factors of efficacy and agency.

Financial efficacy

Efficacy involves self-knowledge as well as general knowledge. Through our various scenarios, we have aimed to prompt you to think more deeply about how you want to structure your longer life. In order to do so from a financial perspective, boosting your financial literacy is crucial.

How much do you understand finance? Are you comfortable making your own investment decisions and reading through the sales literature of financial companies? Perhaps you should approach building your financial competency in the same way that you approach any other process of work-related knowledge acquisition. In fact, a study of financially knowledgeable investors showed they earned an additional 1.3 per cent per annum, even allowing for risk.[11] That makes a big difference: for every $100k invested over ten years, the financially knowledgeable investor will have an additional $16,000; over twenty years they accumulate $42,000; over thirty years it is $84,000; and over forty years an additional $145,000.

You can start to test your own financial literacy by considering what have been termed the 'Big 5' questions (answers at the end of the chapter).

Q1. Suppose you had $100 in a savings account and interest rates are 2 per cent per year. After five years how much do you think you would have in the account if you left the money to grow?

Q2. Imagine that the interest on your savings account was 1 per cent per year and inflation was 2 per cent per year. After one year would you be able to buy more than today, exactly the same, or less than today?

Q3. Do you think that the following statement is true or false: 'Buying a single company stock usually produces a safer return than a stock mutual fund.'

Q4. Do you think that the following statement is true or false: 'A 15-year mortgage typically requires higher monthly payments than a 30-year mortgage but the total interest on the life of the loan will be less.'

Q5. If interest rates rise, what will happen to bond prices?

If you got all five questions right, that puts you very much in the top quartile – only around 15 per cent of Americans surveyed achieved that. What about the first three questions? More people tend to get those questions right. In Germany about half of those asked answered all three correctly; in Japan it is 25 per cent.[12] The results show that people are more likely to get the first three questions right than the last two.

So what can be done to improve financial literacy? There are books aplenty, online courses and financial seminars, and it's wise to take a look at these. Evidence strongly suggests that attending financial seminars is correlated with action and improves investment performance and financial planning.[13] There is some debate about whether the information provided is really what triggers behaviour, or simply that people who attend financial seminars already want to do something about their finances. However financial literacy is too important not to invest in. The evidence does also suggest that experience is the best way of improving financial literacy (hence literacy levels rise with age). This provides another reason to start saving and investing early.

Manage a portfolio

As people become more financially literate, they realize that there are no easy ways of making money through investments. When we talk to finance professors at London Business School and other experts around the world, their investment advice is rarely around specific stocks or transactions. Instead they tend to focus on general principles. Understanding household finances is a growing area of literature, and Harvard Professor John Campbell, in his presidential address to the American Finance Association, identifies some common mistakes households tend to make.[14]

First, households tend to be underinvested in the equity market – even 20 per cent of wealthy households have no exposure to equity markets. Further, even those who do invest in equities tend not to diversify enough; in other words, they invest in just a few specific companies. Second, when households do invest in equities they tend to have a 'local' bias, investing in stocks that are familiar to them or based nearby. Third, households tend to hold concentrated portfolios in the shares of their own employers and, as the collapse of Lehman Brothers demonstrated, by doing so they risk losing both their jobs and their wealth. Fourth, when it comes to selling assets, households tend to sell assets that have been rising in price and hold on to those that have fallen. Finally, there is the question of inertia. Households tend to have a 'status quo bias' and do not revisit their portfolios. For instance, the Teachers Insurance and Annuity Assurance scheme in the USA has 850,000 members, and each year members can costlessly reallocate their funds across different portfolios. In fact, over a twelve-year period, 72 per cent never changed their allocation despite major fluctuations in asset returns, and only 8 per cent changed their portfolio more than once.[15]

People who overcome these failings do so in three ways. They diversify their risk, not just in terms of how they invest their portfolio across assets, but also in terms of pension providers. They realize that as they get older they have less time to make up for financial reversals, so as they near retirement they reduce the riskiness of their portfolio. And, when constructing their financial plan, they seek a secure income during retirement, rather than maximise the market value of their wealth.[16]

It is worth noting that because of the historical dominance of the three-stage life, current long-term financial planning is invariably focused on pension provision. The financing of a multi-stage life requires both saving for the drop in income after retirement, but also the fluctuations in income experienced across the stages and indeed the substantial drop in income during transitions. It is clear to us that lengthening time horizons and more periods of income fluctuation will result in major changes in how the financial sector works and in the products it offers. Take mortgage products, for example: a longer working life means that mortgage repayments can be spread out, but the fluctuations in this longer life require a measure of flexibility in contribution payments. A longer life also creates more time in which to take risks and more time to recover if these go wrong. This means that portfolio diversification and risk taking will alter with a longer life, and this will inevitably result in major structural changes in the industry.

Focus on the costs

Like any industry where consumers know a lot less than producers, it's easy for consumers to make financial decisions they will look back on and regret. This is particularly the case in savings products, where there are financial intermediaries who require some form of cut or payment. As such, it is crucial to keep an eye on the level of fees and charges.

For example, let's assume we have an investment of $10,000 over a forty-year period with an expected return of 7 per cent per annum. With no charges and no taxes this will deliver a sum of $149,744 in forty years. Now imagine an initial charge of 5 per cent ($500) and then an annual charge of 2 per cent. In this case the final figure is $63,877 – $85,000 less than you otherwise would have got. Alarmed by this, you might seek another fund and be attracted by one which offers an initial charge of 1 per cent and an annual fee of 2 per cent. However, even in this case you will only get back $66,567 in forty years' time. The initial charge does matter – but it's the annual fee that is crucial. If you find a fund with an initial charge of 1 per cent and an annual charge of 0.5 per cent then you get back $121,369; find a fund which offers 1 per cent and 0.1 per cent and you will reap \$142,434. Checking the fine print and the charges makes an enormous difference.

Financial agency

Having financial competence is a start – but what of agency? Surveys of retirees show the majority wished they had saved more. So why didn't they?

We cannot help but be reminded of the famous quote by St Augustine who, as a young man, said: 'Lord make me chaste, but not yet.' Most of us intend to be good and virtuous but for some reason we always postpone doing so. We know we should lose weight and exercise more and we intend to do so but we don't. Everyone fights with self-control failures. The point is this: given increases in life expectancy, the cost of self-control issues also increases. The future will last longer now for everyone and so it is crucial to balance current actions with future needs. The importance of self-control and of recognizing the links between current and futures selves is not just specific to finance; it is a thread that runs right through the building of a productive and fulfilling 100-year life.

Understanding these *self-control failures* is currently a rich research vein in social science, combining insights from neurology, psychology and economics. One simple way of thinking about this is to imagine a tussle between different parts of the brain. The prefrontal lobes are a relatively modern (150,000 years) development that helps distinguish humans from other species. The prefrontal lobes play a crucial role in cognitive rational thought and long-term planning. However, this recently developed rational side of the brain is also influenced by other parts, including the older, more established limbic system. It is the limbic system that captures emotional and instinctive responses. To put it simply, what happens is this: the prefrontal lobes tell you to act in your long-term self-interest, while the limbic system pushes you to more immediate decisions and greater immediate gratification. Some have used the metaphor of the elephant and the rider to capture this tussle. Imagine a small rider perched on the back of an enormous elephant, trying to control its actions. There will be times when both want to go in the same direction – but if the elephant chooses a different route, then inevitably its desires will win out.[17]

For much of human existence, it has made sense for the limbic system to dominate and to give in to these immediate claims for gratification. When life is nasty, brutish and short, then giving in to short-term pleasures makes sense. However, as life expectancy increases, wouldn't it be wiser for the rational prefrontal brain to have more force in making better long-term decisions?

Psychologists see this issue of immediate desires from the perspective of the brain; economists see it from the perspective of intertemporal choice and from the existence of 'present-biased' preferences.[18] A popular form of present-biased preference is *hyperbolic discounting*, associated with the psychologist Richard Herrnstein and the economist David Laibson.[19]

Hyperbolic discounting suggests that, in general, people act impatiently in the short term, but exhibit greater patience in long-term planning. Consider the following classic example of hyperbolic discounting. Which would you prefer: $100 today or $105 next week? How about $100 in a year's time or $105 in a year and one week's time? A large number of people prefer the $100 today to the $105 in a week's time but nearly everyone prefers $105 in a year and a week compared with $100 in a year. In other words, we show a short-term impatience but plan to be patient.

However, by the time the long-term happens and plans come around to be implemented, these choices become a short-term issue once more and impatience kicks in again. The result is that plans are revised and virtuous behaviour postponed. So in a year's time, when given the choice between $100 now or $105 in a week's time, you change your previous plan and go for the $100 now.

This is exactly the problem of why people tend to save inadequately for retirement. Saving means postponing consumption – shifting money from today to tomorrow. Hyperbolic discounting suggests that a person would rather spend the money today than later, but that they do intend to save more further down the road. However, as time passes, their present bias kicks in again and they favour consumption today rather than saving. In other words, we all have a natural tendency to say that we will raise our savings later ... we just never do.

The same problem reappears with the challenge of losing weight. Losing weight requires patience, but it takes a while for abstinence to pay dividends in terms of weight loss. The result is that, when faced with the dessert menu, we succumb to the temptations of chocolate gateau but vow tomorrow to forgo such pleasures and instead take a day of exercise and fruit. Of course the story repeats itself the next day. It is as if these near-term decisions are made by the limbic system, but longer-term decisions by the prefrontal lobe.

If hyperbolic discounting is at the heart of why people tend to under-save, is it possible to use this understanding to try and change behaviour? At the heart of hyperbolic discounting are three ingredients: an inability to properly account for a future self; an ability to change plans through future decisions; and short-term impatience vs long-term patience. These can all be tackled.

Account for a future self

Consider again the example of the dessert trolley. Your current self looks at the wonderful puddings arrayed across its shelves and thinks about the pleasure of eating that scrumptious-looking éclair. As you pop it into your mouth, you are in a sense expecting your future self to take the necessary steps to correct the problem.[20] However each future self, when it is their turn to make the decision about what to choose from the trolley, does the same – again passing the problem on to a later self. And so it goes on.

If we were able to plan optimally, then we would do so by coordinating these multiple selves. Creating a sense of identity over a long life, one which recognizes the interactions between yourself today and you future selves, is a crucial component of a successful 100-year life. One way of doing this is called a 'behavioural nudge'. Imagine that, as you sit and plan your finances, it is as if they weren't your plans but someone else's – your future self. Or imagine your 80-year-old self sitting next to you – what would they want you to take into consideration?

One interesting study takes this a step further and uses software (age process algorithms) to forecast how a person will look as they get older.[21] In Figure 7.2 we show the age process algorithm for one of the researchers: you can see his ageing digital avatar. Participants in the study were asked to imagine they had received a windfall of $1,000 and were then presented with four options as to what to do with the money: use it to buy something nice for someone special; invest it in a retirement fund; plan a fun and extravagant occasion; put it in a current account. Those people who were shown their own aged digital avatar decided to save more than twice as much as those who

A: Actual Photo of First Author

B: Nonaged Digital Avatar

C: Aged Digital Avata

FIGURE 7.2 *Age-progressed images of the future self.*

Source: H. E. Hershfield, D. G. Goldstein, W. F. Sharpe, J. Fox, L. Yeykelis, L. L. Carstensen and J. N. Bailenson, 'Increasing Saving Behavior Through Age-Progressed Renderings of the Future Self', *Journal of Marketing Research* (2011) vol. 48, no. SPL: S23–S37.

didn't receive this nudge ($172 against $80). But notice that even with the nudge, there is still a present bias.

Stick with the plan

Preparing for the future requires people, on occasions, to hold off short-term delights in favour of long-term commitments. However, the chances are that they will reverse their decisions or change their plans. Automating financial decisions creates fewer opportunities for reversing commitments, for example, by setting up an automatic shift of funds from current to savings account. Interestingly, what makes this automation work is the very inertia that we earlier described as a problem with household portfolios. Here, however, the inertia acts in a positive way – once committed, the savings plan stays in place.

We expect that as the understanding of savings psychology improves, a number of innovative products will come to market aimed at helping automate savings decisions. For instance, a financial package called *Acorns* will round up any purchases made on a debit or credit card and then put this rounding amount into an investment fund. It's unlikely to fund a retirement, but it does help reduce an under-saving bias.[22]

Economists Richard Thaler and Shlomo Benartzi devised a financial product based around commitment that exploits hyperbolic discounting and turns the status quo bias into a positive. This was a savings plan for employees called Save More Tomorrow (SMarT plan).[23] The plan had four features aimed at overcoming a range of behavioural biases, including hyperbolic discounting. The first feature is that workers are asked to increase the contribution from their salary that goes into their savings plan, but only in the future. The further ahead the scheduled savings increase, the more likely this is to work, according to hyperbolic discounting. The second feature is that the increase in savings will come after a scheduled pay rise; people are generally reluctant to see a fall in their current income, but if a pay rise can help fund a higher disposable income and higher savings, it becomes more acceptable. The third feature is that after each future pay rise the savings rate will ratchet upwards each time until it reaches a preset maximum – this is the automation referred to earlier. Finally, workers always have the option to withdraw from the scheme at any point. Under this scheme, with a trial at a manufacturing plant, participants in SMarT increased their savings from 3.5 per cent of their income to 13.6 per cent. Notice how these schemes try and convert the status quo bias we came across earlier to be a positive advantage in how you save.

We suspect that more and more savings plans will come to market that capture these features. You can of course try and do the same yourself without buying these products – you can just set up instructions with your bank. However, the key for this to succeed is inertia and the costliness of changing your instructions in the future.

Protect your older self

One reason why financial planning is often unappealing is the fact that it requires us to imagine ourselves when we are old. You might find it deeply unpleasant to imagine yourself as old and frail, fragile and vulnerable. As life expectancy increases and morbidity decreases, then the likelihood is that you will be physically and mentally healthier for longer. However, this means that old age has been postponed, not eliminated.

The concept of hyperbolic discounting invites us to make commitments to our future self that would be beneficial – for example, by being fitter or having sounder finances. There are also other ways in which you need to protect your future self through your current actions. This is because there is evidence that financial literacy declines with old age, particularly with regard to analytic thinking. For example, in a study[24] of cognitive skills, different aged participants were asked to answer a range of questions that drew on various cognitive skills. From the age of 50 onwards, there was a continued and marked decline in analytical functioning, with peak financial performance occurring between late 40s and mid-50s.

Obviously these are average results and don't hold for everyone, but they do tell an interesting story. Good financial decision-making is made up of two components: experience and knowledge, and analytic functioning. The young have strong analytic functioning but limited experience of financial products; the old have much experience but declining analytic functioning. This is why financial decision-making in general peaks in the 40s and 50s when people's experience and analytic ability are at a joint maximum.

Therefore it makes sense to financial plan in midlife, rather than relying on a much older version of yourself to do the financial engineering needed to solve any under-saving issues.

Inheritances

In our calculations of how much you should save, we have focused on financing pensions and transitions and have also made mention of mortgages, student loans and healthcare. Another common motivation for savings is the desire to leave an inheritance.

Leaving this world knowing that your children are financially secure is a comfort to most parents, and the desire to pass possessions down through the generations and achieve a form of immortality is also strong. Economics is, however, obsessed with strategic behaviour and offers another – and very bleak – reason why parents leave their children an inheritance: the strategic bequest motive. Put simply, parents can manipulate the behaviour and attentiveness of their children towards them in old age by holding over them the prospect of an inheritance. Famously, King Lear divests his kingdom between his daughters Goneril and Regan (excluding his favourite and youngest Cordelia), as he wishes to enjoy his later years free of the burdens of estate and affairs. However with his wealth now in their hands, their behaviour to him is brutal, outrageous and unnatural. Appealing to Shakespearean tragedy is perhaps not the best empirical evidence, but a study[25] of contemporary American households also points in a similar direction. There are admittedly no evidences of eyes being gouged out, but the data suggests that contact between parents and children is much higher in families where the elderly parent has a substantial amount of bequeathable wealth to offer. It is worth stressing that the wealth has to be in a bequeathable form for this effect to come into play.

These are ugly thoughts and most people find the notion of a strategic bequest motive uncomfortable. Clearly there are other more noble motives behind bequests.[26] A long working career focused on accumulating financial assets but neglecting family may make the strategic bequest motive more relevant. The sad case of Brooke Astor, who died aged 105 in August 2007, shows that being wealthy in old age doesn't guarantee support. The philanthropist, socialite and writer was a member of the wealthy Astor family. In 2009 both her son, Anthony Marshall (then aged 85) and her estate lawyer, Francis Morrissey were imprisoned for forgery. Even worse, Mrs Astor had apparently been living in squalor with restricted medication, and was denied company and medical visits while all this was happening. All the more reason to balance work and life and ensure that the care and support you receive from friends and family is based on affection and not the prospect of a financial windfall. It is good to remember ourselves that it is our intangible assets – our family and friends, interests and passions – that are ultimately the greatest source of lifetime happiness.

Answers to Financial Literacy Questions

Q1: Just over $110

Q2: Less

Q3: False

Q4: True

Q5: Fall

8

Time

From recreation to re-creation

A central theme of this book has been the gift of extra years. We have considered how these extra years can be structured and sequenced and what can be achieved in these new and different blocks of time. Here we turn our attention from thinking about these large blocks of time to considering time in months, weeks, days, hours, and even minutes. The question we address is how will you spend these extra minutes, hours, days and weeks. Will you work long hours to convert your time into cash, or take a class and convert your time into skills, or just lie on the sofa watching television?

Time is inherently egalitarian (everyone has 24 hours a day) and inherently scarce (most people say they don't have enough). So is living a 100-year life minute by minute different from living a 70-year life? *Quantitatively*, of course, it is. There are potentially

168 productive hours in a week: across 70 years that's 611,000 hours, and across 100 years that's 873,000 hours. *Qualitatively* there are sure to be differences when lives elongate, as people make their own decisions about how to spend this extra time. The opportunities are vast: they could spend it working in order to build their financial assets; developing their skills; taking time out with friends, their partner and children; keeping healthy; going on sabbaticals; broadening their networks; or exploring different jobs and different ways of living.

In thinking about how time is spent, it is useful to remind ourselves that while we may think of time as fixed and beyond an individual's control, in reality perceptions of time are very much a social convention. This social convention is obvious with regard to the dominant temporal model of the stages of life, but it is also true for smaller units of time. The length of the working day, the number of working days in the week, the existence of the weekend, the number of days of holiday and the time spent in leisure are not fixed. Rather, they have evolved over time and will no doubt continue to do so.

So it is useful to look back at historical trends of the use of time and then consider how this may change in the future. We believe there will be a fundamental restructuring of time and that this evolution will be a result of the interaction of longevity, the need to invest in intangible assets and a longer-term historical trend towards a decline in working hours.

The paradox of working hours

In general, people are working fewer hours now than they were fifty or 100 years ago. As far back as the ninth century, the English King Alfred sought to divide the day into three lots of eight: eight hours each of work, rest and leisure. It was not, however, until the early and mid-twentieth century that in the Western world the eight-hour working day became a reality for most. During the Industrial Revolution, the standard working pattern was six days a week, and between ten and sixteen hours day were worked by adults and children alike. It was not until 1847 that in the UK, for example, the government passed legislation restricting the working day to ten hours, but even then this was just for women and children.

Take a look at Figure 8.1 to see the rate of decline of the average working week in the US. By 1920, the average hours per

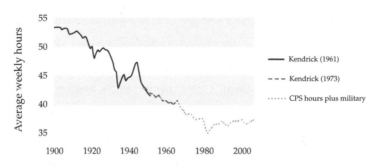

FIGURE 8.1 *Average weekly hours worked per employed person.*
Source: Ramey and Francis, 'A Century of Work and Leisure', *American Economic Journal: Macroeconomics*, 1(2) (2009): 189–224.

week worked by men was fifty hours; by 2005 it had reduced to thirty-seven hours.[1]

In 1930, the famed economist John Maynard Keynes wrote in his *Economic Possibilities of Our Grandchildren* that growing prosperity would bring about such an abundance of leisure that a central problem for humanity would be how to find useful ways to spend all this free time.

> Thus for the first time since his creation man will be faced with his real, his permanent problem – how to use his freedom from pressing cares, how to occupy the leisure which science and compound interest will have won for him, to live wisely and agreeably and well.

What Keynes was referring to was not the windfall of time brought by longevity, but rather the extra time resulting from prosperity. His reasoning was based on the concept of the *income effect*. This says that as people become richer, they want to consume more of most things, including leisure. Therefore, as productivity and wages rise, there will be a fall in working hours, a shorter working week, longer weekends and more holidays. Of course Keynes is not alone in this prediction. There are some contemporary technologists who believe that Keynes' vision could be realized in the decades ahead, as robots raise productivity and free people from the drudgery of labour and work in the home.

It is tempting to believe that Keynes was just plain wrong. It is unlikely that you feel an abundance of leisure to be the central problem you currently face in your life or indeed as you look forward into the future. But Keynes was not totally wrong; he correctly identified that growing prosperity and productivity would lead to more leisure, and so it has. There is indeed an income effect – it just isn't as strong as Keynes predicted. What Keynes underestimated was the development of consumerism in the twentieth century. It is true that as people get richer they want more of most things, including leisure. But it turned out that what people wanted was material possessions and they wanted these a great deal more than they wanted leisure time. So while working time did indeed fall, it didn't fall as sharply as Keynes conjectured. This echoes a comment we have made at several points in this book. The higher your rate of consumption, and the more you like material goods, then the more years you are likely to spend working.

Even if Keynes overestimated the power of the income effect, there has indeed been an effect, and over the years it has led to reductions in average hours worked. Therefore, if we assume that income and productivity will continue to rise, then we would expect further increases in leisure time and further reductions in the working week

But if we take this from the general to the specific, then it may feel rather different. Consider your own life right now: do you feel as if you are working less and do you feel you have more discretionary time? You could be like many other people who feel *time-poor*, and under more pressure than ever before.[2] In 1965, around 25 per cent of Americans reported they 'always felt rushed' and by 1995 this had increased to around 35 per cent. And indeed there is evidence that marital distress, sleep deprivation and stress-related illnesses are increasing. We imagine that this sense of being time-poor contributes to the curse of Ondine. To be told you have more years of life, but that you will spend much of it working for longer when you already feel time-poor is a depressing thought.

But if Keynes was right and people are working less, why do so many feel so time-poor?

The *Downton Abbey* effect

One part of the explanation is that while on average the hours of work have declined, not everyone is working fewer hours. Over the last century there has been an interesting switch. A century ago, the poor and the low-skilled worked longer hours. It was they who toiled in the factories created by the Industrial Revolution. In contrast, the rich and the highly skilled worked fewer hours. In its most extreme form this led to Veblen's notion of the *leisure class*,[3] so aptly portrayed in the popular TV series *Downton Abbey*. The switch between the poor and unskilled and the rich and skilled was completed by around the 1990s. At this point, those on lower wages worked fewer hours, and those on higher wages began to work for a little longer than the low-paid. Moreover, the higher the pay, the more people worked.[4]

This was particularly true of the highest income earners. In 1979, only 15 per cent of men in the US who earned high incomes (defined as the top 20 per cent of earners) worked more than fifty hours a week. By 2006, this had risen to 27 per cent – a near doubling. The reverse was happening for the lower paid. In 1979, 22 per cent of men earning low incomes (the bottom 20 per cent) worked more than fifty hours a week. By 2006 this had fallen to 13 per cent – nearly halving.

Why do higher income earners work longer hours, and why haven't they joined Veblen's leisure class? To understand this, we have to consider another effect that has, over time, offset the influence of the income effect. This is the *substitution effect*, which predicts that as wages rise, the cost of leisure (that is, of working less) also goes up. Look at it this way. The cost of working a shorter week is reduced income as a result of working fewer hours. So as income goes up, so leisure time becomes more expensive. At a certain point, the substitution effect kicks in: an individual's wages are now so high that the cost of leisure is expensive and therefore they decide to work longer hours. Of course taxation matters here, and one of the reasons the switch occurred is reductions in top rates of tax: the greater the tax people pay, the cheaper it is to consume leisure. This is one reason why in Europe, with its higher rates of tax, people tend to have shorter working weeks and take longer holidays.

Of course this is not the only reason why people may choose to work longer hours than predicted by Keynes. There is also the issue of status. When people work long hours then both they and others see them as being busy and in demand, and therefore they may feel better about themselves and externally valued. The context in which people work also plays a role in determining their working hours. One of the implications of the 'hollowing out of work' is that those at the top end of the skill levels are under ever more pressure as they see clearly the implications of a 'winner takes all' labour market. Indeed, there could well be pressure from corporate leaders to work long hours, as they see long hours as crucial to the firm's competitive strategy to maintain its global dominance and marketplace. In a 24/7 working environment, falling short in terms of hours worked runs the risk not just of losing business but of losing a huge amount of business.

Perhaps even more intriguing is that high wage jobs, and the long hours they demand, may also contain aspects that are enjoyable. This is not to deny the stresses and pressures that come with such positions, but it is striking that studies show that job satisfaction increases with the wage attached to a job.[5] It could be that wages are what drive job satisfaction or that the less manual and routine a job, the more enjoyable it is. What seems to be the result is that the more enjoyable a job, the longer hours a person is prepared to work, other things being equal.

The enigma of leisure

But there are other reasons for feeling time-poor. Even if on average people are working less, this doesn't mean they have more leisure. Clearly time spent not working or studying isn't the same as leisure time. For instance, you may work eight hours a day, but if on top of this you have a two-hour commute then shouldn't that be included as part of your 'working' day? Aristotle defined leisure as the freedom from the necessity of labour, but labour is a lot more than just the time spent at work.

Just because you are not at work doesn't mean that when you run errands, do housework or chores, this should count as leisure. Inevitably, definitions of leisure focus on the discretionary use of time, but even this is not quite right. You can, if you want, choose to sleep six rather than eight hours, but does this mean that those extra two hours of sleep should count as leisure?

One way of thinking about leisure and the allocation of time is to consider how much enjoyment people take from different activities. The results of a US survey showed that at the top of the most enjoyable activities are sex, playing sport, fishing, art and music, socializing in bars and lounges, playing with the kids, talking and reading to kids, sleeping, going to church, and going to the movies. At the bottom of the list are work, baby care, homework, second job, cooking and working in the home, child care, commuting, errands, home repairs, laundry, and dealing with children's health issues.[6] We may be working less, but are we spending more time doing the things that give us greatest pleasure?

Right now, how much leisure time do people have? One study estimates that in 1900 people had about thirty hours of leisure a week; by the 1950s this was forty hours; and it increased again in the 1980s to forty-five hours. Since then it has been decreasing and by 2000 was back to forty hours. Other studies suggest even greater gains. Between 1965 and 2003 men benefited from an additional five to eight hours of leisure a week and women between four and eight hours of leisure.[7]

So Keynes was right – many people are benefiting from more leisure, although the magnitude of increase is far from abundant. Moreover, this increase in leisure, weekends and holidays has meant that the twentieth century has witnessed a dramatic increase in the leisure industry; sport, travel, cinema and television have all grown to seek commercial benefit from the additional leisure that people are enjoying.

This leads to the heart of this debate about how much time is allocated to leisure. At the time of writing, most people have more *discretionary time* than at the beginning of the twentieth century.

However, if people feel time poor, what they are thinking about is not discretionary time but *spare time*. In other words, people may be making choices to fill their discretionary time that result in little spare time. As the economists Gary Becker and Staffan Linder have shown, consuming takes time.[8] As people get richer, they own more consumer goods, so their leisure time becomes more hectic, as the rate of accumulation of goods exceeds the increase in available leisure time. The result is people feel they are cramming their leisure into ever shorter blocks of time. How do you squeeze in the theatre, Facebook, a party, a fishing trip and mainlining the latest Netflix mini-series that has just been made available?

Calling time

As you think about how you will spend your time over a long productive life, you may have in mind working eight hours a day and then taking two days off (the weekend). We believe it is time to question this time allocation. If Keynes' logic of the income effect still holds, then it is likely that there will be more leisure and shorter working weeks.

In the much of the developed world, the Industrial Revolution resulted in substantial increases in the number of hours people worked. It is fascinating to consider that across the four centuries from 1200 to 1600, annual working hours in the UK varied between 1,500 and 2,000 hours. Yet by 1840, when the Industrial Revolution was in full swing, annual working hours had leapt to around 3,500, with fifty-two weeks of seventy hours being common in both the UK and US. Not surprisingly, across the industrial world, the desire for a shorter working week became a constant for mass labour organizations throughout the nineteenth century.

As a consequence of this push back from workers, over time Saturday became a half-day of work, but the working week remained substantially in excess of forty hours. It was only in the first half of the twentieth century that the five-day working week and eight-hour working day began to be standardized. Henry Ford introduced the forty-hour week in the US in 1914 but legislation restricting hours wasn't forthcoming until 1938. Europe made progress earlier: Germany restricted hours at the turn of the century, Russia in 1917, Portugal in 1919 and France in 1936. By 2015 the average hours worked per week in Germany was thirty-five, and in France, Italy and UK it was thirty-seven.

Similarly over time, labour movements have campaigned and achieved increases in paid leave, although there are very significant differences across countries in how much employers need to offer. At the time of writing, full-time jobs in the European Union come with at least twenty days' paid leave, although in many countries the reality is more: France and the UK have twenty-five days and Sweden has thirty-three. In other countries, the provision is very short. In the US it is twelve days and in Japan it is twenty.

It is worth pausing to consider just how fundamental this shift to a five-day working week and paid leave has been. It is a long-lost mystery as to why the week is structured into seven days. It mimics no naturally occurring phenomena. Months and years seem to have originated from Ancient Babylon and withstood the efforts of the French Revolution to rationalize them by creating months that were made up of three weeks of ten days each. The existence of a Sabbath, or day of rest, is more recent but still goes back for centuries, even if the day itself varies across nations and the observance of the Sabbath has varied in intensity over time. The seven-day week and a day of rest are therefore long-lasting constants of human history, but the weekend is a far more recent innovation. The *Oxford English Dictionary* dates the common usage of the word 'weekend' to refer to a two-day break from work from 1878. So the concept of a five-day working week and two days of leisure is therefore a relative historical novelty rather than something deeply rooted in our psyche.

In other words, how the week is structured is not a historical constant but has changed over time. Looking forward, if working hours continue to decline, then it seems clear to us that there is likely to be a further restructuring of time and of the working week. The challenge is that when the average working day is seven hours, then further daily reductions may not be optimal. That is because there are fixed costs to working, such as commuting, preparing for the day or making the transition home. These set-up costs mean that it may be better to work longer days but have more days off. From the perspective of this book, the interesting question is whether it is possible to restructure time in a way that supports a 100- year life. There are those who are arguing that it is. For instance, the Mexican billionaire Carlos Slim believes that society should transition towards a three-day working week with each day made up of eleven-hour shifts.[9] His argument is that instead of reserving the majority of leisure for retirement, it makes more sense to spread it throughout life, with a retirement age of 75.

The dilemmas of restructuring time are very apparent in Jane's scenarios. We believe that without fundamental restructuring of time, neither the 3.0 nor the 3.5 scenarios would work. It seemed implausible that Jane would be able to preserve her productive assets and sustain her vitality assets if she worked until the age of 80 in a 9-to-5 job with a two-day weekend and only between two and five weeks' annual leave. She simply would not have the discretionary time available to retrain and revitalize. That is why we created the 4.0 and 5.0 scenarios, and introduced the concepts of stages based around exploration and being an independent producer.

However, what if Jane wanted to work in a corporation for the majority of her working life? It is possible to make the 3.0

and 3.5 scenario a viable option. But to do so Jane would have to work fewer than five days a week and take longer breaks to retrain and revitalize. If the historical trend of more leisure time continues and this is accompanied by a restructuring of time at the weekly level, then Jane will have more potential scenarios to choose from. Indeed this could include a three-stage career with shorter working weeks and longer holiday time.

This means that all the scenarios we created for Jane are built on a way of thinking about work and time that is more flexible than currently practised by most corporations. That is why we anticipate a great deal of experimentation as people attempt to build time into their working lives to reinvigorate and retrain. As they do this, current corporate practices of the structuring of time will come under increasing pressure.

As the economist Claudia Goldin has shown, people who take a career break (most often women with young children) are likely to experience significantly lower lifetime earnings than those who do not.[10] Other studies have shown that people who try to control their time by working from home or working flexibly are less likely to be promoted.[11] So currently those who want to build a fast-paced, highly remunerated career would be unwise to take time out or work flexibly. To requote William Faulkner: 'If you fall out of lockstep you run the risk of being trampled underfoot.'[12] Clearly this will set up tensions as an individual's need for flexibility clashes with the corporate need for long, unbroken, standardized hours of work. This is evidently an area where there will be significant push back on corporate practice and perception. It is impossible to accurately predict how this will play out or indeed the speed of change. However, it is inevitable that growing pressure will result in a greater variety in timing, that highly skilled work will create its unique pattern of time structuring, and leisure will be reallocated from recreation to re-creation.

Greater variety in timing

Clearly the replacement of the three-stage working life with one that offers multi-stages will result in a greater variety of stages of life, and with this will come different needs for how best to allocate time. During those stages where accumulating money is important, we can imagine that people will still work long hours. At other stages of life, there will be times when more leisure and fewer working days will be necessary, for family or education reasons. There is no doubt that the individual's desire for flexibility and a bespoke working week will initially clash with a corporation's desire for standardization and predictability. However, the likely outcome will be a compromise, with firms offering different time packages and responsibilities to different workers.

There are, of course, many ways in which the week could be restructured. The working day could become shorter, the evenings longer, or perhaps the pre-industrial tradition of St Monday, where artisans took an unscheduled break from work, will be resurrected to create a four-day working week and a new three-day weekend. But a three-day weekend is a significant increase in leisure and is unlikely to happen soon. Will it begin, as was the case during the Industrial Revolution, with Friday becoming a half-day? Or will Friday became a day off but in return the other working days increase in length? Right now some firms are experimenting with greater flexibility and variety in the timing of the working week and many alternative suggestions are surfacing.

Not all companies are experimenting and many will resist such diversity and flexibility. This leaves the option of creating flexible discretionary time by working for onself or for small companies where flexibility is more likely to be offered. For the same reason, there will be times when being an independent producer will be highly attractive.

Flexibility for all?

A three-stage working life is more likely to work if there is flexibility around time structures and sequencing. Indeed this flexibility would also support some of the other new stages that are emerging. But what of the intense work periods that the multi-stage scenarios require as a component in order to achieve financial success? In the 5.0 scenario, there are two periods when

Jane is engaged in intense corporate work: first at EatWell and then at TalentFind. Or what of the person who decides to really build up their tangible assets through taking highly skilled or leadership roles? Will the time structuring of elongated weekends and longer holidays work for them?

We doubt it will, for two reasons. It seems to us that skilled and senior leadership roles will always require long and intense hours of work. But it has to be acknowledged that this intensity creates a level of burnout that cannot be continued over a long second stage of sixty years of work. For this group of people, the three-stage working life will not hold. The investment in family and vitality that is required to support a healthy 100-year life will need more consolidated periods of discretionary time than just a longer weekend. Moreover, these skilled roles will require continued investment in skills and technology to counteract the rapid obsolescence of roles and professions. This is not just about topping up knowledge in slivers of time, but rather a more substantial period of retraining and substantial transitions. This investment in new knowledge needs the sort of substantial and sustained focus that cannot be achieved on a one-day-a-week basis.

Therefore, while we could imagine that longer weekends or more holidays will work for some roles, for highly skilled jobs the time structuring we described in the 5.0 scenario makes more sense. In this scenario, two periods of intense corporate activity are bounded by transitional phases where Jane is able to concentrate full-time on building her intangible assets.

One of the audiences for whom this book was written are those who benefit from high levels of education and income and possess some market power in the workplace with their employer and an array of choices and options. Not everyone will be so fortunate, and making the most of a 100-year life will be a challenge for everyone. We can imagine that the three-stage scenario with a much shorter working week will remain a default option for those with fewer skills and options. We can also imagine, over time, governments introducing lifetime transition allowances to help those with low assets to achieve investment in intangibles. Just as paid holidays and maternity (and now paternity) leave are extending in duration through the state, we can imagine the same for these lifetime transition allowances to make sure that it isn't just the well-off who can afford the changes that a 100-year life requires.

Re-creation balances recreation

As well as expecting a restructuring of time, we expect shifts in how time – and especially leisure – is used. A 100-year life puts enormous emphasis on developing key intangible assets that are built around family and friends, skills and knowledge, health and vitality. This requires investment: time with friends and family, time spent in education and retooling, and time spent exercising. Greater longevity requires greater investment in these assets, especially around education.

A three-day weekend would certainly create the time and space for greater investment in each of these intangibles. However, will this be enough? Does a 100-year life need greater investment in intangibles than that which can be provided by a three-day weekend? We believe what will emerge is a fundamental shift in the way people think about leisure time.

Many of our current concepts of time, including how leisure is defined and used, emerged with the Industrial Revolution. The timing of agricultural work – episodic and slow-paced – did not translate well into a factory context. This, combined with the increasing reliability and falling costs of mechanical watches, led to the creation of a clearly structured and defined working day.[13] Factory work demanded the creation of a fixed working day and the separation of work and family. Leisure also became more sharply defined and no longer seasonal, as new blocks of leisure were invented: childhood and retirement, evenings and weekends, Christmas and summer holidays.

With the creation of these new blocks of leisure, people had to decide how to spend this time. The labour movement argued for a shorter working week and a two-day weekend in order to recharge physically and mentally after a long and intense working week. Furthermore, with the separation of work from home and the banning of children from factories, the desire was to use leisure to reconstitute family time.

As leisure time increased, so did the leisure industry. Aided by urbanization and standardized leisure time, entrepreneurs began to develop new forms of entertainment. The music hall, cinemas and the rise of professional soccer are obvious examples. Before the Industrial Revolution, leisure took place in public spaces in an ill-defined way. As the Industrial Revolution proceeded, leisure became privatized and regularized.[14]

The development of the leisure industry has obviously continued throughout the last 100 years, and as leisure time has increased so too has the value of the industry. Consequently, discretionary time is increasingly used for leisure activities: watching television, going to sporting events, shopping, dining out, and taking luxury breaks. These all involve *consuming* time rather than using it.

As people live longer and need to make more investments in their intangible assets, we expect to see a shift in how leisure is used. Rather than consuming time, we expect more time to be spent investing in intangibles. In other words, more re-creation than recreation. As Karl Marx noted, 'To economise on labour time means to increase the amount of free time, i.e. time for the complete development of the individual.'[15] And since re-creation is often an individual pursuit, we can expect to see a more personalized leisure agenda made up of re-creation and recreation. If the last 100 years saw the development of a leisure industry that privatized public entertainment based around consumption, then we can expect a growing leisure industry aimed at the individual, self-improvement and leisure as investment.

Post-industrial time

When life elongates, then time begins to be restructured, both in the new stages we described earlier and in the days and weeks we considered in this chapter. Restructuring time may sound dramatic, but has been done before. That is why we have referred back so often to the impact of the Industrial Revolution. It was during this period that many of the prevailing social conventions were established.

Long, regulated and standardized working hours were a product of the Industrial Revolution. It also ushered in a clear distinction between work and leisure, between where people worked and where they lived, and between the work environment and the family. It led to major changes in gender roles, a greater institutional role in the upbringing of children, and the creation of a three-stage life as children were excluded from the workplace and firms encouraged retirement.

Over the last two decades, many of these features have been challenged and their impact and popularity diluted. Gender roles, the separation of work and leisure, and the standard working week have all come under pressure and shown considerable change. We believe that the social trends that are already in play will be significantly strengthened by the needs of a 100-year life and the profound technological changes many people now face. The Industrial Revolution led to dramatic changes in the structuring of time. Perhaps this new era will usher in even greater changes.

9

Relationships

The transformation of personal lives

Every facet of life morphs as life extends. Marriage and partnerships become longer and experience more change, so they will need to be more flexible if they are to avoid the increasing risk of fracture. Households have fewer children but more grandparents and great-grandparents, so these four-generation families will create opportunities for older generations to challenge and mentor the young, and for the young to support the old. And for parents, once they have brought up their children, there will still be time for friendships to become more central and potentially more diverse as they meet with different ages in shared ideas and passions.

Onto these patterns of transforming personal lives is overlaid the changing context of work. Many family members will work, some into their 70s or even 80s. As more women work, traditional family roles will break down further, impacting on roles within the family and particularly on those fathers who choose to take more responsibility for their children. These effects will be further enhanced as men demand more flexible work patterns to support their multi-stage life.

These are some of the issues addressed in this chapter as we consider the impact longevity has on personal lives. Our interest is in what could happen within the family, what will happen in the interface between work and home, and how multi-generational living could function.

Families

In his 1981 'Treatise on the Family', Gary Becker proposed an economic theory of families based on what he termed *production complementarities*. In this family the husband and wife specialize in the market and domestic spheres respectively, and hence are more productive together than apart.[1]

Marriage

When Jack married, like generations before him, he and his wife simply followed these classic rules of role differentiation. As the Wharton psychologist Stewart Friedman observed: 'Earlier generation men saw themselves as breadwinners and pursued careers with the intention of providing for a family; this was all one seamless, conflict-free mind-set.'[2] Jack specialized in supporting the family with the money he made at work; Jill specialized in bringing up the children and creating a warm, nurturing home for the family. At its simplest, it was Jack's job to build the tangible assets (money, pension, home) and Jill's to build the intangible assets (emotional support, a wider group of friends).

Jack was born in 1945 and although he began his marriage with the model of traditional roles, over the course of his life he saw that much of what he had taken for granted was beginning to change. Across his adult life he witnessed marriage rates falling, cohabitation rates rising, the age for marrying and childbirth ascending, divorce rates rising and then falling again, and an increase in the number of people remarrying.[3] There were many drivers behind these changes: developments in contraception, changes in legislation, changing social and economic attitudes towards gender inequality, and of course greater longevity.

These developments continued more forcefully in Jimmy's life, making a great deal more impression on his own relationships and shaping the expectations of his partnerships. Born in 1971, Jimmy entered what the sociologist Anthony Giddens believes is an age where modern institutions, such as marriage, began to differ from all preceding forms of social order in respect of their dynamism, the degree to which they undercut traditional habits and customs, and in their global impact.[4]

This dynamism is very apparent in Jimmy's case, as the changing norms of family and marriage radically transformed his day-to-day personal and social life. If Jimmy lived in Europe or the US, he would, as a young man, have experienced the sexual revolution that led to both the transformation of female sexual autonomy and the legalization of homosexuality. For Jimmy, the traditional notions of family life and relationships were changing at the very time when geographical mobility and mass media were beginning to undercut many elements of traditional social life. Jimmy was 16 when the Hite report, *Women and Love*, created a storm about the role of women and began a number of cycles of social debate, reinvestigation and further debate. The way in which men and women related to each other and their respective roles became part of the wider public discourse, but also served to alter views about sexuality, the role of men and women, and what constitutes a family.[5]

Jane was born in 1998 into a family where her mother worked and her parents divorced when she was a teenager. How will her own personal life develop? In the 5.0 scenario we built for Jane, we created a rather traditional personal life for her. She works for most of her adult life and has two children with her life partner Jorge. In deciding to work for most of her life, Jane's experience will mirror that of millions of other women across the world, and the elongated dual career partnerships this creates will have a profound impact on these women, on their partners and on their employers.

Over and above these social and economic trends, Jane will also be navigating the effects of longevity and the rise of the multi-stage life. We can expect this to influence her view of options. In a longer life, options become more valuable and so it is no surprise that people are already choosing to marry later, especially women. Yet perhaps the most profound impact of longevity on personal lives and families will be that, across a whole life, a smaller proportion of years will be focused on raising children. People will have more time without the responsibilities of caring for children. This effect is already being felt. In 1880, in 75 per cent of families there were children living at home; by 2005 only 41 per cent of families had children at home. Spending a significant part of your life living without children has become far less unusual.[6] The result has been a slow but significant decline in the importance and perceived appropriateness of Becker's production complementarities and its gender-based specialization of labour.

This specialization of labour has also been undermined by other factors. Women do not have to specialize in working in the home, when vacuums, freezers, washing machines, dishwashers and prepared food do many of the tasks for them. At the same time, the gradual narrowing of male/female wage differentials further undermines the gender separation of activities. When both partners have the opportunity to earn around the same income, this significantly increases the opportunity cost of devoting one member of the household to domestic activities.

If, within a partnership, Becker's production complementarities are becoming less important, what has come in its place? In Giddens' view, what comes in its place is what he terms the 'transformation of intimacy' that approximates the *pure relationship*. These are relationships that are no longer based on the traditional contract but are sought only for what the relationship itself can bring to both partners. Such relationships are reflexively organized and open to constant refashioning and questioning, rather than being static and prone to inertial drag; they have room for manoeuvre. Commitments play a central role in these relationships, as 'the committed person is prepared to accept the risks which sacrificing of other potential options entails'.[7] So it depends on mutual trust between the partners: that each is trustworthy, and that their mutual bond can withstand future traumas. Perhaps most importantly for each partner, self-identity is negotiated through self-exploration and the development of intimacy with the other, creating a shared history. Of course, the great contradiction in this pure form of relationship is that this level of commitment needs some kind of guarantee that the relationship can be sustained for an indefinite period. Yet the feature of a pure relationship is that it can be terminated, more or less at will, by either partner at any particular point. Given these conditions, there are large areas of possible tension and conflict, and over longer periods of time the capacity to work through these tensions and conflicts will be crucial.

At the same time as this transformation of intimacy, there are also important underlying shifts taking place in the economic characteristics of marriage. With the rise of dual income households, there is less focus on production complementarities as both people now work. Instead there is a greater focus on *consumption complementarities.* The relationship argument is that these new forms of partnership work because they create the context for reflexivity and shared history. The economic argument is that these partnerships work in part because it is cheaper for two people to finance a large house, enjoy a holiday or run a household than it is for two single people to live independently. There is also the important advantage of *risk pooling*; this played an important role in the way Jane and Jorge navigated their life, and we expect that more couples will make the same commitments to each other to pool the risk. This may go some way to explaining the significant shift to what has been termed *assortative mating*,[8] where both partners are of similar age, education and income. In Becker's traditional view of marriage, the production complementarities gained most when there is a significant income differential between partners, giving greater scope to comparative advantage. However, when the potential income differential is less, then it makes more sense for partners to pool their risk and this is easiest where the earning capacity of both partners is similar.

Marriage has evolved in Jimmy's lifetime, and Becker's 'production complementarities' are being replaced by 'pure' relationships based more on 'consumption complementarities' and the advantages of risk pooling. There is no doubt that across Jane's long life there will be further changes. In Becker's model, it was the wife who created intangible assets through her focus on the home and the family. In Jane's multi-stage life, the intangible assets that need to be produced extend to productive assets as well. As a result, we believe that there will be a return to the traditional idea of specialization and 'production complementarities', but this time based on the creation of productive assets and involving each partner *switching* as they take the lead at different stages of their life.

Clearly, over a long partnership, this switching will need a high level of complementarity and coordination between partners. These multi-stage lives will involve many transitions and these are difficult to navigate successfully and need support: the updating of skills, and the capacity to take on new challenges and invest in new networks. All of this is a great deal easier with the close cooperation of a partner. That's why these types of high-quality partnerships will be so crucial. Over a long life, they provide emotional support, and a sounding board to discuss tough decisions and make honest criticisms.⁹ Partners help each other to keep their eye on what matters, budget their time and energy, live healthfully, and to make deliberate choices – sometimes tough ones – about work, travel, household management and community involvement. Making these partnerships work will need a great deal more skill and the capacity to make commitments and negotiate resources over a long period of time.

If they can be made to work, these long-lived partnerships create the possibility of deep coordination, enabling the household to maintain an income flow while allowing for re-creation and regeneration of intangible assets. In the three-stage life, those people who were members of dual income households tended to either have one dominant earner and another secondary income, or two-career households with equal earnings. Over a multi-stage life, we expect that more households will be dual income and what will change will be the coordination between the two. This will enable switching between the two partners as each becomes the dominant earner at different stages. Sometimes this switch will be in response to unpredicted events, but more often it will be the result of specific planning ahead, on-going negotiations and commitment making. Dual-career households in a three-stage life have to learn how to juggle and coordinate their domestic obligations between themselves on a weekly basis. In a multi-stage life, this juggling and coordination takes place over decades, not just a matter of weeks, and will require a high level of trust and plenty of planning.

This is clear from Jane's 5.0 scenario. Her partner and family are really important to her and together they will experience many transitions. She is navigating a life where the expectations and norms are changing fast and where she will be experimenting with new ways of living and being. She is also making commitments now that will play out over a long period of time. Given these transitions, what will it take to make these partnerships work?

Like much in the 100-year life, it will be about being prepared to make active choices and understand the consequences. It will also be about making and keeping commitments. This will bring to the fore the importance of negotiation. Not everyone will agree with Sheryl Sandberg's advice to graduating women that 'the most important career decision you're going to make is whether or not to have a partner and who that partner is'.[10] But it is a crucial decision with profound consequences. For Sandberg, a high-quality partnership means arriving at an equitable distribution over the long haul, and having a shared vision of success for everyone at home – not just for oneself.[11] Over a long productive life, it is clear that both men and women will be called upon to make fundamental changes in their outlook on and behaviour towards one another. The adjustments demanded will be considerable.

We have assumed here that marriage will remain a popular choice. This is not to deny that a variety of different types of marriages will emerge, and that there will be many varied and popular alternatives to marriage, such as cohabiting or single parenting. However, we believe that the gains from a long-lasting partnership, the legally binding nature of a marriage contract, and the financial arrangements that are provided in the case of a split will, if anything, be enhanced by the coordination that a multi-stage life requires.

Children

As we developed the scenarios for our three characters – Jack, Jimmy and Jane – we were rather perfunctory about their becoming parents. Children sort of just happened along the way. While a longer life means that proportionally less time is spent raising children, we acknowledge this is inappropriate for such an important topic.

Our focus in discussing a long life has been on the many choices people can make. But one constraint that has remained stubbornly inflexible is the period during which a woman can conceive. No doubt rapid developments in fertility treatments, such as freezing eggs, will widen the time period of fertility, but this is unlikely to ever be completely disconnected from age. So while much of life has elongated and brought with it many new options, the time span for having children is unlikely in the near future to be age flexible. This is important, because there will be a relatively narrow period in which women can answer questions about whether to have children, when to have them, and with whom. These choices become even more profound the longer life lasts.

It is possible to consider these choices by changing the age at which Jane and Jorge have children. In the 5.0 scenario, they were in their late 30s by the time they started a family. We could create another scenario for Jane and Jorge in which they become parents in their 20s, which would give them a chance to build their career in their 30s. But what is the likelihood that they will have met each other in their 20s? And what about the 'explorer' stage that could be so important for them to discover their options? Also, would Jane and Jorge really be able to find a life partner so early in their lives?

That is why, in the 5.0 scenario, they have their first child in their late 30s. The advantage here is that they have spent more time exploring and finding a suitable match, and this has given them time in their 20s and 30s to begin to establish their careers. The disadvantage is that once they have decided to have children in their late 30s, it may prove difficult for them to conceive, and of course they will be older parents.

Naturally, there are many other scenarios around partnerships and children. It depends in part on what sort of partner Jane (and indeed Jorge) is seeking. Is Jane looking for a partner who fulfils the traditional specialized role of breadwinner, leaving her free to bring up the children? And if she wants this match, can she find a man who also wants it? Or perhaps Jane would prefer a match with someone who wants a dual career, where both of them work. Jane can even decide not to find a partner at all but to raise a child on her own, supported by her parents, grandparents and possibly even great-grandparents. With multiple stages to her life, Jane could focus on raising children during an early stage, then have a career, and then later in her 60s think about marriage and companionship. These are questions that Jack and his wife never really had to face. But they are decisions to which young people like Jane are hyper-sensitive, as they try to understand the consequences of the choices they face.

Over a number of decades, the psychologist Stewart Friedman has been surveying his undergraduate students at the Wharton School of the University of Pennsylvania about their partnership aspirations. This is an elite group of young people so it would be foolhardy to draw general global insights from them. However, the changes he has observed in the two decades between the class of 1992 and those of 2012 are profound.

Compared to twenty years ago, fewer young men and women say they are planning to have children, and many are putting vitality and friends as being as important in their lives as long-term relationships and parenthood. In his 1992 survey, Friedman found 78 per cent of students said they planned to have children; by 2012 this had declined to 42 per cent. Will what these students say they want at the age of 22 be an accurate predictor of their actual behaviour? Only time will tell, but it is interesting that their intentions are so different from the earlier cohort.

Another interesting point about this group concerns their intentions about future partnership arrangements. Around a third of the women would like to find a partner and live the traditional specialized roles with them being primary child carers; around a third want a dual career; and around a third want a partnership without children. As Friedman notes, for many of his students 'there is no longer the kneejerk expectation of motherhood, of a mindless march into a predetermined future; nor are they looking through rose-colored glasses'.[12]

These implications are profound for both men and women, and point towards continual shifts in gender roles. Friedman argues that shifting gender roles originate from both sides, pointing out that many educated young men had a working mother as a female role model and see being a father as having a positive social impact. Therefore they appear to be more favourable about a dual-career family and are willing to step outside a traditional breadwinner role, expecting to spend more time with their children and be more involved than their own fathers were with them.[13] All of these changes are needed if marriage is to adapt to the challenges of the 100-year life.

While the age at which people can conceive will in all likelihood remain inflexible, it is probable that the multi-stage life and evolving social institutions will create wider choices than are currently available. The probability is that many people will have a smaller family later in their life. In part this will be an economic decision; saddled with student debt and the need for greater savings, many people are likely to be cautious about undertaking the additional economic burdens of children. Some women will try to delay motherhood so they can explore and discover options before committing to raising a family. This makes sense from an economic perspective, as studies have shown that women who delay motherhood increase their lifetime earnings, with the gains being highest for college graduates.[14]

There will be many other options and greater variability. A women might, with grandparental support and life as an independent producer, choose to be a single mother; or through collaboration with a partner, focus on her career while her partner focuses on child rearing; or raise children while her partner pursues their own career and then, when the children have left home, embark on a new career stage with economic support from her partner. The options for fathers will also be broader; they too can decide to work full-time in a traditional role, be a full-time father, or negotiate different roles over a period of years.

Work and home

An important part of the equation of home and personal lives is work, and particularly the extent to which women work. The twentieth century saw major changes in the role of women in the workplace, and an excellent summary is provided by the Harvard University economist Claudia Goldin.[15]. She shows that there has been a narrowing between men and women in terms of their participation in the workforce and the hours they spend at work – both at home and in the workplace, the type of jobs and sectors in which they work, as well as in terms of wages.

Women and work

However, while differences have narrowed, there still remain substantial gaps and blockages that disadvantage women. This context is important, because if these differences remain then the choices and options facing women over the course of a 100-year life will differ from those facing men. This means that the possible lives men and women can imagine will diverge, and therefore we would have to articulate different scenarios for both sexes. Of course, if it is likely that these differences will narrow over the coming decades, then the scenarios for men and women will be more similar. These are important issues in their own right but also affect the dynamics of the household and partnerships.

Different economic roles in the workplace and different career options will lead to different domestic partnerships. And of course much of the initial negotiation about roles will come at a time when the future is not clear.

So what is the current situation? We know that the number of working women has increased throughout the OECD over the last decades. In 1980, the average proportion of women aged between 25 and 54 who were either in employment or seeking employment was 54 per cent; by 2010 this had risen to 71 per cent. What is particularly striking is the experience of mothers with young children. In the US in 1970, for example, 70 per cent of those with children under the age of five were outside the paid economy – presumably full-time homemakers pursuing the specialized marriage model of Jack and Jill. By 2007 this had reduced to 36 per cent.[16] However, women still remain disproportionately engaged in part-time work (women account for an average of 80 per cent of all part-time work across the OECD) because of their greater involvement in maintaining the home and raising children. All of these changes in work patterns for women have contributed to the profound shifts in marriage and how the household functions.

While in most countries there has been an increase in the proportion of working women, this has not been uniform across countries and substantial differences remain. As a glance at Figure 9.1 shows, the gap between male and female participation

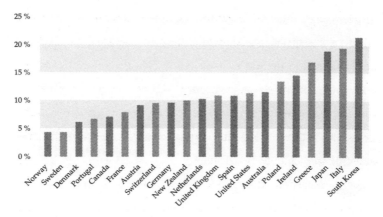

FIGURE 9.1 *Gap between male and female participation rates 2014.*
Source: OECD.Stat

is widest in Japan, Italy and South Korea, and narrowest in
Norway and Sweden. It is interesting to speculate on the speed
at which norms will change in the country in which you live. At
the time of writing, in Japan, for example, there are a number
of government initiatives to bring women into work and, over
time, we can expect more countries to narrow the gap. In those
countries where this gap remains, women will continue to
have less choice over how to construct their 100-year life and
partnerships are more likely to take a traditional form.

The genesis of these differences across countries is complex.
Some reflect social and cultural factors that change over time.
Some reflect significant policy differences in terms of family
benefits, tax allowances and support for childcare. Others reflect

more straightforward economic realities. When the partners within a family plan their life together, our guess is their plans are based on two crucial questions: who does the domestic duties, and who is likely to be paid the most? Of course their challenge is that they have to make important short-term resource allocation decisions without really knowing whether the answer to these question will change over time.

With regard to the first question, we know that in many countries the bulk of domestic and child-rearing duties are carried out by women. A survey of American families in 2013 found that even when both parents work, the women continue to spend more time in child-rearing and domestic activities.[17] This may be US data but it is replicated in most countries of the world. Even in dual-career couples, men spend more hours in work and women more hours at home.[18] Studies show that men spend 11 hours per week more in paid work and have 4.5 more hours of leisure, while women do more childcare and housework.

Looking into the future, if domestic labour becomes more equally assigned between men and women, what would this mean for their careers, particularly if both are working in highly skilled, intense occupations? There is no doubt that if both partners engage equally in the household, this will put a strain on traditional roles. Across a long life it seems inevitable that this will lead to conflict and renegotiation. That is why in the 3.5 scenario for Jimmy we put an emphasis on how he and his partner actively renegotiated their domestic roles so that she had an opportunity to re-skill and to work full-time. In the 5.0 scenario, Jane will need to negotiate even more with her husband so that the domestic workload is spread more evenly, although not necessarily in every stage. It is possible, of course, that over multiple stages each partner can switch in terms of taking the lead in domestic duties.

So that leaves the second question. In a traditional partnership made up of a man and a woman, who is likely to earn the most? This is a hard trend to predict. We know that participation rates are narrowing between men and women across the OECD, and for some countries the gap is nearing closure. In fact, in many occupations, young women are making up more than 50 per cent of the entrants into work. In some occupations, such as medicine and education, it is more than 50 per cent, while in others, such as engineering, IT and investment banking, it is significantly less. It is possible, therefore, that for this cohort of young women (who are around the same age as Jane), this gender balance will continue throughout their working lives and so they will be equal breadwinners in the home

However, while women are catching up with men in terms of participating in the workforce, the pay they receive, even adjusting for differences in education and work experience, is less. Figure 9.2, shows the pay gap between men and women in the US for different ages and over different periods of time and demonstrates that women's pay is catching up with men. The ratio of (mean) annual earnings between male and female workers (working full-time aged 25 to 69 years) was 0.56 in 1980, 0.72 in 2010 and 0.77 by 2014. The bad news is there still remains a significant gap and this difference widens as the career unfolds. In part this reflects the under-representation of women in senior roles. In 2014, in many large corporations, around 30 per cent of middle management roles were occupied by women, while in senior executive roles in many industrial sectors the proportion of women to men was significantly less, at around 15 per cent.[19]

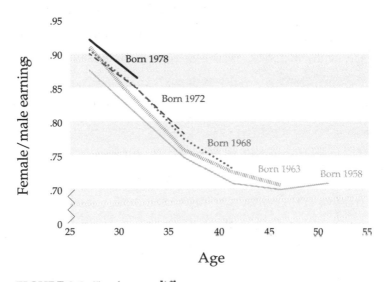

FIGURE 9.2 *Gender pay differences.*

Source: Claudia Goldin, 'How to Achieve Gender Equality', Milken Institute Review http://www.milkeninstitute.org/

As a younger generation of women makes more progress than past generations, there are signs of change. However, the gap is still marked. A study of Chicago MBA graduates,[20] for example, found that on graduating men on average received a salary that was $17,000 more than women. However, after ten years the gap had widened to more than $150,000. The report showed that much of the gap could be accounted for by differences in hours worked, career breaks and employment paths taken prior to enrolling at a business school.

If these are the causes of gender differences in earnings, does this explain why, as noted by Goldin, 'These aggregate ratios [of female to male earnings] have been somewhat sticky for the last ten years or so after greatly increasing in the preceding decades, especially in the 1980s'.[21] Have we reached a limit to the catch-up of women's salaries relative to men's? As we look forward, the question to be addressed is how 'sticky' this pay gap is likely to be. Right now it is likely that when Jane enters her first job she will experience gender parity. But will this continue over her career? For example, will Jane find it as hard to become a senior executive as women in 2014 are finding it? Forecasts from the International Labour Organization (ILO)[22] report 'Women and the Future of Work', published in early 2015, suggest it will take at least seventy years to reach gender wage parity given current rates of change. That's 2085, by which time Jane will be 87. It is a very dispiriting thought.

Flexibility

Goldin's detailed analysis sheds much light on the issue of why women earn less than men. She concludes that the gender gap in pay is largely a result of the value placed on the different characteristics of the work in which men and women have historically engaged. It seems that there are five key choices. Is the person prepared to work in a job that involves significant time pressure? Will they take a job where there is very little autonomy with regard to the times they have to be there? Are they prepared to work in a job where they need to be flexible with regard to their scheduling? Do they want a job where they have to keep in touch regularly with the other members of their team? Will the job be one that only they can do and where it is hard to get someone else to perform the task? These are work choices that command a higher salary and are currently more likely to be embraced by men than women – especially women with children. These are jobs with very little flexibility.

We can illustrate these five work choices by looking at one occupation – law. Typically, this is work that is at the extreme end of all five work choices: significant time pressure; limited time autonomy; no flexibility around scheduling; a need to be constantly in touch with other team members; and limited opportunity for substitution.

Consider a scenario where Jane decides to join the legal profession. After her initial law training, let's imagine that she wants to take a more flexible approach to her work, perhaps because she has small children. Very soon she will find that if she is not available to meet a client when the client needs her, then at that point her value to the firm begins to decline. She may also find that her intangible assets, such as tacit knowledge, begins to erode because she is not constantly in the office to interact with her colleagues and clients in meetings or through random exchanges. So if she is not around, she will be excluded from the ideas that are bouncing around in conversation. As Goldin shows, these types of knowledge-rich occupations (such as law, consultancy, investment banking) impose heavy penalties on people who want to work fewer hours and have more flexible employment.

It's useful at this point to stand back and examine Goldin's argument and also the ILO prediction. Currently, working flexibly is a choice made predominantly by women as they look after their young children or care for elderly relatives. Women are disadvantaged in the labour market because they often have breaks in their career path and they prefer work with greater flexibility. But looking forward, will these be choices made by men as well? If so, what will be the impact on them?

What are the career choices and trade-offs faced by Jane the young lawyer or her male equivalent? She has various options and choices to make, each with a plethora of consequences and trade-offs. Let's imagine that she wants to become a partner in a law firm. We can predict that she will work with little flexibility (as she is available 24/7), under considerable time pressure, in a highly unstructured and unpredictable way, with very little discretion about where and when she works. She has chosen a career path where taking any time off (for example, to have a baby) is heavily penalized. The rewards are, of course, that she will be very highly paid and she may well have a fascinating and meaningful job.

Or Jane could decide to make trade-off decisions. In law, as in other career paths, there are various avenues for this. She could choose to move out of a large law firm where there is a premium for working long and continuous hours, and instead work as a general counsel with a corporation where she can expect to work fewer and more flexible hours. Or she could decide against one of the large firms and instead join a small firm that allows her to work short and discontinuous hours at a lower penalty. We can also imagine that, as the acceptance and technological sophistication of virtual work increases, she will be able to join a virtual law firm and work from home.[23] The trade-offs she faces are clear: as flexibility and autonomy increases, so remuneration decreases (and possibly the work has less variety and excitement).

Or Jane could choose another career all together, one that has greater time flexibility, fewer clients and contact hours, more independence in determining tasks, and more projects with discretion over them. These are jobs that have what Goldin calls *elasticity* and her analysis shows that they are more likely to be found in technology and science, where the gender pay gap is small and does not widen over time. It is interesting, of course, that these are not the occupations to which women are currently flocking. One example would be the profession of pharmacy. Goldin's analysis shows this is an occupation where there is currently a high degree of substitution, so that if one pharmacist is away, then another can take their place with ease. Of course, this is a profession that is paid significantly less than lawyers, consultants or investment bankers. If this substitution were to occur in law partnerships, for example, then partners would have to convince their clients that one partner could be substituted for another, and the lawyers would have to work very closely together to enable substitution and are likely therefore to be paid more.

Goldin's data was published in 2014. Looking forward, can we expect much to change during Jane's lifetime with regard to flexibility and trade-offs? That depends on a range of factors, including attitudes to flexible working around the world, the speed at which virtual technology is adopted, the extent to which tasks become standardized, and the degree to which men in senior roles take time out to spend with their children and therefore act as a role model for others.

What docs this mean for men? What we do know right now is that the depression of pay when people work flexibly is not simply experienced by women. Men tend to work longer hours and earn more after becoming fathers. However, if they choose to reduce their work hours for family reasons, studies have shown they also experience a *flexibility stigma* that depresses their earnings and limits their future career opportunities.[24]

The impact of switching

Let's stand back and look at this in another way. In the 5.0 scenario we created for Jane, we assumed that there would be times in her life when both she and Jorge would be engaged in full-time work, but also times when both took time out from full-time work – to be parents, to build their knowledge or to prepare for transitions. We expected that they would both experience career breaks and flexibility at one or more stages in their working life. We also imagined that there would be times when they switched roles between each other in terms of taking the lead on high-value work, domestic responsibilities and re-creation. Now let's imagine that millions of people have working lives that look like this one. What would be the impact of this switching between men and women?

At present there is a flexibility stigma experienced by both men and women. Would that still be that case if career breaks for men and women became more standard? Isn't it possible that, as a result, the stigma and financial penalties attached to flexibility would reduce? This, combined with the fact that more men will take breaks as part of a multi-stage life, may lead to greater earnings equality. The same argument may hold for flexible working. What happens if, as a result of a multi-stage life, more men pursue flexible working patterns? Here are two possibilities. First, men will work flexibly and in consequence will experience the flexibility stigma and the lower wages associated with this; the result could be greater gender equality in pay as the earnings of both men and women who work flexibly are depressed. Alternatively – and a more radical thought – work will be redesigned so that there is not the same cost, to either firm or individual, from flexible working. In other words, if both men and women prefer more flexible working patterns, then the nature of work is likely to be radically redesigned.

What of the switching scenario? Here, during one stage of the partnership, one person pursues a 24/7 career while the other works flexibly and helps raise the family; at another stage their roles are reversed. Obviously, such a complex joint multi-stage life will require enormous coordination, trust and cooperation between couples, and also major changes from employers in how they view work, age and gender. However, while complex, the advantage is that this would support a convergence across men and women in lifetime income. It may be that at any point in time one is earning less than the other, but across the whole of their working life each makes an equal contribution. Though perhaps an optimistic solution, it does make the most of the interplay possible across a 100-year life, and the impact of the resequencing of stages and of gender equality.

Divorce

One of the assumptions of the 5.0 scenario was that Jane would stay with Jorge for life. Indeed, we assumed the same for Jack and Jimmy and their wives. We did this because building an intangible asset flow with a mid-life divorce is complicated and we did not want to make an already complex picture even more so. But of course this assumption is not realistic.

For some, marriage is a very successful and enduring institution. In fact, current figures suggest that those over 65 are more likely to be married than at any other time in the past – as likely as those aged 16 to 65. This reflects greater life expectancy for both men and women, a decreasing gap in the age difference between males and females at marriage, a rise in remarriage due to more people divorcing, leading to a 'thicker remarriage market', and reduced social stigma.

It is true that when Jack and Jill married they probably had little fear of their partnership ending in divorce. In the

US in the 1950s, only 12 per cent of white female college graduates' marriages ended in divorce. By the 1960s this had roughly doubled. When Jimmy grew up he would have viewed divorce as much more of a social norm. Indeed, in the US, divorce rose through much of the twentieth century and by the 1970s around 48 per cent of marriages ended in divorce within twenty-five years – hence the popular claim that 'half of all marriages end in divorce'. Back in 1981, the American sociologist Andrew Cherlin declared that the new typical life course was 'marriage, divorce, remarriage'.[25] What he described was the phenomenon of marital breakdown that he believed would continue.

However, it turns out that what Cherlin observed was not a continuous increase but rather a peak. As we show in Figure 9.3, divorce in the US was at a peak for those who married between 1970 and 1979. For those who married after 1979, divorce rates have fallen. One explanation for the high divorce rates of marriages that started in the 1970s was that the following period reflected a societal transition. Many people married the right partner for the traditional model of marriage, with clear male and female roles, only to find that the person they married was not able to enjoy the sort of life that they now wanted. Furthermore, the introduction of 'no fault' divorces made divorce easier and created a peak when a backlog of cases came forward.

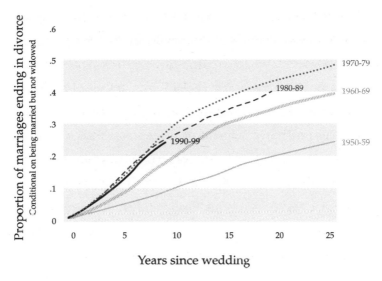

FIGURE 9.3 *US divorce rates across the decades.*

Source: Betsy Stevenson and Justin Wolfers, 'Marriage and Divorce: Changes and their Driving Forces', *Journal of Economic Perspectives*, Spring 2007, 21(2): 27–52.

By 2014, marriage was happening later, divorce was less likely and remarriage was less common. Indeed, certainly in the US, those who have married in recent years have been more likely to stay together than their parents' generation. A potential explanation is that as the basis of a marriage shifts from production to consumption complementarities, people choose on the basis of different criteria and the marriage lasts longer. In addition, people are getting married later in life and therefore divorcing less, since they have more self-knowledge with which to create a stable base for the marriage.

What impact will a 100-year life have on divorce rates? We see forces operating that would potentially result in both increases and decreases.

Clearly a longer life should lead to an increase in divorce rates simply because life lasts longer – more things will happen and people will undergo more transitions and change. Hence it would seem likely that the probability of being divorced over a 100-year life is higher than over a 70-year life. We can also expect that, as people get a clearer view of the length of their lives, they will be prepared to divorce later as well as remarry later. Being in an unhappy marriage when you are 70 and expect to live to 100 is very different from being in the same situation when life expectancy is 75. This is already apparent from the divorce data. While overall divorce rates are indeed declining, they are increasing among the elderly. In the US, for example, one in ten divorces involves people over the age of 60. Compared to 1990, those over 60 are twice as likely to get divorced; in the UK it is three times more. People are realizing that a long life provides more time to recover from a divorce and more time to rebuild both their financial and intangible assets.

However, there are other trends that predict that the divorce rate might decrease. In some of the scenarios we developed, divorce becomes a very costly event. Consider the type of coordinated 5.0 scenario we sketched out for Jane and Jorge. This coordination between them makes a successful relationship extremely valuable over the long term. Of course, it also makes such a relationship hard work and risky, as it puts a great deal of strain on their capacity to negotiate fairly with each other, to make commitments to each other and to trust each other to deliver. The costs of breaking up are high; even if the financial assets are shared equitably, there are sure to be major inequities in each person's intangible assets. Thus, at the point of the break-up, both people will be required to make major revisions of their life plans. So in the 5.0 scenario, the cost of a divorce increases.

Overall, this line of reasoning suggests that over a long life there is a greater probability that people will separate and divorce, and will experience more than one partner. The financial implications of divorce are always significant, but even more so over a 100-year life. The exact impact depends not just on the partnership but also on the law of the country. There are sure to be changes in the distribution of assets after a divorce. In traditional marriages, the man was typically the breadwinner and supported his wife when they were married and for a period after divorce. For dual income households, the outcomes are more complex; across a 100-year life, divorce agreements may become still more complicated. This raises many questions that will have to be considered over the coming decades. For example, if Jane raises a family while Jorge focuses on the finance, with an understanding that in their next stage these roles will switch, what then happens if Jane and Jorge divorce in between stages? Will Jane have to work to finance Jorge's next low-income stage? Should the separation of assets be equal when they divorce or should they reflect the commitments they made to support each other through their different stages?

Multi-generational living

When we consider how personal lives will be shaped as life lengthens, it is clear that this will have a profound impact on how the generations live together. The three-stage life and lockstep helped contribute to the Western pattern of segregation of ages: the young attend educational institutions, the old are retired and in leisure, while the rest interact in the workplace. A multi-stage life, where age is not stage and more mature individuals display juvenescence, should lead to major changes in inter-generational dynamics.

Families

When we visit Asia, particularly India, we are struck by something we rarely see in the West: children, parents and grandparents living together. When we talk to friends in multi-generational families, they talk positively of the many advantages. Children have an opportunity to spend time with their grandparents, the parents feel they have more support when they are working, and elderly relations feel they have a positive role and contribution to make. Indeed, there is a growing body of research that shows that multi-generational relationships can boost longevity. Loneliness in old age is a killer, and there are real advantages for the elderly to be embedded in their families.[26] Of course, our Asian hosts also mention the downside: a lack of privacy and the possibility of caustic relations between the generations.

Western countries have moved away from the constant interaction across the generations that we see in Asia and which would have been the norm in the West four or five decades ago. In its place are smaller family units. Children indeed stay longer with their parents, particularly in high-cost cities, but when they leave the parental home they are likely to set up a relatively small family unit. In some countries, such as Denmark, the household size is getting smaller; in 2013 the average number of people in a household was 2.1 and unlikely to contain an older person. This segregation of ages has been a major societal shift. For example, between 1910 and 1980 in the US, the proportion of people over the age of 65 living alone or with their spouse increased from 20 per cent to 74 per cent, and the proportion living with their children dropped from 61 per cent to 16 per cent.[27] So while older people frequently interact with their children and grandchildren, the intense cross-age interactions of the past have gone. Could it be that this trend will be reversed and Western family units will begin to look more like Asian families?

Let's return to Jane and Jorge, who were born around 1998. By the age of 35, in 2033, it is very likely that their two sets of parents will be alive (they were born around 1973), and so too may their four sets of grandparents (born around 1948). So when their children are young adults, it is possible they will have great-grandparents, grandparents and parents. And since birth rates began to dip from the 1950s onwards, it is also likely that Jane and Jorge have few siblings; their own parents may also be from small families. Moreover, while in our 5.0 scenario Jane and Jorge remained in a partnership, if they had divorced instead then their family would be different again, with step-parents and step-grandparents adding to the breadth and complexity of the family unit.

What will these extended family members be doing? Jane and Jorge's parents are in their early 60s, so it is likely they will either be working full-time or engaged in a series of portfolio activities. Jane's parents divorced when she was a teenager and have both remarried, so her children have two sets of step-grandparents. Jane and Jorge's grandparents are in their 80s, so are likely to be retired and could well be enjoying good health with another decade or two in front of them. They could also be engaged in activities similar to that of Jane and Jorge's children: going to university, travelling the world and learning new skills. This juvenescence could build a strong bridge between the generations. If these extended family networks of grandparents and great-grandparents are enjoying longer, healthy lives, then the overall well-being of the family will rise substantially.

With few role models to act as guides, we can expect a period of experimentation as people negotiate these complex multi-generational relationships. They will be moving into a period of experimenting with cross-generational relationships as the age of the family members extends and the youthfulness of the grandparents becomes more apparent. They will all have to work out what best to do and, as Anthony Giddens observes, construct their own novel ethics for day-to-day life. This will particularly be the case for the commitments they will make within their close and extended family. In the past, tradition decided on commitments – for example, whether to lend money to family members or how to behave as a father. Going forward, people will have to work through a host of questions: how to support four generations, or, if they are a step-parent, what will be their financial commitments to their stepchildren or vice versa?

There is no doubt that these multi-generational families could provide wonderful opportunities for the ages to start to know each other better. As we described earlier, one of the impacts of industrialization has been the segregation of the ages. The segregation of life became normal as the state adopted rules that used chronological age to require children's school attendance while excluding them from the workplace, and to entitle older people to pensions.[28] As the ages became institutionally segregated, they also became spatially segregated. People of different ages no longer occupied the same space and so didn't engage in face-to-face interactions. There are three locations that are potentially important for cross-age interactions: the household, the neighbourhood, and places where routine activities occur (e.g. work, study, recreation, worship). Neighbourhoods – often unintentionally, although sometimes intentionally – segregate ages. The ages are also segmented as a result of many routine activities being structured around age (e.g. youth orchestras, senior citizen activities, senior tour groups) and distinct cultures often grow up around each age group. These age-segregated institutions restrict the opportunity for people to form stable cross-age relationships. Places where people of different ages can interact, become familiar with each other and share personal knowledge are hard to come by. Perhaps the multi-generational family could be one such place?

When relationships span age groups, there is less stereotyping and prejudice about age. What seems to be important here is sustained familiarity – that means stable, lasting interactions over time. Perhaps multi-generations will live together as they do in parts of Asia; perhaps they will simply see more of each other as the ages share and support each other. What is clear is that this sharing could have an incredibly positive impact on both the young and the old.

Friends

As healthy life spans extend, the nuclear family might become less central. Historically, bearing and raising children was the central activity in a lifetime, with no evolutionary advantage being seen in a long life. However, as life extends, child rearing is no longer the all-consuming event it once was, and in its place a phase of friendship could emerge. It's even possible that such friendships could become the new nuclear unit, with friends sharing homes and outgoings.

Stewart Friedman, in his twenty-year study of Wharton MBA students, has seen something of this trend emerging for his students in their 20s. In the more recent studies, he found students placing a great deal more emphasis on friendships as the primary relational link, and wanting to build relationships that would be capable of supporting some of the nurturing more traditionally associated with families.

Just as multi-generational living arrangements could be the place where cross-age connections take place, perhaps friendships that span age groups could also have a positive impact on the current social separation of the old and the young.[29] While in non-industrialized societies age is not a significant locator of a person, in the three-stage life age has become a segmenter of life experiences. Gunhild Hagestad, and Peter Uhlenburg, describe how data from the US and the Netherlands show that when networks of friends are formed, the majority of people choose to form friendships with someone of the same age. For example, a study of the non-kin networks of Detroit men show 72 per cent of their close friends were within eight years of their own age.[30] In a much wider study of where people go to discuss important matters, only 3 per cent of young adults go to a non-kin discussion partner over the age of 53, and about 25 per cent of the older group went to a non-kin discussion partner who was under the age of 36.

When these age-homogenous networks engage with each other, they tend to reinforce their group identity, have the same perspective on life and introduce each other to people of the same age. The authors believe that age segregation is closely connected to ageism, since it sets up sharp distinctions between 'us' and 'them', and leads to stereotyping and associated prejudices. When the three stages become multiple stages, then people from different ages have a chance to engage in similar experiences. As Gordon Allport showed in his classic study, one weapon against stereotypes and prejudices is contact between groups.[31] Perhaps as this happens, the age homogeneity of networks will begin to disintegrate, as people from different ages share experiences and, from this, create friendships. Perhaps old age will become less of a 'separate country'.[32]

Agenda for Change

This book is about what happens when many people across the world live to 100. The most pressing aspect is how to make the finances work, but the real insights come when we focused on intangible assets. Drawing from economics and psychology, we have made the case that living for longer requires a fundamental redesign of life and a restructuring of time. Only then can longevity be a gift and not a curse.

When we looked at possible lives, scenarios and stages, it became clear that even though changes are already underway, there is still a significant amount to be achieved and at myriad levels. Some of these changes are about ourselves and our families; some about the companies we work for and the career environment they offer; some about educational institutions and how they can meet our changing needs; and others about governments and the policies that influence how we decide to live our lives. These are wholesale changes and will be vital in supporting both those who are well placed to live a long and productive life and those who are less fortunate.

Crucially, these changes need to be anticipated today rather than encountered later. Without positive planning and action-taking, longevity has the potential to be a curse. That is why it is so important that there is a wider discourse, so that people can understand their situation more implicitly and consider their options and choices more fully.

As we bring our own thoughts to a conclusion, we are struck by the fundamental impact that longevity has on our *sense of self*: concerned about what it means for the wider society; intrigued by the response of education institutions, corporations and governments; and puzzled why change has been so slow and what it would take to catalyse action. The great advantage of increasing life expectancy is it is happening slowly and is predictable from afar. We need to seize this advantage and make sure we prepare appropriately.

A sense of self

As we consider what it means to live for 100 years, it is clear that there is so much that can be achieved. In the scenarios mapped out for Jimmy and Jane, we segmented their lives into their constituent stages and transitions. Yet fundamentally, a long life is properly conceived as a whole journey. Of course, it is the single journey that defines your life and the key questions you face are: 'What form will this journey take?' and 'What will make it essentially *your* journey?' The answer lies, in part, with the choices you make and the values you live by. It is these that will define and shape the sequence of events, stages and transitions that together become your accumulated sense of self – *your* identity.

Identity

The moral philosopher Derek Parfit[1] defines identity in terms of psychological connectedness and continuity – or what he calls 'Relation R'. As you encounter the flux of a long life, it is the single thread of identity that connects the past to the present and then into the future, and which defines your sense of self. In a three-stage life, this connectedness is relatively easy to manage; in a multi-stage life, this demands more from you.

For much of human history, mankind has faced a battle for existence over a short life and in the face of food scarcity, diseases and a constant threat of violence. As life has extended and people have become richer, especially those living in the advanced economies, so they have evolved to a situation where, for the majority, their children are safe and educated, work provides some financial security, and they can enjoy a retirement with some components of leisure. As life extends even further, people will be forced to move away from the lockstep of the three-stage life and face many more options about how they live their lives. A hundred years provides more time than required by the evolutionary imperative to breed, and more time in which to meet any financial security needs. So what is the purpose of these extra years if not to procreate and accumulate? Might these extra years, distributed throughout a life, bring the time and opportunity to explore who you are and arrive at a way of living that is nearer to your own personal values and hopes than to the traditions of the society into which you were born? If so, then this is perhaps the greatest gift that longevity can bestow.

Achieving this sense of identity and integrity of stages across a 100-year life will not be easy. Some argue that, for the majority of people, such a heightened sense of reflexivity is beyond their grasp. For instance, the sociologist Margaret Archer believes that only a small number of the population are able to muster the required high levels of autonomy and reflexivity. For most people, she argues, life just happens; as a result, most people are incapable of shaping their own lives.[2] We don't see it this way; we believe that the plethora of new role models and the fading of lockstep will create social norms in which people will be forced to make their own choices. Taking these actions will develop deeper self-knowledge and stronger reflexivity capabilities. The forces that are already profoundly transforming society in this way will be greatly enhanced by the restructuring shifts created by a 100-year life.

Much has already changed. For past generations, tradition would have dictated many of the responses to questions such as: 'How should I behave?', 'What should I wear?' and 'What do I want?' People behaved how their parents behaved, perhaps how their social class or occupation dictated; they wore what was socially appropriate; and they wanted the same things as their parents.

Consider, for example, the flows of psychological and social information that are available to you right now. You probably live in a world of globalization, where you have genuinely worldwide social connections and are inevitably confronted with ideas that are both local and global. So at any point of time, in place of the traditions and rituals that helped your parents and grandparents to understand who they were and could be, you are now presented with a plethora of role models. Global media has enabled most of us to be part of a direct audience for performances that happen in other places, and has given us access to role models that are not physically present. The result is that, as you think about who you are and what you can become, you are able to view many possible selves.

In this book we have considering these issues and described the consequences, but ultimately, only we as individuals can answer the questions: 'Who am I?' and 'How shall I live?' Over the course of a long life, these questions will become impossible to ignore.

Planning and experimentation

At the centre of building a productive 100-year life are plans and experiments. Planning and preparation are crucial in ensuring that the flux of a long life doesn't destroy financial and intangible assets. Experimentation is required so that possible selves are considered and examined. Together, these plans and experiments provide both purpose and individuality, and the psychological connectedness that shapes identity.

Planning and preparation are crucial, since there is so much scope for individual choice: there are more stages to be connected; more time for bad decisions to have dire consequences; and fewer standardized role models to follow. Planning for a 100-year life forces everyone to make key decisions about what they want to do and how they want to do it. The danger is that they fail to make the *right* key decisions. Instead, in the words of the economist Daniel Kahneman, they are driven by delusional optimism. People don't act or plan appropriately, not because they are terrified about the consequences of their action, but rather because they are ridiculously optimistic about the future and about themselves.[3] We are all prone to what Margaret Heffernan calls 'willful blindness'.[4] The challenge of a longer life is that the impact of mistakes potentially lasts for longer, even if there is time to claw situations back from the edge. This is why we have placed such emphasis on planning and preparation.

It is also why experimentation is so important. Devoid of traditional role models, and with a plethora of possible selves, you need to experiment to find what works for you, to understand what you enjoy and value, and to be insightful about what resonates with your own character and personality. Experimentation is not just for the young – it will be crucial at all ages. It is experiments that guide us to where we want to be next and reveal how we should navigate that transition. Indeed, it is this sense of experimentation and exploration that is part of the thread that runs through life.

In Jane's scenario we can see this sense of self as a journey play out. To the question 'Who am I?', Jane's answer will change over the course of her long life; indeed, in principle, at any point in time there could be many possible future Janes. For Jane's age cohort, these are strong behavioural shifts compared to past generations. We believe that these reflect the realization of a long life rather than any mysterious 'Millennial' or 'Gen Y' effect resulting from the specific year in which they were born. A common criticism of this age cohort is their lack of commitment and a sense of entitlement. But viewed from the perspective of a long journey, it is clear they are investing more in a sense of self at the start of their journey, because they realize it is this identity that will be a crucial factor in structuring their stages and transitions.

Mastery

Over a long life, dedication and focus are crucial. If mastery is to be achieved, there will be many occasions when you will have to determinedly put in hundreds, perhaps thousands, of hours of learning, rehearsal and repetition to acquire a level of mastery. Whether or not you are prepared to do that speaks in part of your motivation to learn. There will be times when you are faced with what may look like an easier path ahead, rather than jumping into the turmoil involved in navigating any transitions. In Jimmy's three-stage scenario, we took a closer look at the default scenarios where he simply repeated past actions and routines. They led to an uncomfortable old age.

We argued earlier that the key for mastery was efficacy (knowledge and competence) and agency (the propensity to take action). With regard to efficacy, there is much that can be done to ensure that everyone has a better idea of what is happening in their world and a clear idea of the ways in which they can respond to their changing world. We hope that books like this one will create a context in which people can talk more openly and think more concretely about life planning. It is clear that educational institutions, corporations and governments also have a key role to play in building the general awareness of what is to come, and also in creating the tools of navigation. More conversations about intangible assets will be crucial. It worries us that much of the debate has been dominated by tangible assets: pensions, retirement savings, home loans, etc. There are other topics that are equally as important – for example, the use of leisure time, or commitment-making within partnerships.

In terms of agency, the challenge of a longer life is that there are many more possible future selves to be considered. A 100-year life needs more saving rather than spending, more recreation time converted into re creation, and more capacity and willingness to engage in challenging conversations with partners about roles and commitments. It involves making tough decisions now for potential gains in the future. This is usually referred to as self-control, although when faced with a long life and the array of possible future selves, the phrase 'self-control' is ambiguous. Perhaps 'self-sharing' is a better way of thinking about this challenge.

There is evidence that people differ in their capacity to exercise self-control and these differences manifest themselves from an early age. For example, studies of young children show that even by the age of three, some are more able to exercise self-control and defer gratification than others – in this case, to hold back eating a marshmallow now with the promise of two marshmallows in 30 minutes.[5] Being able to defer gratification can be important in mastery, since acquiring a skill often entails deferring short-term pleasure (watching the next episode of a mini-series) for long-term gain (being able to speak Italian).

However, there is also evidence that this self-control is a learned behaviour and that people can be taught to defer immediate gratification in order to achieve personal mastery. Carol Dweck of Stanford University[6] discovered that people differ in their capacity to cope with tough challenges and achieve mastery or complete a project. Those who have what she calls a *growth mindset* are able to stick with future plans by pushing themselves out of their comfort zone and focusing on the path ahead. Those who don't tend to experience what she refers to as the 'tyranny of the now'; they are always looking for short-term rewards and become fazed when confronted with something more stretching. She believes that learning methods play an important role in this. Those children who are taught and encouraged to attempt tasks that stretch them and that they find hard, if not impossible, to complete are more likely to have this growth mindset. We imagine that her advice to those determined to be productive over a longer life would be to set tough, challenging learning goals and then be focused and determined to persevere.

Clearly, encouraging people to plan, experiment and achieve mastery through efficacy and agency will become increasingly important, and both educators and governments will attempt to play a role in this.

What does this mean for education?

Over a long life, learning and education are crucial. For many people there will be more education and learning, more years at college as undergraduate degrees expand to include more experiential content, more people taking postgraduate qualifications, more vocational training and more innovations in learning. This won't simply be extra years of education at an early stage, but also serious investment in later life as people learn new specialisms, so as to adapt to a changing employment landscape and to mentally refresh and stimulate. As a consequence, it is very likely that the range of educational institutions and academic or professional credentials will widen significantly.

How education institutions respond will be interesting to observe. As an industry, education is relatively conservative; it is, after all, based on teaching the current generation the ideas created by previous generations. Furthermore, elitism and selectivity are seen to be crucial in bestowing an external market value on education. This reputational signalling feature of education – particularly by elite institutions – makes it hard for new institutions and new forms of certification to establish themselves. Of course, educational institutions do evolve but historically they have tended to do so gradually, with only minor changes in products and a stability of providers.

It is clear that the combination of technological innovation and longevity poses a substantial threat to this traditional sector; as a consequence, there will be new providers, new products and new ways of achieving existing aims. In order to support those destined to live long lives, the agenda faced by educational institutions is fourfold: how to incorporate new learning technologies and experiential learning; how to break down boundaries between age groups; how to think more deeply about ways to teach creativity, innovation, humanity and empathy; and how to rapidly expand practical specialisms in order to ensure that education wins in its race against technology.

It is no surprise therefore that Harvard Business School Professor Clayton Christensen argues that technology makes education ripe for 'disruptive innovation', and that this will have a positive impact on lifelong learning. Investments in digital innovations will transform the classroom, with online teaching, MOOCs, digital degrees and certifications with new providers and new entrants. Looking forward, Jane and her cohort will find an ever-increasing array of options for how, what and where they study, and at what price. If Christensen is right, then this disruptive force will leave existing incumbents slow to change and increasingly superseded and replaced.

Digital technologies offer tremendous advantages for supporting learning over 100 years. Take, for example, the participation in the courses on Coursera, one of the major providers of MOOCs. They surveyed[7] over 50,000 participants and found 72 per cent were taking the course in order to achieve a career benefit, with 87 per cent saying that they succeeded in this aim. Of those registered, 83 per cent already had a college degree or higher, and had a median age of 41 (with a range of 31 to 55 between the first and third quartile). There is no doubt that the flexibility of the course makes it an ideal form to help people update their specialist academic knowledge.[8] Given the need for workplace learning, we expect more of these MOOCs to become vocational, building portable, certified skills that can be taken from job to job. Over time, we can expect more colleges and online providers to create credits that have some of the reputational cachet of elite institutions.

Of course, most traditional educational institutions operate in ways that reflect the three-stage view of life. Just as pensions and retirement are seen as 'end of life' issues, education is about 'start of life'. Like communities and friendship groups, the majority of educational institutions are 'age stratified', putting distinct age groups in each course: school, undergraduate, postgraduate or 'mature student'. The result is age homogeneity, as classes are made up of people in a very narrow age band. Inevitably, this increases boundaries between the ages, creates greater distinctiveness between age groups, and encourages stereotyping and prejudice. Young people are separated from the potential for mentoring and sharing life experiences with older people, while older people lose the opportunity to engage meaningfully with the young.

There is no doubt that age segregation will come under pressure from many angles. As those pursuing a multi-stage life want and need to re-skill and re-invigorate at many ages, they will look to educational institutions to support them. This will put pressure on the formatting of learning. For those who take a couple of years of transition in order to learn, the standard existing degree format might work. But what of those who don't want this, and who aspire instead to convert their chunks of recreation into re-creation? As people have more time available during the week and at different stages of life, there is sure to be an increase in the relative importance of part-time education.

These forces will break down age homogeneity and usher in an era of cross-generational blending. This is all for the good. As people from different ages mingle, they develop deep friendships and the boundaries between 'us' and 'them' begin to break down; this in turn encourages people to take multiple perspectives and stretch their view of the world. In the words of the social scientist Valerie Braithwaite, schools, colleges and universities could create 'spaces where young, middle-aged and older people from all walks of life can get to know each other enough to build mutual respect, develop cooperative relationships, and reignite the norm of human-heartedness'.[9] Currently such places are hard to find – perhaps education could construct such a place.

Longevity will also no doubt put pressure on the interface between education and work. In the traditional three-stage life, a short period of education was followed immediately by entry into work. Employers typically looked for people who would commit to staying with them and working full-time, and expected colleges and universities to ensure their future employees were 'fully formed' with their kitbag of skills and capabilities already developed. This hope is already not being fulfilled. Indeed, an increasing proportion of employers are reporting that the graduates they recruit do not have the skills they need, particularly with regard to creativity and innovation, humanity and empathy. They want schools and colleges to focus more on these life skills. The impact of this pressure will be felt in a variety of ways. From a curriculum perspective, there will be more emphasis on experiential learning whereby students experience first-hand those activities that develop deeper empathy or creativity, and are able to learn judgement and decision-making in conditions of ambiguity and uncertainty. At the same time, more people will decide to manage their own learning experiences before they join a corporation. They will keep their options open by becoming an explorer or an independent producer, gathering up experiences and honing their skills, sometimes before embarking on full-time education, sometimes afterwards. Educational institutions are well set up to provide the needs of the traditional first stage of the three-stage life, but we suspect they will find themselves continuously in catch-up mode, as they try to meet the aspirations of multi-stagers while remaining competitive with the rapidly emerging MOOC sector.

What does this mean for corporations?

The context of working lives is not only framed by our desires and wishes, but is also shaped by the practices, processes, culture and values of corporations. The coming decades will see a process of negotiation and bargaining between firms and individuals as society seeks to reshape life. In order to meet the demands of their workforce, corporates will have to substantially redesign their policies.

Starting with the positive agenda, what is it that corporations must do in order to support those who will live for 100 years? We would like to make six suggestions.

First, there is a need to rebalance the corporate rhetoric between tangible and intangible assets. Right now the relationship between employer and employee is mediated by tangible assets: how much to pay, what pension to make available, car and housing allowance, etc. Yet as we saw from the scenarios of Jimmy and Jane, tangible assets, while important, are only part of a life balance and will not be the main concern within all future stages of work.

How can this balance be shifted? It would be useful to acknowledge and identify intangible assets. We have made a start here but it could be that there are more corporate-specific intangibles that are appropriate. It would be useful to understand the contribution of intangible assets for each job category: will performing this job lead to the creation of intangibles such as productivity or vitality? Does it help the employee build their intangibles outside the workplace? Once this is achieved, it will be possible in the selection and development of employees to use this intangible asset narrative as a way of describing to others what the deal is and to make this as clear as possible.[10] This narrative will make it easier for individuals to make educated choices about which job to go for in the light of where they are in their life. At any point, their motivation for working will reflect the multi-dimensional aspect of their life and the role that intangible assets play in it.

Next, corporations need to support and acknowledge employee transitions and the profound requirements they will have to develop and protect their transformational skills. It is inevitable that most employees will, at some point in their career, make a transition, and there is a great deal that firms could do to support them in this. Such help could take the form of training to boost skills in transformation; it could be ensuring that people are able to develop dynamic and diverse networks; or it could be that self-knowledge is developed through the use of peer-based feedback. We know that transformational assets are boosted through crucible experiences, so corporations should consider the possibility of exposing employees to the 'edges of the system' as part of corporate learning and development. Firms will need to do this both as a process of onboarding for multi-stage entrants to the firm but also as a way of attracting new workers.

Third, firms will have to re-frame the practices and processes of corporate careers from three stages to multi-stages. A glance at the scenarios for Jimmy and Jane shows the diversity of their experiences and their needs. Jimmy wants and needs to work beyond the age of 60. He wants to stay alert and would like to build a portfolio that will take him to the next stage of his life. So he wants to craft a new deal: he wants attitudes to retirement and ageing to change; he needs support in staying productive; he would like the corporation he joins to think more creatively about how it pays him; and he would be willing to see his pay level off or even fall. Jane is an explorer in her early years, so she needs corporations to reach out to find her, and other skilled people like her; she would like the opportunity to take a sabbatical, or to ramp up and down at various times in her life; she'd like support to manage the transitions she will go through and to be working in a way that enhances her vitality. Many firms are already confronting these challenges, but often in a piecemeal manner as they respond to the individual demands of retiring workers or newly started employees. Firms will increasingly need to shift from such one-off deals to something more transparent, predictable and fair.

Next, firms will have to consider the evolving role of the family at work. In the last chapter we laid out the impact that longevity will have on partnerships and family structures. Among a greater diversity of structures, the dual-career partnership will become more popular. It will also be used as a means of managing the finances of a family, by enabling each partner to switch between high- and low-income roles. With a greater variety of household structures and more multi-stagers, firms will need to be clearer and more specific about the demands of different jobs. As Goldin shows, there are jobs that are very tough (significant time pressure, limited time autonomy, limited flexibility around scheduling, a need to be in constant touch with team or clients, and limited opportunity for substitution) and therefore highly paid. Be clear about this: these are jobs that are unlikely to work at a stage in life when either men or women want to be active, deeply involved parents. Secondly, corporates will need to be gender-agnostic in capability and resource planning. If the current trends of young men are to be believed, many of them will want to be active parents and will be prepared to shape their work around this choice. This means that flexibility will not just be something that women want – it's something that *many* people will want.

Fifth, we believe that one of the toughest challenges will be to change corporate attitudes to age and initiate a shift to age-agnosticism. Business is one of the institutions that have helped cement the separation of the young and the old. Corporate support for retirement played an important role in this, as firms tried to free up jobs for more physically able workers in a non-confrontational way. Even job titles reinforce this separation of ages: labels such as 'junior' and 'senior' are both age-related titles. This made sense in a three-stage life, where there was one major career stage, but it makes no sense in a multi-stage life. As we have shown, there will be times when people of different ages will embark together on remarkably similar experiences. Corporations will do themselves a disservice if they don't understand and accept this.

There is growing legislation that is forcing firms to adopt anti-ageist policies, but it is clear to us that firms will have to go beyond this. In a multi-stage longer life, nominal measures such as a person's age no longer have the same resonance as they had in a three-stage life with fixed transition dates. When a three-stage life was the primary model, it was appropriate for HR policies to implicitly use age as a shorthand way of capturing performance and incentives. It is not appropriate, however, when the model moves towards multi-stages. It will be a major challenge to unpick the implicit rather than explicit ageism in recruitment, promotion and salary setting, and replace them with objective criteria not linked to age and age-based peer assessment. As an example, consider the ease that comes with the fact that age in a three-stage life is a simple proxy for experience, and this feeds directly into promotion and pay. In a multi-stage life, age and relevant experience will become increasingly disconnected.

Finally, corporations will have to be prepared to accept and appreciate experimentation, both in the working practices they are prepared to accept and in the CVs of those they recruit. Over the next couple of decades, people will be adapting to their changing lives and some of them, like Jimmy, will be making these adaptations mid-career. They have few role models to guide their path so they will be pushed into experiments. Some of these experiments will work and others will not. Those that work will quickly gain attention and then traction, and we can image that they will rapidly scale as others see what can work and want to copy their lead. So it will be for corporations to be aware of these experiments and be prepared to incorporate them into their thinking. At present, under the current rules of a three-stage life model, an individual with a CV that shows 'gaps', whether for experimentation or other reasons, is treated with suspicion. In a world where increasing numbers have such periods as a way of managing intangibles, firms will need to be more tolerant.

These suggestions represent a substantial reworking of current HR practices and will demand much reform. As such, we expect considerable resistance. In part, this will reflect a reluctance to shift from the low dimensionality and predictability of current policies, because age alone is a sufficient proxy indicator for much of what an employee needs and wants. When this shifts, then rather than a small set of fixed policies with standard times and gateways, there will need to be a much wider range of options involving individual negotiations. These are both complex to manage and open to concerns of procedural injustice, as some employees will be able to negotiate better terms than others. Inevitably this move away from standardization, and the resultant increase in complexity, will be resisted by many firms, simply because this type of change is challenging and the way forward is insufficiently defined.

There are other reasons why these shifts will be resisted. Complexity often comes at a price. At times of financial pressure, there is much valuing of standardized practices. The flexibility required by a 100-year life may be simply uncommercial for some. This is not the first time that flexibility has been on the agenda. A key feature of the Industrial Revolution was demand by firms for standard and uniform working hours. For most companies, the episodic and irregular pattern of pre-industrial work was too expensive; they had made substantial capital investments in factories and machinery and these were best used constantly and uniformly. The result of this demand was the introduction of a six-day, 72-hour week which became the defining model for the original 'working week'. No doubt workers resented the change in their working patterns and the loss of flexibility that had transformed their personal and family life. But at that time, the corporate will prevailed. While firms and labour organizations then spent several decades renegotiating the deal, the corporate desire for standardization remained and the working week was simply shortened rather than made more flexible.

Might the same desire for standardization win out today? Regardless of what Jimmy and Jane may want from their employers, the firms that employ them may simply not oblige for commercial reasons. However, while some firms will undoubtedly resist and refuse to let go of standardization, we think most will make some form of adaptation.

To a certain extent, this is because the modern economy is very different from that of the Industrial Revolution. Today the highest value-added industries are based around human not physical capital, and this gives greater scope for skilled workers to have their demands met. It is for precisely this reason that so many high-value-added sectors are beginning to adopt flexible working and retirement practices. There is no doubt they have further to travel down this route. The war for talent and the growing importance of creativity and innovation all mean that many firms have strong interests in attracting and retaining good workers, and will be prepared to listen and respond to their needs and requirements.

Moreover, machines are increasingly embodying intelligence. While this is leading to a greater hollowing-out of the centre, it is also widening the gap between types of work and greater diversity in how the workforce is engaged. For those jobs where man and machine work together, there may be more opportunity for flexibility, as the routine aspects of the work can be carried out by a machine. And if technology means less standardization is required in the workforce, it also helps in terms of coordination within the organization. The promise of data analytics is that it will enable executives to move beyond standardization to being able to cope with different work patterns without the associated costs. It's easier to work flexibly when collaborative technology keeps team workers connected and individual performance is constantly measured and monitored.

There is no doubt that some firms will persist with simple standardized policies that are optimal for them but not optimal for employees. However, we predict that many firms will attempt to change. They will increasingly see offering more diverse employment policies as a major strategic advantage, especially in high-value-added industries where human capital plays a crucial role. The fact that not all firms will find it profitable to do so does, however, raise major issues for government and society. The scarcer your talents, the stronger your negotiation hand and therefore the more choices you have to structure your life and make the most of your 100 years. Not everyone will have this negotiation hand or access to choice.

How far along on this agenda are corporations? As part of this 100-year study, we took a sounding of what corporations are currently doing to prepare for these new ways of working. This became a theme of the *Future of Work Consortium* that Lynda directs and which brings together executives from around the world. In a series of interviews, and then in a workshop in London in October 2014, we discussed their plans to make the most of this 100-year bonanza. We found that, with a few exceptions, most are doing very little.

Many firms simply don't currently have the practices and processes to deal with the complexity of Jimmy's and Jane's lives. Most have kept with the traditions of recruitment and development that were created more than fifty years go. They are using graduate recruitment as the primary entry point, thereby excluding anyone who decides to enter into a phase of exploration, or indeed to move into corporate life mid-career. The learning processes are typically front-loaded training, so there are fewer learning and educational opportunities for those over the age of 30. Very few corporations have any systematic process of sabbaticals or time out, thus forcing people to resign rather than take a break. With regard to families, in many workplaces the tacit assumption is that women will be the main carer in families, which offers little support to fathers who want to take on more parental responsibility. Perhaps the greatest challenge is the prevailing attitude to retirement. In most companies, the assumption is that employees will want to leave full-time work in their early 60s. The result is that those who want to work longer are seen as the exception rather than the norm, and anyone over 60 is viewed as 'old' and probably unable to cope with the intellectual challenges of the job. Retirement is then followed by a 'hard stop', which of course removes any opportunities for older workers to enter into more flexible mentoring and supporting roles, or indeed to actively build a portfolio.

Of course, this will change. Companies will reach out to the explorers; they will provide learning opportunities throughout a career; they will encourage sabbaticals and help fathers be involved parents; they will enable employees to stay longer and build in pathways that create more varied work; and they will develop 'soft stops' that encourage older people to actively engage in some aspects of work. But to do so they have to be prepared to confront various barriers to change.

The government agenda

Corporations create the context for work, while government policy builds much of the broad context for living. Where do governments stand and how long will it take for them to catch up with the emerging realities of longevity? The agenda for governments is huge. Just as individuals will be redesigning life, so too will governments need to reconfigure the legal system, the tax and benefit systems, and a host of employment legislation, along with the institutions that deal with education and marriage. For people to reconfigure their lives successfully, governments will need to reconfigure their rules and institutions.

In one sense, the debate and agenda for what governments need to do in order to tackle longevity has been ongoing for decades. The unsustainability of public finances based on an unchanged retirement date, greater longevity, and higher pensions and healthcare costs has led to substantial analysis and policy in the macroeconomic and fiscal spheres. Just as we did in our initial response in Chapter 2, the immediate response of governments when faced with the prospect of a 100-year life is to focus on sorting out the finances. However, as we have shown, the real challenge comes in the management of intangible assets and this is an area where much government policy lags behind.

When we consider the challenges of planning for tangible and intangible assets, one important data point is the probability of how long life will last. Here there are mixed messages. As we described earlier, there are two ways of estimating life expectancy: period estimates and cohort estimates. We strongly recommend that governments and the actuarial industry reconsider their use of period estimates of life expectancy as their core assumption.

This is not only a misleading assumption for the macroeconomic policy debate, it also creates confusion and a false sense of security in the mind of citizens. In our earlier analysis, we described how period estimates assume that an 8-year-old born today has the same survival probabilities when they reach 40, 50 or even 70 years of age as does a 40-, 50- or 70-year-old today. In practice, this estimate rules out the probability that over the next 40, 50 or 70 years there will be progress in nutrition, public education and medical technology. That is why period estimates of life expectancy are, for rich nations, currently around 80 to 85 years. In contrast, cohort estimates, which factor in future increases in longevity, put life expectancy at over 100. A glance at Figure 1.2 shows the constancy of the gains from the 1800s onwards. The discrepancy between the two methods of estimates is important as well as alarming. It means that not only are governments likely to be underestimating the future strain on public finances, but they are failing to communicate the urgency of the challenge to citizens.

Beyond fiscal policy there are other profound challenges that a long life creates for government policy. Much current policy is viewed through the lens of a three-stage life where certain ages have a particular significance. Indeed, chronological age is a central feature of policy in education, government bureaucracies and firms. Examples abound of how government legislation and regulation is age-dependent. Take government statistics around the labour market. Currently, most government statistics view those aged 0–15 as 'children', 16–64 as 'working age', and 64+ as 'retired' (and implicitly 'old'). The reality is that as life lengthens, so perceptions of young and old change. These categories fail to capture juvenescence or the shuffling of age and stage that we've predicted. Just as it will take time for educational institutions to catch up with this emerging reality, so it will be the same for governments.

To understand the dangers of three-stage thinking, consider the macroeconomic policy debate around how public finances can be made sustainable. Most governments are trying to implement policies to increase the age of retirement. Yet as Figure 10.1 shows, a major problem for many countries is low levels of employment among those aged 55–64.

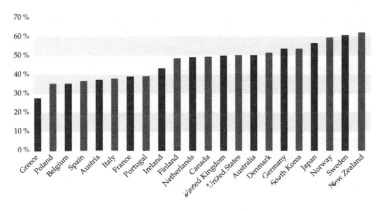

FIGURE 10.1 *Employment rates of 55-64-year-olds.*
Source: OECD.Stat

The age at which people retire (what the OECD terms the 'average age of transition into economic inactivity') varies substantially across nations. Why do Greeks, Italians and French retire around a decade earlier than Norwegians, Swedish and New Zealanders? Studies suggest that government legislation and fiscal policy play a significant role. Do pensions increase with additional years of work or are they capped? How are pension savings and pensions treated for tax purposes? What is the availability of disability benefits before retirement? Most governments are trying to tackle these discrepancies by removing incentives for early retirement in order to achieve fiscal sustainability. However, the challenge is more complex than this; the multi-stage life requires much less focus on key factors such as retirement age and instead support for greater flexibility of working practices across all ages. Rather than fix the dates of key transitions, governments must provide a framework that enables people to choose their own milestones.

The emergence of a multi-stage life, the disconnect between age and stage, and the breaking of lockstep will all create opportunities for people to make individual choices about how they structure their life. Governments, like companies, will need to shift their policies. This isn't just about changing retirement dates and contribution rates, all of which reflect three-stage thinking. The reforms to tax and benefits will need to be much more profound than governments currently entertain. This will include a greater focus on lifetime allowances and lifetime credits, rather than the current excessive focus on age-related schedules and the decade immediately before retirement. Lifetime allowances will provide people with greater flexibility and choice about how they manage the different stages of their life. Governments will have to show greater flexibility over how people use pensions and savings schemes. We have emphasized the value of everyone learning how to balance the books and the importance of saving. But to make this happen, governments will also have to make major efforts to encourage savings and support greater financial literacy. Of course, it is not just governments who will have to change but the financial sector too. Financial planning and financial products will alter radically, as tens of millions of people shift from a three-stage to a multi-stage life, and this in turn will require major changes in government regulation.

The deconstruction of the three-stage life has other challenges for governments. Many have established legislation for the second stage of life – the working stage – and assume that workers are either in full-time or part-time work, with each category clearly defined. As our discussion about leisure and the working week showed, governments will need to allow for a significant range of lifestyle and work-style choices, and simple characterizations of full-time and part-time will make little sense. This is already apparent in what has been called the 'sharing economy'. The growth of sharing businesses, such as Uber and Airbnb, has already brought to the fore complex questions such as 'What is an employee?' and 'Who is responsible for benefits such as healthcare and pensions?' In the past, trade unions have spoken for the collective rights of their members. The profiles of these unions are only just emerging in the sharing economy and we can expect more battles as the rights of these flexible workers are contested in the courts.

Our discussion of transitions and partnerships is also challenging for governments. Currently, the unit of analysis for legislation is the typical familial household. With blended families and frequent transitions, governments will not only have to offer greater flexibility in financial, tax and employment legislation across different periods of life, but will also have to offer similar flexibility across individuals who are in alternative forms of partnerships and parenting households.

The agenda for governments is far-reaching and complex and will be ongoing for decades. Just as the Industrial Revolution saw decades of government legislation in response to changing patterns of work, so we can expect decades of legislation in response to longevity. However, some of the changes will be more subtle than just reconfiguring legislation. One of the fascinating aspects of longevity is the rise of the four-generation family. We wonder if this cross-age blending will affect the time frame over which people consider the impact of their actions and the policies of governments. In Lampedusa's *The Leopard*, the Prince believes he can only be expected to care about the world in which those whom he can physically touch and love (his children and perhaps grandchildren) will live. Many would echo his words. It is hard to care about the welfare of yet unborn children. But longevity brings people into contact with more generations. Consider Jimmy; if he becomes a grandparent in 2031, his grandchild would probably have a 50/50 chance of living beyond 2140. Some scientists working on modelling climate change estimate potential warming occurring by 2100. That date seems too far away to consider now, but they are describing an impact on climate which those whom we can touch and love will experience.[11]

The inequality challenge

One of the most significant impacts of longevity that will face governments is around inequality. There are two major challenges here. The first is that although life expectancy is increasing, it is not increasing at the same rate for all. Right now there are sizeable differences opening up that are determined by income level, with the rich living significantly longer than the poor. In other words, not everyone will have the prospect of a 100-year life. The second challenge is that making a 100-year life a gift rather than a curse requires a great deal of self-knowledge, considerable skill and education, the financial resources required to support transitions and a negotiating strength with employers. These are attributes found in the top quartile of the income distribution, especially in professional and technical occupations, but are not necessarily found across the whole population. Not everyone, given current government policies, has access to the options we have outlined.

Figure 10.2 illustrates the first challenge. It shows how life expectancy has increased for those born in the US in 1940 compared to 1920, and how the gains differ between men and women and by income. Notice that life expectancy is not increasing at the same rate for all and a sizeable gap is opening up between the rich and poor. This isn't just a US phenomenon but a global problem. Even worse, for low-income men, life expectancy actually *decreased* over those twenty years. Across the board, life expectancy for the rich exceeds that of the poor by more than twelve years. With growing life expectancy occurring at different rates, health inequality will continue to rise and we expect these growing health inequalities to become a subject of increasing debate and policy focus. How governments will respond is not clear. However, we would expect major policies aimed at directing resources towards the poor and increased public education aimed at narrowing this health gap. This will not eliminate the gap, but it will narrow it. A long life should not be accessible only to a privileged minority.

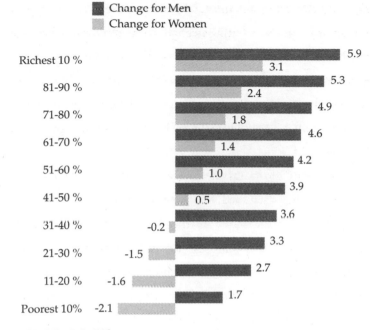

FIGURE 10.2 *Life expectancy across income groups.*

Source: B. Bosworth and K. Burke, 'Differential Mortality and Retirement Benefits in the Health and Retirement Study', Brookings Institution mimeo 2014.

The second challenge is that those with lower (lifetime) income will be disadvantaged when it comes to the flexibility and skills needed to deconstruct the three-stage life. For them there is a real danger that – to steal from Hobbes, as we did earlier – life will be nasty, brutish and long. Those who lack skills and knowledge will be unable to support a long retirement and will be ill equipped to deal with transitions. They face the real risk of losing, and not gaining, from the potential benefits of longevity. Their lives could look more like those of our ancestors – working for most of their life until their end approaches, and facing declining income and living standards as they age.

Part of a government's response will be to preserve the gains to welfare brought about by the introduction of retirement. For citizens to have an old age of leisure and financial security was a tremendous social achievement. One solution would be a divergence of government policy. For those on a lower income, it makes sense to keep the state pension and target it towards them; they are more likely to have a three-stage life, with a longer second working stage and a longer retirement. For those on higher incomes, pensions will be self-funded and sufficiently flexible to deal with a multi-stage life. Sadly, because lower income households have lower life expectancy, then the increase in retirement age will be more modest for this group and their retirement will therefore be shorter.

While this is a likely outcome, given the rich variety of options that a 100-year life offers, it doesn't seem a socially desirable outcome. A long continuous working career between the ages of 16 and 70 or even longer is bad for intangible assets, irrespective of income level, and is probably one of the reasons why life expectancy is lower for those on a low income. The problems of burnout, physical exhaustion, mental boredom and difficulties in balancing work with family and friends are not unique to the rich. However, the rich have the resources to deal more successfully with this stress in terms of their spending power and their capacity to live healthy lives. Moreover, technological innovations displace unskilled workers more frequently than skilled workers, so a long career will see repeated instances of technological obsolescence at the bottom end of the income distribution.

It seems probable that governments will therefore have to offer support to those on a low income to fund transitions, prepare for future stages, and take time out to build their intangible assets. In many countries, the twentieth century saw the introduction of unemployment insurance, sickness and disability pay, maternity and increasingly paternity leave, and state pensions. All of these policies helped to provide the poor with resources that enabled them to deal with transitions and shocks – something that had previously only been available to the rich. If transitions become more important and a crucial part of re-creation, then it is possible to imagine the introduction of state-provided lifetime allowances that enable people to draw down on in order to fund paid leave, up to a fixed length or value. Perhaps the voice of the labour movement will again be heard – a mass movement representing lower income groups and calling for government legislation to support workers in availing themselves of free time and avoiding the blight of endless work.

The lengthening of life holds great potential in overcoming inequality; a longer life with many stages gives people more chances to overcome initial bad starts or negative events in early life. However, if differences in investment – in health, education, contacts and networks, savings – are what drives inequality, then over a longer life, where investment in a wider range of assets is more important, the danger is that inequality will increase. In the twentieth century, there was significant state investment in free education and infant health care, which were the key periods of investment for the three-stage life. If increasing life expectancy produces a multi-stage life, then there will be plenty of other periods when similar investments are required. In the decades to come, we can imagine significant debate about the level of government involvement in these later years.

These are speculative thoughts, but the logic is familiar – so much that is focused on longevity concerns finances, earnings and savings. The real challenge, as we see it, is how to manage intangible assets in order to support a longer life. Currently, social policies aimed at inequality focus primarily on financial issues. With longer lives this focus will have to be extended. The issue is urgent and challenging, if as many people as possible are to experience longer life as a gift. In many countries, current social policies have helped boost welfare by creating a three-stage life; if the three-stage life is now being undermined, then so too are the landmark social policies created in the twentieth century.

Why is change so slow?

What is striking is the contrast between the magnitude of change that society will embark upon as people live longer, and the relatively limited response from corporations and governments. Even more remarkable is the general lack of awareness of the agenda and issues. Saying that corporates and governments are 'behind the curve' doesn't even come close.

Given that greater longevity will bring profound economic and social change, why has there been such limited change to date? The first explanation is the simplest. Social change simply takes a very long time. Increases in longevity have accumulated slowly across each decade, rather than suddenly. It's a perfect example of the much-used frog story. Put a frog in a slowly heating pan of water and it will not jump out, staying until it is boiled; throw it into boiling water and it will jump out. The moral of the story is that when something accrues slowly, it is more difficult to take radical action. It's no surprise then that social change, backed up by government legislation, tends to accrue slowly. For instance, during the Industrial Revolution in the UK it wasn't until 1802 that Parliament passed an act attempting some form of regulation of child labour. After 1802, it took over four decades for a variety of Factory Acts to restrict working hours for those aged 8–13 to six-and-a-half hours a day. So rather than a quick fix, there is more likely to be a raft of government legislation unfolding over the coming decades that will enable individuals and society to adjust to greater longevity.

The second reason behind the delayed nature of change is perhaps more profound. It is a problem also linked to issues of environmental sustainability – the question of short-termism. Like those changes required to reduce CO_2 emissions, the costs of change are felt now while the benefits accrue later. Thankfully, the problem for longevity is not as severe as for sustainability, where many of those who will benefit from current change have not yet been born. At least members of the current generation aged 18–30 have a vote and so can influence governments to make changes that will benefit them in later life. However, in many countries this generation is smaller than previous ones and often less engaged with politics. Take, for example, the 2012 US election voting patterns, which saw a turnout of two-thirds of people aged 45 and over, 50 per cent of those aged 25–44, and slightly over a third of those aged 18–24. It seems that young people are becoming increasingly disillusioned with politics. In 1964, half of them voted; by 2012 it was little more than a third. A smaller cohort that votes less will struggle to have its voice heard. The larger, more politically active baby boomers will focus government attention on retirement and ageing healthcare. The opinions of the young could go unheeded on subjects such as lifetime education, skill development, flexible work and transitions. A theme of our argument is that living for longer isn't just about what people do when they are old. But if older voters have the ear of politicians, then reforms will take longer and are likely to be flawed.

A further reason why we can expect the response of governments and corporates to be slow is the social heterogeneity that will emerge as society tries to work out how best to respond to this gift of longevity. With the emergence of each new stage or transition, society has to experiment first before change can occur. It is only over time that it becomes clear how best to structure the corporate and government practices and policies that these new stages of life require.

Significant change is unlikely to emerge without some kind of consensus. We could imagine that over the next decade there will be a growing awareness that current practice and regulations aren't effective. But it may be that no clear sense emerges of how best to tackle this. Moreover, the other problem for policymakers is that, even once a social consensus begins to emerge, there will be considerable heterogeneity among individuals. The three stage life created lockstep and could only be sequenced in one way; by contrast, a multi-stage life can be sequenced in many different ways depending on individual preferences and circumstances, and this deep variety makes it ever more difficult to come to a consensus view of action.

What will be the catalysts for change?

So is all of this hopeless? Will people be forever destined to live longer and longer in a context of corporate policies and government regulations ill suited for this emerging reality? It is our view that, fundamentally, the agent of change will not be corporations or governments – it will be people. Faced with the challenges and opportunities of longevity, it is individuals, partners, families and networks of friends who will experiment, deconstruct, reconstruct, discuss, argue and become frustrated.

What will emerge from the actions and discussions of these millions will not be a new preferred model for how to live a productive life. Rather, it is likely to be a shared desire for flexibility and individual freedom. Of course, it is this desire for flexibility and individual freedom that will be one of the reasons behind the slow responses of corporates. We think this will be the battleground for a major social tussle in response to longevity. Firms and governments will want to persist with simple standardized models, but individuals will be pushing for greater flexibility and individual discretion. Society will have to decide where it wants to position itself in terms of a trade-off between bureaucratic efficiency and individual preferences. Our own view is that the bias will lie towards the individual rather than the organization. This will particularly be the case in high-value-added industries where corporate success is determined by an engaged and motivated workforce.

So how will change emerge? Governments are already starting to respond, although mostly by focusing on the third stage with changes to the retirement age, the level and availability of pensions, and the introduction of anti-ageist legislation. However, governments are also beginning to amend the tax and financial systems to focus on lifetime rather than annual measures of income, wealth and allowances. These movements towards greater individual flexibility will also be backed by businesses, in particular financial institutions, which will see the commercial advantages of fee income from helping people restructure their finances. As governments introduce greater lifetime flexibility, they will also start to adjust legislation to remove the implicit ageism that the three-stage life has supported.

What about firms? Corporations have many resources that can be put into play to keep some of the realities we have discussed at bay. It could be, for example, that there are sufficient graduates who will happily join straight from college, so that it's not necessary to reach out to the explorers. Or that there are enough fathers who are prepared to leave the bulk of parenting to their partners, so that it's not necessary to introduce more equitable ways of working for those at a senior level. Indeed, it could be that there are sufficient skilled younger people that it's fine to let those over 60 go and not bother to re-employ them in more creative ways.

So change will be piecemeal. For example, while sticking to their current policies, firms will start to develop exceptions and variations to support the different requests from individuals. This is already apparent in those firms who are offering some variation over retirement age, letting individuals take several months off before coming back into work, or supporting some workers to shift to a three-day weekend or half-day working. Over time, the number of exceptions and the increasingly bespoke nature of requests will trigger a more fully fledged response from the HR departments of firms. Cracks will start to appear, as wages rise because workers are scarce, and as talented and experienced workers threaten to leave unless their requests are met. It will be under these circumstances that firms begin to realize the positive advantages of restructuring their working week and career path settings.

In fact, cracks are already appearing. There is a growing realization that some highly talented people want to build their own companies and then re-engage with bigger companies later. What a shame never to use these talents. Some highly skilled men and women are demanding that their responsibility as parents and caregivers is acknowledged. And there are huge swathes of 60-year-olds who are currently retiring and leaving extraordinary holes in the skill pools of industries such as aeronautical engineering and pharmaceuticals. Such skill deficits are putting these sectors at real risk.

So these pressures will mean that change will come – but it will probably be slower, lumpier and more tentative than many would hope for. As such, it will ultimately be up to every individual to make it clear what they want and need and to accelerate corporate change. And it will be up to corporate leaders to realize that a corporation built for a three-stage working life is profoundly ill equipped to cope with what is coming.

Faced with the frustration of government and corporate norms, people – both individually and collectively – will want to set out themselves to experiment with different ways of working and living. This will all be for the good. It is our view that this arc of experimentation will create opportunities for many people to really explore what is important to them and that individuality and diversity will be encouraged and celebrated. There will be lots of variety out there – and from this variety will spring the gift of a 100-year life.

Engaging with the 100-Year Life

Writing this book has been a very exciting journey for us both and has given us much thought about our own lives and how we plan our future. We really hope that it has had the same effect on you and started you thinking and engaging in conversations with your family. We want this book to trigger many such conversations as well as a wider debate with corporations and governments. The 100-year life will only prove a gift for society if those wide-ranging discussions happen. It is the responsibility of us all to ensure they do.

If you are interested in seeing how these conversations are going and also to contribute to them and learn more, then please go to our website *www.100yearlife.com* for updates.

When you arrive at the website you will see that there is a diagnostic that you can use to assess your current situation and help you plan more clearly for your future. The diagnostic takes a closer look at the flow of your tangible and intangible assets now and into the future. We think this will be a great opportunity for you to learn more about yourself and start your thinking about how to engage.

We'd love to hear about how you and your family and, indeed, your company are experimenting with making this work so we and everyone else can learn from one another. On the website you'll see that there is a space for you to upload your stories and share your thoughts with the community that we hope will form around the book.

NOTES

Introduction

1   Oeppen, J. and Vaupel, J., 'Broken Limits to Life Expectancy', *Science* 296 (5570) (2002): 1029–31.

2   From 'A Letter to Jean-Baptiste Le Roy (13 November 1789)', first published in *The Private Correspondence of Benjamin Franklin* (1817).

Chapter 1

1   Deaton, A., *The Great Escape: Health, Wealth and the Origins of Inequality* (Princeton University Press, 2013).

2   Preston, S. H., 'The Changing Relation Between Mortality and Level of Economic Development', *Population Studies* 29 (2) (July 1975): 231–48.

3   The oldest person to have ever lived (officially confirmed) was Jeanne Calment, who passed away at 122.

4   Kurzweil, R. and Grossman, T., *Fantastic Voyage: Live Long Enough to Live Forever* (Rodale International, 2005).

5   Fries, J., 'Ageing, Natural Death and the Compression of Morbidity', *New England Journal of Medicine* 303 (3) (July 1980): 130–5.

6   Freedman, V. A., Martin, L. G. and Schoeni, R. F., 'Recent Trends in Disability and Functioning Among Older Adults in the United States: A Systematic Review', *Journal of the American Medical Association* 288 (24) (December 2002): 3137–46.

7   A recent global study focusing on 188 countries suggests that life
    expectancy is increasing faster than healthy life expectancy for
    most countries. For instance, in Japan over the last twenty years life
    expectancy has increased by 4 but healthy life expectancy by 3, in
    South Korea the numbers are 7 and 6 respectively, in the US 3.5 and
    2.5, and for Western Europe 5 and 3.5. See 'Global, regional and
    national Disability Adjusted Life Years (DALYs) for 306 diseases
    and injuries and Healthy Life Expectancy (HALE) for 188 countries,
    1990–2013: Quantifying the epidemiological transition', GBD 2013
    DALYS and HALE Collaborators, *The Lancet* (2015).

8   Lafortune, G., Balestat, G. and the Disability Study Expert Group,
    'Trends in Severe Disability Among Elderly People: Assessing the
    evidence in 12 OECD countries and the future implications', OECD
    Health Working Paper no. 26.

Chapter 2

1   See for example the work of our colleagues Campanale, C., Fugazza,
    C. and Gomes, F., 'Life Cycle Portfolio Choice with Liquid and
    Illiquid Assets', *Journal of Monetary Economics* 71 (2005): 67–83; or
    Cocco, J. Gomes, F. and Maenhout, P., 'Consumption and Portfolio
    Choice over the Life Cycle', *Review of Financial Studies* 18 (2) (2005):
    491–533.

2   The advantage of our stripped-down model is its simplicity, which
    hopefully makes our calculations easier to comprehend. It is worth
    pointing out, though, that this is a *very* stripped-down model. We
    assume that you save a constant amount of income each year, whereas
    the standard life cycle and permanent income hypothesis models in
    economics would have you saving when your income is high and
    borrowing when your income is low. We also have income growing
    at a constant rate throughout your working life. In reality what
    economists call 'earnings profiles' are hump-shaped: rising initially
    fast, then levelling out at a peak, before declining. Ignoring these

assumptions makes our calculations easier and also makes it much easier to compare across our three personas. We also in this chapter completely abstract from issues such as housing or other forms of debt that need repaying – see Chapter 7 for why. Undoubtedly these simplifying assumptions miss important features and this is again why this isn't intended as a substitute for personal financial advice. However our stripped-down model does successfully capture the basics and is what we need to make our point.

3   https://publications.credit-suisse.com/tasks/render/ file/?fileID=AE924F44-E396-A4E5-11E63B09CFE37CCB

4   Again this is a major simplification. Growth rates of income vary from sector to sector and from decade to decade: exactly how fast the salaries of Jack, Jimmy and Jane grow depends on where they work. (See Miles, D., 'A Household Level Study of the Determinants of Incomes and Consumption', *Economic Journal* 107 (1997): 1–25 for estimates across different professions of how income varies with age, which we use to calibrate our calculations.)

5   While Jack is fictional, we try and give ourselves some discipline. The US government estimate (http://www.ssa.gov/oact/NOTES/as120/ LifeTables_Body.html) of cohort life expectancy measures for males born in 1945 is around 72. We use 70 so as not to give the impression of spurious accuracy.

6   As noted earlier, we assume that income grows continually over your working career and that you save a fixed percentage every year. Jack almost certainly didn't save 4.3 per cent every year but focused his savings on the period of his life where he was earning the most and his children had left home. Obviously if you spend some years not saving, then you need to save more than 4.3 per cent when you do in order to compensate. However because early years of a working life have low income compared to middle years, it is not the case that the savings rate needs to double for each year you don't save.

7   See Office for National Statistics, 'Pension Trends', Chapter 7: Private Pension Schemes Membership 2013 Edition, http://www.ons.gov.uk/ ons/dcp171766_314955.pdf

8   Ellis, C.D., Munnell, A.H. and Eschtruth, A.D., *Falling Short: The Coming Retirement Crisis and What to Do About It* (Oxford University Press, 2014).

9   Using official UK ONS data, if Jimmy is born in 1971 his cohort based measure of life expectancy, given he is currently 45, is actually 87.

10   Crossley, T. and O'Dea, C., 'The Wealth and Savings of UK Families on the Eve of the Crisis', Institute for Fiscal Studies Reports (July 2010).

11   UK government data for cohort measures of life expectancy suggest that if Jane is born in 1998 her life expectancy is 93 under central projections, or 99 under more optimistic assumptions. These are of course averages for the whole population. If Jane is born into a top quartile income family, her life expectancy will be greater than either of these.

12   Even these simple calculations raise lots of issues. We assume that income continues to rise at a constant rate over your working career. The good news about that is that it means you have more money to help finance retirement. The bad news is that because we assume that you want a pension worth 50 per cent of your *final* salary, a growing income also raises the amount you need to save. The faster your income grows, the greater your final salary. This is why, in our simulations, as the income growth rises, people need to save more. Another assumption would be to say that you want to achieve a pension worth 50 per cent of your salary at 65 regardless of when you retire. This stops you needing to save more and more as you work longer by cutting the link with your final salary. If we do this for Jane, then she can retire at 75 with a pension worth 50 per cent of her salary at 65 if she saves around 10 per cent a year. At this point we are getting into deep waters. Once again, if Jane bases her pension at retirement on a salary of ten years ago (let alone thirty-five years ago by the time she reaches the age of 100) it is going to be very low compared to other members of society. Further, a better assumption is probably to assume that income may fall after 65 (as most earnings profiles do bend down with age). In this case, with Jane earning less in later years, she has to have a higher savings rate throughout her lifetime to finance the pension. So if we assume that her earnings remain the same after she reaches 65, that she wants to retire on a pension worth 50 per cent of her salary at aged 65, and she wants to keep her savings at the 10 per cent level, then she would have to work to 77 to achieve this. If her salary declines after 65, then if she wants to keep savings at the 10 per cent level, she will now basically work until she is 80. We said right at the outset that our model was simple and you needed to seek detailed financial advice to really make your choices. This note is showing the limits of some of our simple assumptions.

Chapter 3

1　Most economic analysis of longevity focuses on the expected fall in the size of the working population and the increase in pensions and health care costs that come from ageing. The macroeconomic effects of ageing and falling birth rates are significant: upward pressure on wages, downward pressure on rates of return, falls in savings and investment and changes in current account deficits. See Magnus, G., *The Age of Aging: How Demographics are Changing the Global Economy and Our World* (Wiley, 2008).

2　Gratton, L., *The Key: How Corporations Succeed by Solving the World's Toughest Problems* (Collins Business, 2015).

3　See for example Richard Florida's view of the rise of the city, *Who is your City? How the creative economy is making where you live the most important decision in your life* and *The Rise of the Creative Class* (Basic Books, 2002).

4　Deloitte, *London Futures: London crowned business capital of Europe* (UK Futures, 2015).

5　Moretti, E., *The New Geography of Jobs* (Mariner Books, 2013).

6　Costa, D. and Kahn, M. E., 'Power Couples: Changes in the Locational Choice of the College Educated 1940–1990', *Quarterly Journal of Economics* 115 (4) (2000): 1287–315.

7   Johns, T. and Gratton, L., 'The Third Wave of Virtual Work', *Harvard Business Review* (2013).

8   The fears over robots and artificial intelligence (AI) are much broader than just employment. In spring 2015 Lynda facilitated a discussion at the World Economic Forum at Davos on the question 'Will machines make better decisions that humans'. On the panel were four professors from the University of California, Berkeley, experts in AI, neuroscience and psychology. Later that week the UK *Telegraph* reported on the session with the headline: 'Sociopathic robots could overrun the human race within a generation', accompanied by a particularly scary picture of aggressive, demonic-looking fighting robots. The headline didn't capture the nature of the debate but it did capture the growing unease people feel about the impact that AI and robotics will have on their work and concerns about what will be left. When even Professor Stephen Hawking worries that the rise of AI represents a fundamental threat to the future of humanity, it is perhaps not surprising that such widespread concerns exist.

9   See for instance Ford, M., *The Rise of the Robots* (Basic Books, 2015); Brynjolfsson, E. and McAfee, A., *The Second Machine Age* (W. W. Norton & Company, 2014).

10   Ford, *The Rise of the Robots*.

11   Brynjolfsson and McAfee, *The Second Machine Age*.

12   Autor, D. H., Levy, F. and Murnane, R. J., 'The Skill Content of Recent Technological Change: An Empirical Exploration', *Quarterly Journal of Economics* 118 (4) (2003): 1279–334.

13   Beaudry, P., Green, D. A. and Sand, B.M., 'The Great Reversal in the Demand for Skill and Cognitive Tasks', NBER Working Paper 18901 (2013).

14   Frey, C.B. and Osbourne, M.A., 'The Future of Employment: How Susceptible are Jobs to Computerization?' (Oxford University mimeo, 2013).

15   Polanyi, M., *Personal Knowledge. Towards a Post Critical Philosophy* (Routledge, 1958/98).

16 Moravec, H., 'When Will Computer Hardware Match the Human Brain?', *Journal of Evolution and Technology* 1 (1) (1998).

Chapter 4

1 See for example Johns, T. and Gratton, L., 'The Third Wave of Virtual Work', *Harvard Business Review* (2013).

2 Oscar Wilde's famous quote (from *Lady Windermere's Fan* [1892]), 'A cynic is a man who knows the price of everything and the value of nothing' comes to mind here – a quote often thrown at economists.

3 New Testament, Matthew 19.24: 'And again I say unto you, it is easier for a camel to go through the eye of a needle than for a rich person to enter the kingdom of God'; Qu'ran: 'Let not your worldly goods or your children make you oblivious of the remembrance of God: for if any behave thus – it is they, they who are the losers.' We do not explicitly deal with spiritual or religious issues in this book. For the religiously inclined, faith is clearly an overriding intangible asset that needs to be supported, nourished and invested in and would form the backbone of a good life.

4 Vaillant, G. E., *Adaptation to Life* (Little, Brown, 1977).

5 This statement is not uncontroversial, with more recent studies questioning whether this is true. See Stevenson, B. and Wolfers, J., 'Economic Growth and Subjective Well-Being: Reassessing the Easterlin Paradox', *Brookings Papers on Economic Activity* 1 (2008): 1–87.

6 Hamermesh, D. S., *Beauty Pays: Why Attractive People are More Successful* (Princeton University Press, 2011).

7 Schick, A. and Steckel, R.H., 'Height as a Proxy for Cognitive and Non-Cognitive Ability', NBER Working Paper 16570 (2010).

8 Greenstone, M. and Looney, A. http://www.hamiltonproject.org/assets/legacy/files/downloads_and_links/06_college_value.pdf

9   Goldin, C. and Katz, L., *The Race Between Education and Technology* (Harvard University Press, 2008).

10   For example, a number of people born around 1955 in California had early access to computers because their fathers worked at the Palo Alto campus of Xerox and brought these insights and some equipment home to their children. These 'outliers' such as Bill Gates and Steve Jobs gained incredibly valuable skills from their upbringing in these unusual historical conditions.

11   Kremer, M., 'The O-Ring Theory of Economic Development', *Quarterly Journal of Economics* 108 (1993): 551–75.

12   Groysberg, B., *Chasing Stars: The Myth of Talent and the Portability of Performance* (Princeton University Press, 2012).

13   Coleman, J. S., 'Social Capital in the Creation of Human Capital', *American Journal of Sociology* 94 (supp.) (1998): S95–120.

14   Gratton, L., *Hot Spots: Why Some Companies Buzz with Energy – and Others Don't* (FT Prentice Hall, 2007).

15   Gratton, *Hot Spots*.

16   Polanyi, M., *Personal Knowledge* (Routledge and Kegan Paul, 1962).

17   Sennett, R., *The Craftsman* (Yale University Press, 2008), 62.

18   Burt, R., 'Bandwidth and Echo: Trust, Information and Gossip in Social Networks', in J. E. Ranch and G. G. Hamilton (eds), *Networks and Markets* (Russell Sage Foundation, 2001).

19   For accounts about shaming by social media and its consequences, see Ronson, J., *So You've Been Publicly Shamed* (Riverhead Books, 2015).

20   Aleman, A., *Our Ageing Brain* (Scribe Publications, 2014).

21   'Stressed Out? A Study of Trends in Workplace Stress Across the Globe', Regus Research Institute (November 2009).

22   Wolfram, H. J. and Gratton, L., 'Spillover Between Work and Home, Role Importance and Life Satisfaction', *British Journal of Management* 25 (1) (2014): 77–90.

23 Gratton, L., *The Shift: The Future of Work is Already Here* (HarperCollins Business, 2011).

24 Buettner, D., 'Blue Zones: Lessons for Living Longer from the People who've Lived the Longest', *National Geographic* (2008).

25 *liminality* (from the Latin līmen, meaning 'threshold').

26 Ibarra, H., *Working Identity: Unconventional Strategies for Reinventing Your Career* (Harvard Business Review Press, 2004).

27 Schein, E., 'Organizational Learning: What is new?', MIT Working Paper 3192 (1965).

28 Stroh, L. K., Brett, J. M. and Reilly, A. H., 'A Decade of Change: Managers' Attachment to Their Organizations and Their Jobs', *Human Resource Management* 33 (1994). 531–48. They authors found that job mobility increased between 1979 and 1989.

29 See for example Douglas Hall and his concept of the 'Protean careers': Hall, D. T., 'Protean Careers of the 21st Century', *Academy of Management Executive* 10 (1996): 8–16; Hall, D. T., *Protean Careers In and Out of Organizations* (Sage, 2002).

30 Giddens, A., *Modernity and Self-Identity: Self and Society in the Late Modern Age* (Stanford University Press, 1991).

31 Kegan, R., *In Over Our Heads: The Mental Demands of Modern Life* (Harvard University Press, 1994).

32 Markus, H. and Nurius, P., 'Possible Selves', *American Psychologist* 41 (9) (1986): 954–69.

33 Linde, C., *Life Stories – The Creation of Coherence* (Oxford University Press, 1993).

34 Granovetter, M., *Getting a Job: A Study of Contacts and Careers* (University of Chicago Press, 1974).

35 Openness to experience (Costa, P. T. and McCrae, R. R. *NEO-FFI: Neo Five-Factor Inventory* [Psychological Assessment Resources, Inc, 2003]) is a long-established construct of the 'Big 5' personality model

related to one's posture toward ambiguous situations and willingness to try new things.

36   Giddens, *Modernity and Self-Identity*.

37   Hall, D. and Mirvis, P., 'The New Career Contract: Developing the Whole Person at Midlife and Beyond', *Journal of Vocational Behavior* 47 (1995): 269–89; Mirvis, P. H. and Hall, D. T., 'Psychological Success and the Boundaryless Career', *Journal of Organizational Behavior* 15 (1994): 365–80.

Chapter 5

1   With a 5.0 stage life the number of assumptions required is multiplying rapidly. We assume that when Jane starts at EatWell she earns twice what she had been bringing in as an independent producer, that when she starts with the search firm in her third stage her starting salary is 150 per cent of her final salary at EatWell, and that during her portfolio stage she earns 50 per cent of her final salary at the search firm. Her pension is based on 50 per cent of her earnings during the portfolio stage.

Chapter 6

1   Nachmanovitch, S., *Free Play: Improvisation in Life and Art* (Penguin, 1990), 150.

2   For historical accounts of the development of childhood, see Aries, P. *Centuries of Childhood* (Pimlico Press, 1960); Cunningham, H. *Children and Childhood in Western Society Since 1500* (Pearson Longman, 1995); Heywood, C., *A History of Childhood* (Polity Press, 2001).

3   For fascinating accounts of how the concept of a 'teenager' developed, see Palladino, G., *Teenagers: An American History* (Basic Books, 1996); Savage, J., *Teenage: The Creation of Youth 1875–1945* (Pimlico Press, 2007).

4   There is, surprisingly, relatively little literature on the emergence of retirement either in the economic or sociological fields. It is perhaps indicative of a broad lack of interest in this third stage of life. For a historical analysis of the institutional development of retirement, see Graebner, W., *A History of Retirement: The Meaning and Function of an American Institution 1885–1978* (Yale University Press, 1980); Costa, D., *The Evolution of Retirement: An Economic History 1880–1990* (University of Chicago Press, 2000).

5   Harrison, R. P., *Juvenescence: A Cultural History of Our Age* (University of Chicago Press, 2014).

6   Hagestad, G. and Uhlenberg, P., 'The Social Separation of Old and Young: A Root of Ageism', *Journal of Social Issues* 61 (2) (2005): 343–60.

7   Nachmanovitch, S., *Free Play: Improvisation in Life and Art* (Penguin, 1990).

8   Miller, S., 'Ends, Means and Galumphing', in *American Anthropologist* (1973). The term 'galumphing' is taken from Lewis Carroll's poem 'Jabberwocky' in *Through the Looking-Glass* (1871).

9   Rainwater, J., *Self-Therapy* (Crucible, 1989), 9.

10 Giddens, *Modernity and Self-Identity* (Stanford University Press, 1991).

11 Scharmer, O., *Theory U: Leading from the Future as it Emerges* (Berrett-Koehler, 2009).

12 Bennis, W. and Thomas, R., 'Crucibles of Leadership', *Harvard Business Review* 80 (9) (2002): 39–46.

13 Mirvis, P., 'Executive Development Through Consciousness-raising Experiences', *Academy of Management Learning & Education* 7 (2) (2008): 173–88.

14   Deal, J. and Levenson, A., *What Millennials Want from Work: How to Maximize Engagement in Today's Workforce* (Center for Creative Leadership; McGraw-Hill, 2016).

15   Scharmer, *Theory U.*

16   The novel *The Makers* by Corey Doctorow is a good fictional explanation of this lifestyle and accreditation process although that novel focuses on how these trends subvert existing organizational trends.

17   http://www.kauffman.org/~/media/kauffman_org/research%20 reports%20and%20covers/2015/05/kauffman_index_startup_ activity_national_trends_2015.pdf

18   See Moretti, '*The New Economic Geography of Jobs*' for a detailed analysis of this specific issue; or Glaeser, E., '*Triumph of the City*' (Macmillan, 2011) for the general advantages of cities in terms of innovation and creativity from connectedness, scale and competition.

19   http://www.economist.com/news/leaders/21573104-internet-everything-hire-rise-sharing-economy

20   Ibarra, H., *Working Identity: Unconventional Strategies for Reinventing Your Career* (Harvard Business School Press, 2003).

Chapter 7

1   HSBC, *The Future of Retirement: A Balancing Act* (2014) https://www. google.co.uk/url?sa=t&rct=j&q=&esrc=s&source=web&cd=1&ved= 0CCEQFjAAahUKEwi_usPx58nIAhUFShQKHf2zCVo&url=http%3 A%2F%2Fwww.hsbc.com%2F~%2Fmedia%2Fhsbc-com%2Fabout-hsbc%2Fstructure-and-network%2Fretirement%2Fglobal-reports%2F150119-en-global.pdf&usg=AFQjCNHqnTTn6X-Ts8_ kJH-F6btYYp2HQg&sig2=1rMAiGNK9r7QQbA6hgiFVg

2   Aguair, M. and Hurst, E., 'Lifecycle Prices and Production', *American Economic Review* 97 (5) (2007): 1533–59.

3   Quoted in Prelec, G. and Weber, R., 'What, mc worry? *A Psychological Perspective on Economic Aspects of Retirement*', in Aaron, H. J. (ed.), *Behavioral Dimensions of Retirement Economics* (Brookings Institution Press, 1999), 215–46.

4   Skinner, J., 'Are You Sure You're Saving Enough for Retirement?', *Journal of Economic Perspectives*, 21(3) (2007): 59–80.

5   Binswanger, J. and Schunk, D., 'What Is an Adequate Standard of Living During Retirement?', *Journal of Pension Economics and Finance* 11 (2) (2012): 203–22.

6   HSBC, *The Future of Retirement.*

7   Mitchell, O. and Lusardi, A. (eds), *Financial Literacy: Implications for Retirement Security and the Financial Marketplace* (Pension Research Council Series, 2011).

8   Venti, S. and Wise, D., 'But They Don't Want to Reduce Housing Equity', NBER Working Paper 2859 (1989).

9   Palumbo, M., 'Uncertain Medical Expenses and Precautionary Saving Near the End of the Life Cycle', *Review of Economic Studies* 66 (1999): 395–421.

10 Given that 3 per cent is the historical average, this implies that for every Warren Buffett there must be someone who is doing worse than the 3 per cent average. So while it's important to find a good investor to look after your money, it's also important to avoid those who perform below average. The trouble is knowing who is who and distinguishing between luck and judgement.

11 Clark, R., Lusardi, A. and Mitchell, O., 'Financial Knowledge and 401(k) Investment Performance', NBER Working Paper 20137 (2014).

12 Hastings, J. S, Madrian, B.C. and Skimmyhorn, W. L., 'Financial Literacy, Financial Education and Economic Outcomes', NBER Working Paper 1841 (2012).

13 Allen, S. G., Clark, R. L., Maki, J. A. and Morrill, M.S., 'Golden Years or Financial Fears? Decision Making After Retirement Seminars ', NBER Working Paper 19231 (2013).

14 Campbell, J. Y., 'Household Finance', *Journal of Finance* LXI(4) (2006): 1553–604.

15 Samuelson, L. and Zeckhauser, R., 'Status Quo Bias in Decision Making', *Journal of Risk and Uncertainty* 1 (1988): 7–59.

16 A point Nobel laureate Robert Merton stresses in 'The Crisis in Retirement Planning', *Harvard Business Review* (2014).

17 Heath, D. and Heath, C., *Switch! How to Change Things When Change is Hard* (Random House Business, 2011).

18 O'Donoghue, T. and Rabin, M., 'Doing It Now or Later', *American Economic Review* 89 (1) (1999): 103–24.

19 Properly understanding discounting requires us to go way beyond the financial literacy levels of the Big 5 questions outlined earlier. In fact this footnote is probably being read only by the Business School Finance professors. Under exponential discounting you discount an event in N years' time at the rate e-rN where r is the discount rate. If r is zero then you have complete patience and the higher is r the more impatient you are. Hyperbolic discounting is so called because it doesn't use a simple exponential like e-rN but instead a hyperbolic form 1/(1+rN). The key punchline is that with standard exponential discounting the relative weight between the outcome in two different periods is always the same no matter how far ahead the periods are. Therefore, in the absence of new information, what you say you will do now in those later periods is what you actually do when the time arrives. Under exponential discounting, as the future dates gets closer to today, you weight things differently and don't carry out the plan you earlier said you would.

20 In the episode 'The Glasses', Seinfeld touches on this problem of multiple selves in his discussion of Night Guy and Morning Guy. 'I never get enough sleep. I stay up late at night cause I'm Night Guy. Night Guy wants to stay up late.' 'What about getting up after five hours' sleep?' 'Oh that's Morning Guy's problem. That's not my problem, I'm Night Guy … So you get up in the morning … you're exhausted, groggy, oooh I hate that Night Guy! See, Night Guy always screws Morning Guy.'

21 Hershfield, H. E., Goldstein, D.G., Sharpe, W. F., Fox, J., Yeykelis, L., Carstensen, L .L. and Bailenson, J. N., 'Increasing Saving Behavior Through Age-Progressed Renderings of the Future Self', *Journal of Marketing Research* 48 (supp.) (2011): S23–37.

22 www.acorns.com

23 Thaler, R. and Benartzi, S., 'Save More Tomorrow: Using Behavioral Economics to Increase Employee Saving', *Journal of Political Economy* 112 (supp.) (2004): S164–87

24 Salthouse, T., 'Executive Functioning', in Park, D. C. and Schwarz, N. (eds), *Cognitive Aging: A Primer*, 2nd edn (Psychology Press, 2008).

25 Bernheim, D., Shleifer, A. and Summers, L., 'The Strategic Bequest Motive', *Journal of Political Economy* 93 (1985): 1045–76.

26 Although clearly aspects of the strategic bequest motive have always been in operation. See for a historical account Hartog, H., *Someday All This Will Be Yours: A History of Inheritance and Old Age* (Harvard University Press, 2012).

Chapter 8

1 Ramey, V. and Francis, N., 'A Century of Work and Leisure', *American Economic Journal: Macroeconomics* 1 (2) (2009): 189–224.

2 Schor, J., *The Overworked American* (Basic Books, 1993) and *Plenitude: The New Economics of True Wealth* (Penguin, 2010).

3 Veblen, T., *The Theory of the Leisure Class: An Economic Study of Institutions* (The Macmillan Company, 1899).

4 Costa, D., 'The Wage and Length of the Work Day: From the 1890s to 1991', *Journal of Labor Economics* (1998): 133–59.

5 See for instance Grund, C. and Silwka, D., 'The Impact of Wage Increases on Job Satisfaction – Empirical Evidence and Theoretical Implications', IZA Discussion Paper 01/2001.

6   Ramey, V. A. and Francis, N., 'A Century of Work and Leisure'
     (National Bureau of Economic Research, 2006).

7   Aguiar, M. and Hurst, E., 'Measuring Trends in Leisure: The Allocation of
     Time Over Five Decades', *Quarterly Journal of Economics* 122 (3) (2007).

8   Becker, G., 'A Theory of the Allocation of Time', *Economic Journal*
     (1965): 493–517; Linder, S., *The Harried Leisure Class* (Columbia
     University Press, 1970).

9   http://www.ft.com/cms/s/0/4899aaf8-0e9f-11e4-ae0e-00144feabdc0.
     html#axzz3nJ2crVXm

10   Goldin, C., 'A Grand Gender Convergence: Its Last Chapter',
     American Economic Review 104 (4) (2014): 1–30.

11   Elsbach, K. and Cable, D. M., 'Why Showing Your Face at Work
     Matters', *MIT Sloan Management Review* 53 (2012): 10–12.

12   Faulkner, W., *The Wild Palms* (Random House, 1939).

13   For more detail on these historical trends, see Cross, G. S., *A Social
     History of Leisure Since 1600* (Venture Publishing Inc., 1990);
     Cunningham, H., *Leisure in the Industrial Revolution* (Croom Helm,
     1980).

14   For instance, in the UK, the ancient day-long, sprawling, violent
     football matches were replaced by the mass spectator sport of
     Association football, a well-defined 90-minute game with a fixed
     number of players policed by a referee and occurring in stadia.

15   Marx, K. *Grundrisse* (1858).

Chapter 9

1   Becker, G., *Treatise on the Family* (Harvard University Press, 1981).

2   Friedman, S., *Baby Bust: New Choices for Men and Women in Work
     and Family* (Wharton Press, 2013), 33.

3 Stevenson, B. and Wolfers, J., 'Marriage and Divorce: Changes and Their Driving Forces', NBER Working Paper 12944 (2007).

4 Giddens, *Modernity and Self-Identity* (Stanford University Press, 1991).

5 Hite, S., *Women and Love* (Viking, 1988).

6 Stevenson and Wolfers, 'Marriage and Divorce'.

7 Giddens, *Modernity and Self-Identity*, 93.

8 Wolf, A., *The XX Factor* (Profile Books, 2013).

9 Groysberg, B. and Abrahams, R., 'Manage Your Work, Manage Your Life', *Harvard Business Review* (March 2014).

10 Friedman, *Baby Bust*.

11 Giddens, A., *The Transformation of Intimacy: Sexuality, Love and Eroticism in Modern Societies* (Stanford University Press, 1992).

12 Friedman, *Baby Bust*.

13 Friedman, *Baby Bust*, 33.

14 Buckles, K., 'Understanding the Returns to Delayed Childbearing for Working Women', *American Economic Review* 98 (2) (2008): 403–7.

15 Goldin, 'A Grand Gender Convergence: Its Last Chapter', The American Economic Review 104(4), 1–30.

16 Isen, A. and Stevenson, B., 'Women's Education and Family Behaviour: Trends in Marriage, Divorce and Fertility', NBER Working Paper 15725 (2010), http://www.nber.org/papers/w15725.

17 *Modern Parenthood*, study by the Pew Center (2013). *Dual income couples* – men spend 11 hours per week more in paid work, have 4.5 more hours of leisure; women do more childcare and housework.

18 *Modern Parenthood* (Pew Center).

19 McKinsey research programme examining gender diversity: see for example 'Gender diversity in top management: Moving corporate culture, moving boundaries' (McKinsey, 2013); 'Unlocking the full potential of women in the U.S. economy' (McKinsey, 2012); *Women*

Matter. Gender diversity at the top of corporations: Making it happen (McKinsey, 2010).

20 Bertrand, M., Goldin, C. and Katz, L., 'Dynamics of the Gender Gap for Young Professionals in the Financial and Corporate Sectors', *American Economic Journal: Applied Economics* 2 (2010): 228–55.

21 Goldin, 'A Grand Gender Convergence: Its Last Chapter'.

22 'Women and the Future of Work', ILO (International Labour Organization) (2015) http://www.ilo.org/wcmsp-132/groups/public/@dgreports/@dcomm/documents/briefingnote/wcms_347,950pdf

23 Law firms such as Clearspire in the US or Obelisk in the UK are already developing an online platform that enables home-based lawyers to practise their skills in a more flexible way.

24 Coltrance, S., Miller, E., DeHaan, T. and Stewart, L., 'Fathers and the Flexibility Stigma', *Journal of Social Issues* 69 (2) (2013): 279–302.

25 Cherlin, A., *Marriage, Divorce, Remarriage* (Harvard University Press, 1981).

26 Buettner, P., The *Blue Zones: lessons for living longer from the people who have lived the longest* (National Geographic, 2008).

27 Ruggles, S., 'The Transformation of American Family Structure', *American Historical Review* 99 (1994): 103–28.

28 Kohli, M., 'The World We Forgot: An Historical Review of the Life Course', in Marshall, V. W. (ed.), *Later Life* (Sage Publications, 1986), 271–303.

29 Hagestad, G. and Uhlenberg, P., 'The Social Separation of Old and Young: The Root of Ageism', *Journal of Social Issues* 61 (2) (2005): 343–60.

30 Fischer, C. S., *Networks and Places: Social Processes in Informal Places* (Stanford University Press, 1977).

31 Allport, G. W., *The Nature of Prejudice* (Addison-Wesley, 1954).

32 Smith, P., *Old Age is Another Country* (Crossing Press, 1995).

Agenda for Change

1   Parfit, D., *Reasons and Persons* (Clarendon Press, 1984).

2   Archer, M., *The Reflexive Imperative* (Cambridge University Press, 2012).

3   Kahneman, D., *Thinking Fast and Slow* (Penguin, 2011).

4   Heffernan, M., *Willful Blindness: Why We Ignore the Obvious at Our Peril* (Simon & Schuster, 2011).

5   The original experiments on delayed gratification took place at Stanford in the late 1960s and early 1970s. Mischel, W., *The Marshmallow Test: Mastering Self-Control* (Bantam Press, 2014).

6   Dweck, C., *Mindset: The New Psychology of Success* (Random House, 2006).

7   Zhenghao, C., Alcorn, B., Christensen, C., Eriksson, N., Koller, D. and Emanuel, E. J., 'Who's Benefiting from MOOCs, and Why', *Harvard Business Review* (September 2015).

8   Sebastian Thun, a former Stanford University professor, vice president of Google and founder of online educational company Udacity, puts it well: 'The education system is based on a framework from the 17th and 18th century that says we should play for the first five years of life, then learn, then work, then rest and then die. I believe we should be able to do all those things all the time.' http://www.theguardian.com/education/2013/sep/05/google-glass-creator-testing-regimes-technology

9   Braithwaite, V., 'Reducing Ageism', in Nelson, T. D. (ed.), *Ageism: Stereotyping and Prejudice Against Older Persons* (MIT Press, 2002), 311–37.

10   Erickson, T. J. and Gratton, L., 'What It Means To Work Here', *Harvard Business Review* (March 2007).

11   We thank Adair Turner for both the reference to *The Leopard* as well as this specific example.

INDEX

The letter *f* following an entry indicates a figure